Cultural Influences in Coping with Grief

Frank E. Eyetsemitan

Cultural Influences in Coping with Grief

Impact of Social and Psychological Factors

Springer

Frank E. Eyetsemitan
Department of Psychology
Roger Williams University
Bristol, RI, USA

ISBN 978-3-031-86816-0   ISBN 978-3-031-86817-7 (eBook)
https://doi.org/10.1007/978-3-031-86817-7

This Springer imprint is published by the registered company Springer Nature Switzerland AG
The registered company address is: Gewerbestrasse 11, 6330 Cham, Switzerland

Preface

Cultural influences in coping with grief: *Impact of social and psychological factors* is a unique book that discusses in different chapters, cultural influences in grief in death contexts that include widowhood, abortion, dying, death anxiety, and the workplace. This book also discusses culture's influence in disenfranchised grief and in developing resilience. It looks at culture beyond religion and how culture impacts on age, gender, acculturation, finances, and identity in the wake of death. Lastly, while not explicitly stated in conventional grief models, this book highlights the impact of grief rituals in coping with bereavement around the world. At each chapter's end, there are "key take-aways"; and "critical cultural thinking" vignettes are provided to stimulate both self-reflection and chapter comprehension.

A compelling reason for writing this book is to contextualize grief and to approach culture's influence in bereavement beyond religion.

Chapter 1 discusses the importance of the cultural meaning attached to death in influencing grief outcomes. Death meaning could be personal or based on a collective experience at familial and societal levels—which could change over time. Death meaning is embedded within the following general perspectives people take on death:

- Death is a certainty, but the difference is *when* it will happen.
- Death is a certainty, but it depends on *how* it will happen.
- Death is a certainty, but can it be *delayed*?
- Death is a certainty, but *why* think about it?
- Death is a certainty, yet a *continuation of life* in another form.

Chapter 2 reviews conventional bereavement theories and models. Some theories and models are descriptive while others are prescriptive. All the grief theories and models believe that a person's emotion and cognition are involved in bereavement outcomes, and that grieving is a process. Yet, some individuals are never allowed the process. For some bereaved individuals, the grief process never comes to an end and would require the help of a professional. This is known as complicated grief or prolonged grief disorder. This chapter includes "The disruption in daily functioning scale in bereavement" to help monitor progress made in coping with grief.

Chapter 3 discusses culture's impact on thinking, emotions, and actions. When a death occurs, attributions are made as to its cause, based on cultural beliefs and values. And this invariably affects grief outcomes.

Chapter 4 discusses culture's impact on the dying experience. Dying could occur *with hope* or *without hope*. In dying with hope, medical intervention is used; but in dying without hope, palliative care becomes an option after medical intervention is deemed as futile. In Elisabeth Kubler-Ross' 5-stage model of dying (denial, anger, bargaining, depression, and acceptance), some stages may not apply to every dying person. Also, a dying person may go back and forth the stages. The emotions of anger and sadness associated with dying are universal; yet are influenced by cultural factors. Furthermore, between the dying person and loved ones, farewells are exchanged; but not included in Kubler-Ross' 5 stages. Verbal instructions from the dying person to their loved ones are socio-cultural factors that contribute to the dying experience; and so is the communication about dying by a medical doctor to the patient and to the patient's loved ones. The *how* and *to whom* the "bad news" is shared by the medical doctor is a culturally sensitive issue. Generally, in Western cultures, a doctor communicates the bad news directly to the dying patient; but in non-Western cultures, the preference is for the doctor to communicate the bad news to the dying person's family, first. There are cross-cultural benefits to both approaches.

Chapter 5 discusses spousal loss. Following spousal loss, two types of grief by the survivor spouse occur: a) grief for the deceased spouse; and 2) grief by the survivor spouse for himself or herself. The survivor spouse may have to contend with loneliness, living arrangement, and identity. After a death, the survivor spouse's identity changes from "married" to "widowed." In some cultures, a married woman's identity is tied to her husband's. For some bereaved spouses, therefore, moving forward self-identity could pose a challenge.

Chapter 6 discusses abortion and bereavement. An abortion act comes with two types of stigma: a): stigma from society and b): stigma from family members/friends. Each individual is affected differently by an abortion stigma: society (and not family/friends); family/friends (and not society), or both society and family/friends. To cope with the shame and guilt associated with abortion, *concealment* from others (or disenfranchised grief) could occur. Yet, as a cultural value, *individualism* allows for personal responsibility in an abortion decision, whereas as a cultural value *collectivism* expects the sanction of others in an abortion decision. Also, *pre-abortion meaning* or a *post-abortion meaning reconstruction* is impacted by gender identity and gender roles in grief outcomes. An abortion act results in the de-attachment between the woman and the fetus; with physical, cognitive, and emotional implications.

Chapter 7 discusses bereavement in the workplace. Grief is common in the workplace, as most adults spend a good amount of time at work. Workers experience a variety of loss that includes the death of a child, a parent, a grandparent, a companion animal, or a friend. A blanket bereavement policy may not include a worker's peculiar attachment experience to the deceased. Some bereaved individuals have "hidden" grief because of their belief that the organization's formal bereavement policy does not apply to them on who should be bereaved (e.g., a lesbian with a miscarriage). Also, hidden grief occurs when a bereaved employee believes that taking time away from work on bereavement leave would reinforce stereotypes about their incompetence (e.g., a minority group member); or if the bereaved employee perceives that their job is insecure (e.g., a probationary worker or a sportsman/sportswoman). A commonly asked question of the bereaved of the deceased is: "what caused her death?" Also, in talking to a bereaved worker, a commonly used term is "death" or "loss." These may be culturally inappropriate. Suggestions are made on culturally sensitive approaches to interacting with bereaved employees in a diverse workplace.

Chapter 8 discusses cultural influences in death anxiety. Cultural factors that influence death anxiety include a society's life expectancy; available resources (e.g., healthcare and access to it); and risky occupations. Others include concerns by ethnic minority group members in interacting with law enforcement officers; after-life beliefs; beliefs about death causation; dependence on others; approaches to coping with grief; and cultural expectations of what constitutes a fulfilled life.

Chapter 9 discusses culture's impact on resilience in coping with a loss. Resilience is the process that enables a person to adapt well in the face of adversity, trauma, tragedy, or a significant source of stress. Resilience is a way of thinking, believing, and acting which could be learned. Psychologically, US minority group members face persistent trauma which could lead to learned helplessness. Yet, in the face of persistent trauma that causes individuals to become helpless, cultural norms can provide directions in how to become resilient. Cultural norms provide guidance through grieving rules, beliefs, and practices. Furthermore, culture acts as a "looking glass" to a grieving person, whose resilience can be measured against adherence to culture's grieving rules, beliefs, and practices.

Chapter 10 discusses the impact of culture on disenfranchised grief—a grief denied and not publicly acknowledged. People who experience disenfranchised grief may be limited in obtaining social support, in expressing distress, or in coping with a loss. Cultural expectations are relative, however: a grief recognized in one culture may be denied in another. Also, a cultural environment is not monolithic. Based on Bronfenbrenner's (1979) environmental ecological model, a grief denied at one cultural level (e.g., government/society) may be acknowledged at another cultural level (family/ friends) or vice versa.

Historically, a culture undergoes change. Therefore, a grief that is currently recognized could have been disenfranchised in the past. Yet, humans are not entirely at the mercy of their environment. They can exercise agency and "niche-pick" their environment. To circumvent grief rules that disenfranchise their grief, a bereaved individual could selectively interact with aspects of their environment that recognize their grief.

Chapter 11 discusses the impact of rituals on grief. Around the world, grief rituals are an important part of the cultural (and religious) lives of people.

Yet, conventional grief models do not *explicitly* point to the roles of grief rituals, in helping the bereaved to cope with the pain of their loss and/or in making it less burdensome on the bereaved to move on with their lives. A ritual is not a random act, but has meaning to the person performing it. In a situation of uncertainty, as happens after a death, a grief ritual helps to provide control and reassurance. A ritual is a learned behavior and could be verbal or non-verbal. When a survivor has more than one belief system (e.g., traditional religion and Christianity), grief rituals could conflict with each other. However, it becomes easier when the survivor finds a common ground between both belief systems, in grief rituals. Through the help of a bereavement counselor/healthcare professional, a survivor could explore common grounds on belief systems or the saliency of one belief system over the other, in grief rituals. Some grief rituals are never late if not done at the appropriate time, but could serve a *redemptive* function to a survivor. A bereavement counselor/healthcare professional could help with exploring a *redemptive* grief ritual, with the survivor. A prospective act by the deceased when alive (e.g., a last will and testament, a living will, or a verbal instruction) could become a grief ritual, as it enables a survivor to gain control and reassurance after a loss. With the help of a bereavement counselor/healthcare professional, a survivor could explore the decedent's prospective acts when alive, in coping with grief.

Bristol, RI, USA Frank E. Eyetsemitan

Acknowledgments

I want to thank Springer Nature for bringing this book to fruition; and Rachel Daniel, Editorial Director (Behavioral and Health Sciences), for taking the lead. My gratitude also extends to Pradheepa Vijay, Production Editor; and the other production team members, for a wonderful job. And, to my wife Francisca and son Tosan, whose sacrifices and support I always count on, I say a big thank you!

Competing Interests The author has no competing interests to declare that are relevant to the content of this manuscript.

Contents

Chapter 1
The Human Experience of Death, Dying, and Bereavement

This chapter discusses the finality of death that leads to a separation between the living and the dead. Humans have different understanding of death, based on their peculiar experiences and developmental stage in life. The understanding of death forms the bedrock for coping with loss. Some people believe that they have experienced a death and not a loss. Others believe that with death comes a loss also. Based on death meaning, some bereaved individuals continue to maintain bond with the deceased, whereas others do not. Yet the meaning that death portends to the survivor would impact on the different approaches to coping with death.

What Does Death Mean?

Psychologist Erich Fromm is noted as suggesting that *life has no meaning except the meaning that one gives to life* (e.g. Allen, 2005).

Similarly, death has no meaning except the meaning that one gives to death.

Therefore, death meaning is embedded within the following general orientations that people have toward death:

- Death is a certainty, but the difference is *when* it will happen.

In most societies, some deaths are regarded as "off time," while others are regarded as "on time." Generally, death in childhood is regarded as "off time," whereas death in late adulthood is perceived as "on time." Therefore, an off-time death in childhood is perceived as bad and is least preferred, whereas an on-time death in old age is regarded as good or is most preferred.

- Death is a certainty, but it depends on *how* it will happen.

Depending on how it happens, a death could trigger different emotions in the survivor. For example, a death from a house fire or from a drive-by shooting is likely

F. E. Eyetsemitan, *Cultural Influences in Coping with Grief*,
https://doi.org/10.1007/978-3-031-86817-7_1

to trigger the emotion of anger, whereas a death from a protracted illness with lots of discomfort may be perceived as a relief to the deceased instead and not engender anger in the bereaved (Eyetsemitan & Eggleston, 2002). In the United Kingdom, researcher Jane Fleming and colleague (Fleming et al., 2016) noted that about 50% of the deaths that occurred involved people ages 85 years and older and that prior to death these individuals developed multiple, protracted ailments. Therefore, due to the burdens of their ailments, death was perceived as a relief. Also, in the state of Oregon in the United States, individuals who seek physician-assisted suicide are more welcoming of death over life. In a 2019 report of residents who took advantage of the state's Death with Dignity Act, the following reasons were given for their decision: inability to participate in enjoyable activities, loss of autonomy, and loss of dignity (Oregon Government Health Authority, 2020).

- Death is a certainty, but can it be *delayed*?

With some individuals, the issue is not *if* death would occur but *when* it should occur. With this perspective, efforts and actions are made to delaying death for as long as possible. People with this orientation demonstrate a heightened sense of *death anxiety*. Death anxiety happens when the dying process or ceasing to be is contemplated (Fraley & Bonanno, 2004). Death anxiety has been described as the precursor to almost all anxieties (Klein, 1948). To delay death, therefore, people manage death anxiety in the following ways (Hayes et al., 2010):

- Proximal defenses: These are actions that people take *now* to reduce death anxiety from conscious thought. They include denial, suppression, or distraction. An example would be participating in a wellness program or taking on membership in a gym or a health club.
- Distal defenses: These are actions that people take to reduce death anxiety with the *future* in mind. They include beliefs in an afterlife (e.g., heaven) or involvement in legacy issues (e.g., establishment of a foundation).
- Death is a certainty, but *why* think about it?

While some individuals acknowledge that death is a certainty, they do not include death or dying in their conscious thought. Young people with much to look forward to in life are likely to fall into this category. Any reminder of death, including having a will or having a discussion about death in general, is avoided.

- Death is a certainty, yet is a *continuation of life* in another form.

For some individuals, belief in an afterlife is a reminder that death is a transitional phase into an imagined future. A survey by the Pew Research Center (November 23, 2021) reports that two-third of American adults believe in heaven with a relatively fewer number who believe in hell. Heaven is believed to be a place where people are free from earthly pain and suffering, are reunited with deceased loved ones, and can monitor what is happening on earth. Hell is the opposite of heaven, and it is a bleak future.

This survey also reports that while some people may not believe in heaven or hell, they believe in an afterlife where the spirit goes to dwell after death (Pew Research Center, November 23, 2021).

Death Meaning at Personal, Familial, and Societal Levels

Death meaning could hold at personal, familial, or societal levels because survivors are influenced by personal beliefs as well as by the beliefs of others.

Personal: As earlier mentioned, for some individuals death is final, whereas for others death is not final as they maintain continuing bonds with deceased loved ones (e.g., letter writing or verbalizing to the deceased). In death meaning, the *attribution* made as to death causation is also important. Psychologist Julian Rotter (1966) describes how people make attributions to events in their lives. They make attributions based on *situational* cause or *dispositional* cause. In situational cause, people make attributions to external factors (e.g., the action of others), whereas in dispositional cause, they make attribution to internal factors (e.g., personal actions). Generally, people who make attributions to situational causes are regarded to have an *external locus of control*, whereas those who make attributions to dispositional causes are said to have an *internal locus of control*. For example, a survivor with an internal locus of control may attribute death's causation to their own action or inaction, whereas a survivor with an external locus of control may attribute death's causation to God's sovereign will.

Researcher Jule Specht and colleagues (Specht et al., 2010) examined the influence of locus of control in coping with the death of a spouse, an extremely stressful life event. Over a period of 4 years, this study followed 414 widowed individuals before and after their loss and found that external locus of control (or beliefs in situational causes) was a buffer against declines in life satisfaction. Also, researcher Ara Norenzayan and colleague (Norenzayan & Lee, 2010) note that people tend to explain life outcomes that are impossible as "meant to be," which aligns with an external locus of control. These researchers found this behavior to be common among people with religious beliefs than among those of nonreligious beliefs.

Family: Death meaning could be influenced by the collective experience of family members who share a common heritage and socialization experience. In some families, death experience could be due to genetic factors or "faulty genes." Here, for example, across generations family members die at a young age from similar ailments, such as heart disease or breast cancer. In contrast, in other families, death occurs mostly in old age. Thus, whereas in some families death is "off time," in others it is "on time."

Yet an "off-time" death could be perceived as "meant to be" (Norenzayan & Lee, 2010), if it involves "faulty genes." Family members might say words like "our grandmother died from breast cancer, our mother died of breast cancer, and we have other relatives who died of breast cancer, as well. So, it runs in our family." In other words, a life that comes to an end at a relatively young age is a common family occurrence, and therefore little can be done to stop it. Yet, depending on the family members' socialization experience or locus of control, to die at a relatively young age could be perceived as *not meant to be*. Family members with faulty genes could take preemptive measures to delaying death. Oscar-winning star Angelina Jolie, at age 37, had preventive or prophylactic double mastectomy because her mother died of breast cancer at 56. After the surgery, her chances of developing breast cancer dropped from 87% to 5% (BBC News; May 14, 2013).

Angelina Jolie, a mother of six children, acknowledged that throughout the process she enjoyed the support of her partner and family members. By her action, Angelina Jolie might have influenced her children to take a similar step in the future.

However, how well a family functions would influence its collective death meaning. A family that functions well, with open communication, is more likely to have a similar outlook to death than a family that experiences strife and dysfunction (e.g., Schuler et al., 2012).

The concept of *possible selves* reflects on one's hopes, fears, and expectations for the future (Markus & Nurius, 1986). It is a state of goal setting that enables individuals to structure their behaviors and internal resources to propel them into an imagined future state. In pursuing certain lines of action, possible selves can enable the individual to avoid other lines of actions (Cross & Markus, 1991; Markus & Nurius, 1986). While considered an individual resource, *possible selves* could be a shared resource as well, for family members that function well together.

Society: Societies have different meanings attached to death, and these meanings may change over time. Several factors, including the following, could influence the meaning a society ascribes to death:

- Life expectancy.
- Technology and biomedical advances.
- Dominant religion.
- Final act on the decedent's body.

Life expectancy: Life expectancy is the average length of time a person is likely to live from the point of birth in a society. Life expectancy varies from one society to another, and within a society, it varies among different groups. It also changes across historical times. In 2023, life expectancy in the United States is 80.75 years, but in Chad it is 59.57 years (CIA: The World Factbook; accessed May 17, 2023).

Expectations can influence behaviors, attitudes, and beliefs. Therefore, life expectancy in a society could provide a benchmark for the meaning of death. For example, in 2023, whereas death in the United States at age 70 may be "off time," death in Chad at age 70 may be "on time."

Technology and biomedical advances: In developed societies, due to technological and biomedical advances over the years, life expectancy has improved, resulting in the delaying of death. According to the United States Census Bureau (Medina et al., 2020), between 1960 and 2015, life expectancy in the United States increased by almost 10 years: from 69.7 years in 1960 to 79.4 years in 2015.

With improvement in life expectancy, however, comes changes in expectations regarding death meaning. Thus, an "on-time" death in 1960 becomes an "off-time" death in 2015.

Dominant religion: Due to *cultural religiosity* (cultural beliefs merging with religious beliefs), a society's dominant religious practice could have a pervasive influence on that society's death meaning. For example, in Middle Eastern societies where Islam is the dominant religious practice (Pew Research Center, 2017), the pervasive death meaning is only the will of God (Allah) that can make a death to occur. Therefore, a person's attitude toward death should be peaceful (Britannica.com; May 17, 2023).

In the United States, Canada, and Mexico, the dominant religion is Christianity (Pew Research Center, 2011). Christians believe in an afterlife in heaven or in hell. Based on Christian beliefs, therefore, death is perceived as a transitional phase which is likely to encourage continuing bond with deceased loved ones, in heaven. In Asia, Hinduism or Buddhism is the dominant practice of majority of the people (Pew Research Center, 2012). Either religion teaches rebirth of the human soul after death. Based on religious beliefs, life continues in another form after death. Continuing bond with the deceased is blended into child-rearing practices (Neimeyer et al., 2014). Hinduism recognizes that good or bad rebirths does occur, based on good or bad acts of the deceased prior to death (Lipner, 2012; Sharma et al., 2013). These religious beliefs are likely to influence a survivor's coping trajectory. However, as religious beliefs become part of cultural beliefs, changes that occur at the cultural level (due to acculturation or modernity) could affect religious beliefs, as well. This impact that cultural shift has on attenuating religious beliefs was observed among Japanese students (Neimeyer et al., 2014).

Final act on the decedent's body: The final act on the decedent's body, including funeral rites and burial methods, reflects a society's approach to death meaning. In most cases, a society's pervasive religious beliefs reflect these acts. For example, in Asian societies where Hinduism is the dominant religion, cremation is the common body disposal practice. Cremation allows for a quick release of the decedent's spirit in rebirth. However, the final act on the decedent's body could reflect more than one death meaning. It could indicate the rejection of other meanings, as well. For example, part of the Christian belief is bodily resurrection. Thus among Christian practitioners, cremation may not be popular. However, in the United States, with earth burial becoming expensive, cremation is becoming popular for cost-saving reasons (National Cremation, 2015).

In the United States, the Organ Procurement and Transplantation Network (OPTN) maintains a national database of patients that are awaiting organ transplant. Through organ donation, death can bring forth life. Therefore, a dead person's heart, lungs, liver, kidney, intestine, or pancreas can be donated to save a life. This final act on the decedent's body is devoid of religious beliefs, yet it provides an understanding to death meaning that is altruistic.

Evolution of Death Meaning

Death meaning has evolved over historical times. According to researcher Janet Starkey (2009), the technological era has brought a new meaning to death that is neither circumscribed to religion nor to tradition. To highlight the change of death meaning over historical times, French historian Philip Aries (1974) identifies four seasons of death meaning in Western societies: (1) tamed death, (2) one's own death, (3) thy death, and (4) forbidden death. In tamed death, before the seventeenth century, death meaning was that death was part of life. In one's own death, during the eleventh and twelfth centuries, death meaning included what happened to the individual after death. In death meaning, the afterlife as in heaven and hell became prominent. In thy death, which began in the eighteenth century, death was not embraced. Death was an interloper; therefore, it triggered excessive emotions. In forbidden death, which represents the current era, death occurs mostly in the hospital and not at home. Therefore, based on technological and biomedical advances, there is the need to delay death as much as possible.

Death Meaning in Context

Context does provide a basis for death meaning (Walter, 2017). This includes religion, family, and material issues. Meaning making based on contexts that include religion, family, and materialism reflects a collectivist value system, whereas meaning making based on personal attachment to the deceased reflects an individualist value system. Yet in both collectivist and individualist societies, meaning making from both context and personal attachment to the deceased can occur. This highlights the cultural complexity of societies (Walter, 2017). For example, in a study of Senegalese people, researcher Jane McCarthy and colleagues (McCarthy et al., 2020) report on how contexts such as religion, family, and materialism provide meaning to death. Grief response to death was mediated by religious beliefs that only God could allow a death to occur. It was also mediated by family through the deceased person's lost roles such as the go-to person in resolving family disputes and by materialism by sliding into poverty occasioned as a result of the loved one's death. So, to the Senegalese, death meaning is better understood from a contextual lens.

Researcher Tania Ka'Ai (2004) notes that for the Maoris of New Zealand, death meaning can only be understood within the following contextual frameworks: tribal identity, land, importance of elders, kinship structure, culture, and spirituality.

Death meaning is also reflected in a funeral's location. Funerals conducted in secular locations (that are not religious locations) are increasingly becoming popular. In New Zealand secular locations include outdoors, community halls, and school buildings. Over 60% of funerals take place in non-church locations (Raudon, 2011). Instead of a clergy, a paid *funeral celebrant* (without religious affiliation) presides over the funeral event, in accordance with the decedent's lifestyle, beliefs, and values (e.g., Schwass, 2005). Thus, people no longer turn to religion or culture in death meaning. Rather, death meaning is based on their personal values.

Yet, within a religious setting, funerals should be sensitive to the aspirations of survivors. For example, in the United States, an officiating priest at a funeral of a teenager who took his life said suicide was wrong in the sight of God. The parents of the teenager had a different death meaning to their loss. They sued the Catholic Diocese in a court of law for compensatory damages for pain and suffering caused on the family (Yan & Bowman, 2019).

Death Meaning and Coping with Bereavement

Researchers James Gillies and Robert Neimeyer et al. (2006) note that death meaning can form the basis for coping with bereavement. These researchers suggest that in coping with bereavement, death meaning would do the following: (a) make sense of the death, (b) seek benefit from the death, and (c) change the survivor's identity. Also, these researchers suggest a *pre-death* meaning and a *post-death meaning*. The pre-death meaning stems from a preexisting cognitive framework for coping with a loss. In the case of a pre-death meaning being inadequate, a post-death meaning (or meaning reconstruction) becomes necessary. Earlier, Swiss psychologist Jean Piaget (1936) proposes an existing cognitive framework for processing new information in cognitive development. When this happens successfully, it is known as *assimilation*. However, a failure in assimilation would require that the existing cognitive framework be adjusted, in order to comprehend the new information. This is known as *accommodation*. Yet to make this cognitive adjustment would be the individual's choice. For example, some bereaved parents hold on to a pre-death meaning of loss even if inadequate, because they believe that a post-death meaning reconstruction of loss would justify their child's death (Toller, 2008).

Pre-death Meaning: Core or Peripheral

To the bereaved person, a pre-death meaning could be either *core* or *peripheral* in essence. A core pre-death meaning is more established than a peripheral pre-death meaning. When a pre-death meaning is core, the death experience is easily explained within an existing cognitive framework (Gillies & Neimeyer, 2006) or the death experience becomes easily assimilated (Piaget, 1936). Therefore, to evaluate a pre-death meaning, a bereavement counselor could determine if it is core or peripheral to the survivor. As earlier discussed, the Islamic religion teaches that God (Allah) is the ultimate decider of what happens in death, whether expected or not. To some followers of Islam, this belief could become a core pre-death meaning, whereas to others it could just be a peripheral pre-death meaning. Not all followers of a particular faith accept or comprehend the tenets of their belief at the same level. In the loss of a loved one, studies show that some people question their religious faith. Researcher Wendy Lichtenthal et al. (2011) explain what they call *spiritual struggle* among a sample of homicide survivors. Spiritual struggle among bereaved individuals negatively impacts on meaning making (e.g., Lichtenthal, Burke, & Neimeyer, 2011). This has led to anger toward God, questioning of God's authority, and feelings of disaffection toward God (Burke & Neimeyer, 2014).

Yet, for some homicide survivors, in coping with bereavement spirituality is a potent resource (e.g., Bailey et al., 2013; Sharpe, 2015). In other words, spirituality provides a bulwark for resilience in difficult times for these survivors (Bailey et al., 2013). Therefore, in pre-death meaning a bereaved individual's spirituality could be a core trait or a peripheral trait.

A core trait is more pervasive than a peripheral trait and is more likely to have controlling influence over other traits than a peripheral trait. In his seminal work on impression formation, psychologist Solomon Asch (1946) points to the importance of central (or core) versus peripheral traits. In Asch's (1946) experiment, when a central trait (e.g., warm) was substituted with a peripheral trait (cold), the impression that others had of a person was changed. Additionally, stereotyped persons are cognizant of the impression that others have of them. For example, a female is aware of stereotypes associated with their gender. As a core trait in pre-death meaning, therefore, a perceived gender stereotype can influence a survivor's death meaning and how to cope with bereavement. For example, based on perceived gender stereotype, following his father's death, a young male may view himself as "the man of the house." According to researcher Kevin Roy and colleagues (Roy et al., 2014), this means that the young man assumes adult roles and responsibilities, especially in economically disadvantaged households.

Based on stereotypes also, as a core trait the pre-death meaning in an individual is reinforced by his or her perceived expectations of others. A young man who assumes *the man of the house* role may do so, based on the belief that others expect such of him. Thus, a survivor working with a bereavement counselor/healthcare professional could provide a list of three core traits that best describes them (with 1 being the most important and 3 being the least important). Within this framework, core traits in pre-death meaning could be explored.

Post-death Meaning

As discussed earlier, a survivor can either *assimilate* the death experience into an existing pre-death meaning (e.g., Park & Folkman, 1997) or *accommodate* it within a post-death meaning reconstruction (e.g., Neimeyer et al., 2006). Years after experiencing a loss, studies on bereaved individuals point to those who were able to find meaning to their loss or struggle to find meaning to their loss, (e.g., Keesee et al., 2008). A post-death meaning would lead to personal growth through the assumption of new roles and responsibilities (e.g., Calhoun et al., 2010). This is viewed as positive. However, a post-death meaning could be negative as well. It could lead to the questioning of one's ability/competence or to being cynical and less trusting of one's world. A *negative* post-death meaning reconstruction could end up with a narrative of oneself that is not uplifting.

Therefore, the outcome of a post-death meaning reconstruction could be either positive or negative. As a first step, therefore, an exhaustive exploration of a pre-death meaning based on core versus peripheral traits is important, before a post-death meaning consideration.

Pre-death Meaning, Dual Beliefs, and Coping with Death

A survivor could subscribe to more than one belief system. For example, some professed Christians or Muslims also believe in evil eye, sorcery, or witchcraft (which is not part of their religious teaching) as cause of death. Therefore, in pre-death meaning, belief systems may be core or peripheral. From a study of 17 Brazilian families who had experienced the death of a loved one, researcher Regina Bousso and colleagues (Bousso et al., 2011) noted the saliency of one belief system over another. One of the study respondents said that Catholicism or Protestantism could not help provide a meaning to their loved one's death, but Spiritism did instead.

In Brazil, most of the people profess Christianity, but about half of the population also subscribe to Umbanda. Anthropologist Guilherme Velho (2003) notes that:

> "The vast majority of Brazilian society is made up Roman Catholics. However, there are endless and frequent examples of Catholics attending spiritist centers and umbanda and candomblé rituals." (Velho, 2003, p. 25)

A post-death meaning reconstruction could be found in a different belief system. If existing belief systems are adjudged to have failed them, a survivor may take on a new belief system on the recommendation of close friends or relatives.

The Structure of Death Meaning: Global Versus Specific

Death meaning could be *global* based on the generally acceptable meaning ascribed to death in a society, in one's family, or in one's religion. A global structure could provide a survivor a mental framework for pre-death meaning or post-meaning in coping with bereavement. However, a global structure could come up short because two deaths may not have the same meaning to a survivor. For example, the death of a male child could proffer a different death meaning from that of a female child. Also, the death of a firstborn child (perceived as successor of the parent's business venture) could connote a different death meaning from that of a middle born child or an only child whose death could proffer a different meaning.

Therefore, some bereaved individuals may fall through the cracks if death meaning is approached from a global (e.g., religious beliefs) perspective.

Studies report that in an average of over 6 years, 47% of bereaved parents are unable to find meaning to their children's loss (Keesee et al., 2008). When the child's death is sudden or violent, 64% of bereaved parents are unable to find meaning (Lehman et al., 1987).

Thus, death meaning could be specific. This includes no meaning at all, which should be validated. In reviewing 124 parents who lost infant children, researcher Christopher Davis and colleagues (Davis et al., 2000) noted that a significant number of bereaved parents did not find meaning to their loss. Yet, in adjusting to their situation, these parents were not significantly different than those who found meaning.

Key Takeaways

1. The meaning attached to a death could influence grief outcomes. Death meaning could be influenced by historical times, by cultural factors, by contexts, and by life expectancy in a society. Also, death meaning does occur at personal, familial, and societal levels. However, some individuals refuse to attach meaning to not validate their loss.
2. Death meaning could occur either prior to a loss or after a loss. It could be core or peripheral to the individual. A core death meaning is less likely to change than a peripheral death meaning.
3. Death meaning could be general or specific. Death meaning that is general could be derived from societal norms (e.g., off-time death or on-time death) or from religious teachings (e.g., God's will in affecting death's timing). However, death meaning is specific to each survivor and could be influenced by the deceased based on gender, age, sibling position, or if an only child.

Critical Cultural Thinking

With the COVID-19 pandemic, several people experienced multiple deaths of loved ones. Let us assume you are aware of two family members who died from COVID-19: Tom, from not wearing a mask, not following social distancing, and not washing of hands, and Brandon, regardless of taking all those precautions. Based on death meanings, what possible reactions could result from both losses?

References

Allen, B. P. (2005). *Personality theories: Development, growth, and diversity*. Psychology Press.
Ariès, P. (1974). The reversal of death: Changes in attitudes toward death in western societies. *American Quarterly, 26*(5), 536–560.
Asch, S. E. (1946). Forming impressions of personality. *The Journal of Abnormal and Social Psychology, 41*(3), 258.
Bailey, A., Hannays-King, C., Clarke, J., Lester, E., & Velasco, D. (2013). Black mothers' cognitive process of finding meaning and building resilience after loss of a child to gun violence. *British Journal of Social Work, 43*(2), 336–354.
BBC News. (2013, May 14). *Angelina Jolie has double mastectomy due to cancer gene*. www.bbc.com/news/world-us-canada-22520720
Bousso, R. S., Poles, K., Serafim, T. D. S., & Miranda, M. G. D. (2011). Religious beliefs, illness and death: Family's perspectives in illness experience. *Revista da Escola de Enfermagem da USP, 45*, 397–403.
Britannica.com (2023, May 17). *Islam*. www.britannica.com/topic/Islam
Burke, L. A., & Neimeyer, R. A. (2014). Complicated spiritual grief I: Relation to complicated grief symptomatology following violent death bereavement. *Death Studies, 38*(4), 259–267.
Calhoun, L. G., Cann, A., & Tedeschi, R. G. (2010). The posttraumatic growth model: Sociocultural considerations. In T. Weiss & R. Berger (Eds.), *Posttraumatic growth and culturally competent practice: Lessons learned from around the globe* (pp. 1–14). Wiley.
CIA. *CIA: The world factbook*. Accessed May 17, 2023., from www.cia.gov/the-world-factbook/countries/
Cross, S., & Markus, H. (1991). Possible selves across the life span. *Human Development, 34*(4), 230–255.
Davis, C. G., Wortman, C. B., Lehman, D. R., & Silver, R. C. (2000). Searching for meaning in loss: Are clinical assumptions correct. *Death Studies, 24*(6), 497–540.
Eyetsemitan, F., & Eggleston, T. (2002). The faces of deceased persons as emotion-expressive behaviors: Implications for mourning trajectories. *OMEGA-Journal of Death and Dying, 44*(2), 151–167.
Fleming, J., Farquhar, M., Brayne, C., Barclay, S., & Collaboration CCo-sCS. (2016). Death and the oldest old: Attitudes and preferences for end-of-life care-qualitative research within a population-based cohort study. *PLoS One, 11*, e0150686.
Fraley, R. C., & Bonanno, G. A. (2004). Attachment and loss: A test of three competing models on the association between attachment-related avoidance and adaptation to bereavement. *Personality and Social Psychology Bulletin, 30*(7), 878–890.
Gillies, J., & Neimeyer, R. A. (2006). Loss, grief, and the search for significance: Toward a model of meaning reconstruction in bereavement. *Journal of Constructivist Psychology, 19*(1), 31–65.
Hayes, J., Schimel, J., Arndt, J., & Faucher, E. H. (2010). A theoretical and empirical review of the death-thought accessibility concept in terror management research. *Psychological Bulletin, 136*(5), 699.
Ka'Ai, T. (2004). *KI Te Whaiao: An introduction to Maori culture and society*. Longman.
Keesee, N. J., Currier, J. M., & Neimeyer, R. A. (2008). Predictors of grief following the death of one's child: The contribution of finding meaning. *Journal of Clinical Psychology, 64*(10), 1145–1163.
Klein, M. (1948). A contribution to the theory of anxiety and guilt. *The International Journal of Psycho-Analysis, 29*, 114.
Lehman, D. R., Wortman, C. B., & Williams, A. F. (1987). Long-term effects of losing a spouse or child in a motor vehicle crash. *Journal of Personality and Social Psychology, 52*(1), 218.
Lichtenthal, W. G., Burke, L. A., & Neimeyer, R. A. (2011). Religious coping and meaning-making following the loss of a loved one. *Counseling and Spirituality, 30*(2), 113–135.
Lipner, J. (2012). *Hindus: Their religious beliefs and practices*. Routledge.
Markus, H., & Nurius, P. (1986). Possible selves. *American Psychologist, 41*(9), 954.

McCarthy, J. R., Evans, R., Bowlby, S., & Wouango, J. (2020). Making sense of family deaths in urban Senegal: Diversities, contexts, and comparisons. *Omega, 82*(2), 230–260.
Medina, L., Sabo, S., & Vespa, J. (2020). *Living longer: Historical and projected life expectancy in the United States, 1960 to 2060 population estimates and projections*. Current population reports. www.census.gov/content/dam/Census/library/publications/2020/demo/p25-1145.pdf).
National Cremation. (2015). *Why is cremation becoming more popular in the US?* Retrieved April 25, 2024, from https://www.nationalcremation.com/cremation-information/why-is-cremation-becoming-more-popular-in-the-us
Neimeyer, R. A., Baldwin, S. A., & Gillies, J. (2006). Continuing bonds and reconstructing meaning: Mitigating complications in bereavement. *Death Studies, 30*(8), 715–738.
Neimeyer, R. A., Klass, D., & Dennis, M. K. (2014). A social constructionist account of grief: Loss and the narration of meaning. *Death Studies, 38*, 1–14.
Norenzayan, A., & Lee, A. (2010). It was meant to happen: Explaining cultural variations in fate attributions. *Journal of Personality and Social Psychology, 98*(5), 702.
Oregon Government Health Authority. (2020, March 6). *Oregon death with dignity act: Annual report.* https://www.oregon.gov/oha/ph/providerpartnerresources/evaluationresearch/deathwithdignityact/pages/ar-index.aspx
Park, C. L., & Folkman, S. (1997). Meaning in the context of stress and coping. *Review of General Psychology, 1*(2), 115–144.
Pew Research Center. (2011, December 19). *Regional distribution of Christians*. www.pewresearch.org/religion/2011/12/19/global-christianity-regions/
Pew Research Center. (2012, December, 18). *The global religious landscape*. www.pewresearch.org/religion/2012/12/18/global-religious-landscape-exec/
Pew Research Center. (2017). *Why Muslims are the world's fastest growing religious group*. www.pewresearch.org/short-reads/2017/04/06/why-muslims-are-the-worlds-fastest-growing-religious-group/
Pew Research Center. (2021, November 23). *Views on the afterlife*. www.pewresearch.org/religion/2021/11/23/views-on-the-afterlife/
Piaget, J. (1936). O trabalho por equipes na escola. *Tradução De Luiz G.Feiure.Revista De Educação–Diretoria do Ensino do Estado De São Paulo Set/Dez.*
Raudon, S. (2011). *Contemporary funerals and mourning practices: An investigation of five secular countries*. Winston Churchill Memorial Trust.
Rotter, J. B. (1966). Generalized expectancies for internal versus external control of reinforcement. *Psychological Monographs: General and Applied, 80*(1), 1.
Roy, K., Messina, L., Smith, J., & Waters, D. (2014). Growing up as "man of the house": Adultification and transition into adulthood for young men in economically disadvantaged families. *New Directions for Child and Adolescent Development, 2014*(143), 55–72.
Schuler, T. A., Zaider, T. I., & Kissane, D. W. (2012). Family grief therapy: A vital model in oncology, palliative care and bereavement. *Family Matters, 90*, 77–86.
Schwass, M. (2005). *Last words: Approaches to death in New Zealand's cultures and faiths*. Bridget Williams Books.
Sharma, I., Pandit, B., Pathak, A., & Sharma, R. (2013). Hinduism, marriage and mental illness. *Indian Journal of Psychiatry, 55*(Suppl 2), S243.
Sharpe, T. L. (2015). Understanding the sociocultural context of coping for African American family members of homicide victims: A conceptual model. *Trauma, Violence, & Abuse, 16*(1), 48–59.
Specht, J., Egloff, B., & Schmukle, S. C. (2010). *The benefits of believing in chance or fate: External locus of control as a protective factor for coping with the death of a spouse* (SOEPpaper No. 317).
Starkey, J. (2009). Death, paradise and the Arabian nights. *Mortality, 14*(3), 286–302.
Toller, P. W. (2008). Bereaved parents' negotiation of identity following the death of a child. *Communication Studies, 59*(4), 306–321.

Velho, G. (2003). In J. Zahar (Ed.), *Anthropology of complex societies: Project metamorphose* (3rd ed.).

Walter, T. (2017). *What death means now: Thinking critically about dying and grieving*. Bristol University Press/Policy Press.

Yan, H. & Bowman, R. (2019). A priest condemned suicide while speaking at a teen's funeral. Now a grieving mother is suing him. https://www.cnn.com/2019/11/20/us/michigan-mom-sues-priest-for-condemning-suicide-at-funeral/index.html

Chapter 2
Culture and Bereavement Theories/Models

In this chapter, bereavement theories and models for understanding and coping with loss will be discussed. Some theories and models are stage based, whereas others are not. The following would be reviewed: grief work, the four tasks of mourning, the dual process model, continuing bond with the deceased, meaning reconstruction, and intuitive versus instrumental grievers.

Grief Work

Sigmund Freud (1917) suggests that bereaved persons cannot hold on to deceased loved ones while trying to move on with life at the same time. That would be counterintuitive. Additionally, the pain and suffering from not letting go of the deceased could lead to unresolved grief. Therefore, the bereaved person has to break ties with the deceased, in order to move on with their life or enter into new relationships. By holding on to thoughts of the deceased, the bereaved would not become "free and uninhibited again" (Freud, 1917/1957, p.245). To break ties with the deceased would therefore require a conscious effort, hence *grief work*.

Following his daughter's death, however, Sigmund Freud had to reverse his initial thoughts, as he found it completely difficult to move on from the thoughts of his deceased daughter. In a letter to Leonard Binswanger, a colleague, Freud noted:

> *Although we know that after such a loss the acute state of mourning will subside, we also know that we shall remain inconsolable and will never find a substitute [for the person who died]. No matter what may fill the gap, even if it be filled completely, it nevertheless remains something else*. (E.L. Freud, 1992, p. 386)

As Freud (1960) would later acknowledge, to forego the memories of a deceased loved one is a difficult task.

F. E. Eyetsemitan, *Cultural Influences in Coping with Grief*,
https://doi.org/10.1007/978-3-031-86817-7_2

Personal and cultural dimensions: To forego the memories of the deceased loved one could be a personal or cultural imperative. A study of bereaved persons in Ecuador by researcher Terrah Foster et al. (2012) found that majority of their study respondents (71%) said they found comfort by keeping the memories of their deceased loved ones. These included keeping personal belongings/photographs, talking/praying to the deceased, enjoying activities the deceased participated in while alive, and visiting cemetery.

Yet 55% of the respondents said they felt uncomfortable keeping reminders of their deceased loved ones as they elicited pain, especially when the death was unexpected or the result of violence. Unexpected death from an accident or from drug overdose was said to cause much discomfort (Foster et al., 2012).

Among Indigenous Australians (Aboriginals) who make up about 3.3% of the Australian population, researcher Kate Jones (2015) notes that certain cultural practices are put in place to help reduce the pain of bereavement. These include destroying personal belongings of the deceased, relocating from the house where the deceased person had died, and changing one's name if a namesake to the deceased. Thus, any cue that triggers the deceased person's memory is viewed as discomfiting (Jones, 2015).

The Four Tasks of Mourning

Psychologist William Worden (2018), in his four tasks of mourning, lays out the stages a bereaved person has to go through in coping with a death. Similar to Freud's (1917) grief work, the survivor has to make a conscious effort in going through these stages:

Acknowledge the loss: There has to be a conscious acceptance of the loss, in order to move on. Otherwise, the survivor might remain hopeful that the loved one is still alive somewhere. Thus, viewing of the decedent's body would be helpful.

Feel the pain of the loss: Due to attachments formed, death brings about a painful separation, even when it is expected (e.g., Neimeyer et al., 2014). Therefore, the survivor should feel free to experience the discomfort caused by the loss. Each person reacts differently to pain caused by a death. Also, the pain experience could be expressed differently across sociocultural groups. Most cultures are permissive to females in the outward expression of pain, unlike their male counterparts who are expected to be less demonstrative of their pain experience.

Pain experience appears to be a healthy approach to coping with bereavement (Worden, 2018). However, the general attitude of friends and family members is to try and minimize, placate, or distract the bereaved person from experiencing pain. This is done through their constant presence, by sharing in the pain experience by crying, and/or by distracting the bereaved with positive stories or having the presence of little children needing attention. Usually, this is done at the initial stage of bereavement when the pain experience is intense. Researcher Kate Jones

(2015) notes that among Indigenous people of Australia, the pain experience in bereavement is a collective experience. It is referred to as a "sorry business," whereby in sharing the pain of the survivor community members gather to eat, drink, talk, and cry. However, some bereaved persons prefer their pain experience be private and would request for privacy, accordingly. In individualistic cultures (mostly Western societies), this request would be acceptable or honored. However, in collectivist cultures (mostly non-Western societies), such a request would be unacceptable. For example, in the United States, following death by suicide at age 55 of fashion designer Kate Spade, family members of the deceased issued the following statement:

> *We are all devastated by today's tragedy. We loved Kate dearly and will miss her terribly. We would ask that our privacy be respected as we grieve during this very difficult time.* (Simmons, June 5, 2018)

As earlier noted, children help to distract the survivor with positive thoughts. Distraction or avoidance behavior is adaptive, especially when it allows the individual to maintain control over his or her environment (e.g., Hofmann & Hay, 2018).

Yet certain cultural and/or religious practices ensure that distraction or avoidance behavior does not stand in the way of the griever in experiencing the pain of their loss. In Jewish tradition, for example, certain actions are prescribed in the grieving process. In the 7 days following a death, known as *shiva*, the bereaved person sits on a low stool or on the floor to demonstrate the emotional low caused by the death. During this period, the survivor pays little attention to personal hygiene, including bathing or shaving (Lamm, 1969).

Also, the Bapedi ethnic group of South America believes that the experience of pain restores the harmony disrupted by death. Thus, in the 6 months to 1 year following a death, a widower is forbidden from having intimate relationships (Baloyi, 2019).

<u>Replace the role of the deceased:</u> With death comes lost roles, e.g., breadwinner. Therefore, to successfully cope with a loss, the decedent's roles should be replaced. As an implicit benefit, replacement of the decedent's role could lead to personal growth (e.g., Calhoun et al., 2010). Being thrust into a new role (e.g., a breadwinner), the bereaved could acquire new skills and experience, resulting in a transformative experience (Triplett et al., 2012). To step into the role left behind by the deceased, however, could be a voluntary or an involuntary act. For some bereaved persons, to take on the deceased person's role could be a daunting task, especially if they are lacking in self-efficacy and/or competence in the new role (Bandura, 1977). Most societies segment roles along gender lines. As noted by Eyetsemitan (2022), it may not be culturally acceptable to cross gender lines to take on the opposite gender's role. Thus, a third party may have to assume the role left behind by the deceased, if it is gender prescribed. For example, through a remarriage a widower could have a surrogate mother for his little children or get help from female family members or friends.

Yet roles can be difficult to replace because they can be personified. A former student once reminded this author that "Nobody can replace my mom."

After the loss of a child, an interesting discussion on what becomes of the parent status ensues: Is he or she no longer a *parent* of the deceased child or does the dead child becomes parentless? Does the parent include the dead child in counting his total number of children (Eyetsemitan, 2022)? In roles, this addresses the issue of *continuing bonds*.

<u>Memorialize the deceased and move on with your life</u>: During this stage the bereaved finds ways to keep alive the memory of the deceased while also moving forward with his or her life. An example would be to keep alive the memory of a deceased spouse while also entering into a new relationship. Stephanie Petit (2018) reports that American journalist Katie Couric still memorializes her deceased husband 20 years after his death, even though she has since remarried (Petit, January 24, 2018).

Some bereaved individuals find it difficult to do both, however. They hold on to their loss and do not move on with their life with new relationships. This might lead to *complicated grief or prolonged grief disorder*; that is, the inability to integrate one's grief into normal functioning. In the United States, about 7–10% of bereaved individuals experience complicated grief that affects both physical and mental health (Dutton & Zisook, 2005). In complicated grief, psychiatrist Katherine Shear (2012) notes that the survivor constantly ruminates on the circumstances of the death and persistently avoids reminders of the deceased. There is also a continuous concern about what the future holds without the deceased and an inability to find meaning to their loss. Another factor likely to contribute to complicated grief is that the bereaved person is unable to give up on their *memory of habits* that involves the deceased. For example, they eat or watch a particular television program together (Eyetsemitan, 2022).

The Dual Process Model (DPM)

The dual process model of bereavement, proposed by researcher Margaret Stroebe and colleague (Stroebe & Schut, 1999), suggests that the bereaved oscillates between attending to the pain of their loss (loss orientation (LO)) and moving forward with life in filling the void created by their loss (restoration orientation (RO)). This is contrary to the stage sequence in William Worden's (2018) four stages of grief. In other words, the bereaved is not focusing on the pain of their loss *all the time*, neither is he/she focusing on moving on with his/her life *all the time*. During the oscillation period, an indication that the bereaved is coping well with their loss is when he/she spends relatively less time in loss orientation than in restoration orientation.

However, the bereaved could spend relatively less time in loss orientation yet more time in restoration orientation because of the necessity to be "strong for others" (Eyetsemitan, 2021). In this case, the bereaved is forced to *stifle* her grief

(Eyetsemitan, 1998). Also, due to cultural norms (e.g., shiva in the Jewish tradition), the bereaved may be restricted to loss orientation, even when the need to move on to restoration orientation.

Researcher Ruth McManus and colleagues (McManus et al., 2018) reviewed two disaster incidences in New Zealand (the New Zealand's Christchurch earthquake and the Pike River mine disasters) against the backdrop of Stroebe and Schut's (1999) dual process model of grief.

These researchers report that more emphasis is placed on restoration orientation (RO) than on loss orientation (LO), especially when government agencies are involved and when a disaster brings about material disruptions that could affect the survivors' day-to-day living. Additionally, these researchers note that authorities could manipulate restoration orientation to downplay personal loss experience, especially when the grief is a collective experience. These researchers cautioned that with the desire to emphasize restoration orientation, less attention could be given to loss orientation. The same situation could apply in bereavement counseling when more attention is given to loss orientation over restoration orientation (McManus et al., 2018).

Continuing Bond with the Deceased

As researcher Dennis Klass and colleagues (Klass et al., 1996) note, memories of the deceased should not hinder the bereaved from moving on with his or her life. People like Katie Couric, mentioned earlier, are able to do so successfully (Petit, 2018). Psychiatrist John Baker (2001) explains that the internal state of the bereaved can be transformed from mourning and, therefore, allows for the physical absence of the deceased to be accommodated. However, for some bereaved persons, to forego the memories of the decedent would lead to a change in identify. It is for this reason that some widows/widowers refuse to remarry. According to John Bowlby (1980): "For many widows and widowers it is precisely because they are willing for their feelings of attachment to the dead spouse to persist that their sense of identity is preserved and they become able to reorganize their lives along lines they find meaningful" (Bowlby, 1980; p.98). There is a reason to maintain continuing bond with the deceased but not necessarily to keep one's identify. In non-Western cultures, belief in the supernatural powers of the deceased over the living is a reason to maintaining continuing bond with the deceased. In African culture, for example, the death of a child could be attributed to the wrath of an angry deceased ancestor (e.g., Maboea, 2002). Therefore, to appease the deceased, continuing bond with the deceased is maintained *through ancestor worship* (Eyetsemitan, 2022).

Meaning Reconstruction

The *meaning* ascribed to a death helps to make sense with a loss (Gillies & Neimeyer, 2006). For some deaths, no word adequately describes or explains the loss. A loss from suicide could have a very profound impact on the bereaved. Yet if a suicide note is left behind, this helps with sensemaking. In most societies different types of death are experienced (e.g., suicide, homicide, genocide). Therefore, the meaning an individual ascribes to a death could reflect the normative meaning his or her culture ascribes to death. Reflecting on the difference between the European culture and the Chinese culture in a death by suicide, researcher Zhao Xiurong (2020) notes that suicide among the Europeans in the early modern times is condemned and is a crime and the survivors are humiliated. During the same period, however, suicide in the Chinese culture is handled differently; the survivors or the body from a suicide death is not despised. Besides, unlike the Europeans, the Chinese have different classifications for suicide: suicide for moral reason, suicide to redress a wrong, or suicide to admonish others. Based on Christian ideology, the Europeans believe that nobody but God has the right to take a life, irrespective of the motive for suicide. However, with time the European culture has evolved. Now, suicide is understood as a mental health issue (e.g., Windfuhr & Kapur, 2011).

Grieving rules may change due to modernization influences but may also reflect what is convenient for a community. The Auhelawa tribe in Papua New Guinea abandoned traditional practices in mourning and instead embraced government ideas and Christian teaching (Schram, 2007). They realized that traditional practices were time-consuming and slowed down their return to normal life. They were spending too much time on loss orientation and less time on restoration orientation (e.g., McManus et al., 2018). Researcher Ryan Schram (2007) reported on how the death of a prominent community leader caused the cancellation of a future sporting event that the community had looked forward to enjoying, due to the observance of traditional burial rites, which also affected church attendance on Sunday. This did not sit well with most members of the community which led to a change in grieving rules.

Intuitive Versus Instrumental Grievers

Researchers Kenneth Doka and Terry Martin (2011) identify two types of grievers: The *intuitive* griever is more emotional, and the *instrumental* griever is more cognitive. In most cultures, the intuitive griever is the female, whereas the instrumental griever is the male. Culturally, females are allowed more expression of their emotion than males. Yet emotions could be internally experienced and males could be intuitive grievers as well. The same applies to females as instrumental grievers. These grieving styles are not gender specific (Doka & Martin, 2011).

Grieving styles could also reflect how each individual copes with a stressful situation. Stress is from internal or external demands beyond an individual's available resources to cope. Therefore, to cope with stress requires the management of these excessive demands (Lazarus & Folkman, 1984). The following approaches are suggested for coping with stress:

Problem focused: In a *problem-focused* approach, coping efforts are made to solving, minimizing, or reducing the impact of the stressful situation (Schoenmakers et al., 2015). The instrumental griever in bereavement makes an effort to filling the void or solving the problem created by the loved one's death, including taking on new roles and responsibilities or being "strong for others."

Meaning focused: In a *meaning-focused* approach, an existing belief, value, or philosophy provides a perspective for coping with the stressful situation (Folkman & Moskowitz, 2007). For example, a meaning could be based on the belief that a death is "on time" or "off time" and that a death is "God's will" or "not God's will." The instrumental griever could cope with death in this manner as well.

Emotion focused: In an *emotion-focused* approach, efforts are made to regulate the emotional consequences of the stressful situation (Schoenmakers et al., 2015). The death of a loved one brings about emotional reactions. By taking on new roles and responsibilities or being "strong for others," this could regulate emotional reactions. Also, the belief that a death is on time or is God's will could regulate emotions as well. However, if emotions are not adequately regulated, these could have adverse impact on cognitive thoughts. Yet the experience of pain is part of the bereavement process (e.g., Worden, 2018; Stroebe & Schut, 1999) and should be encouraged (McManus et al., 2018).

The dual process model (DPM) by Stroebe and Schut (1999), discussed earlier, suggests that the survivor oscillates between loss orientation (similar to intuitive grieving) and restoration orientation (akin to instrumental grieving). In other words, the bereaved moves in and out of both coping styles (intuitive and instrumental). In William Worden's (2018) four stages of mourning, the bereaved engages in both intuitive and instrumental grieving but in a sequential manner.

Disenfranchised Grief

Researcher Kenneth Doka (1987) suggests that the bereaved becomes a *disenfranchised* griever when his or her loss is not acknowledged by society. This makes it difficult to cope with a loved one's death. As examples, losses from the following situations result in disenfranchised grief (Kenneth Doka, 2002, 2008):

(a) A relationship that is not socially approved (e.g., extramarital affair).
(b) A relationship not based on recognizable ties (e.g., neighbors, friends, coworkers, companion animals).
(c) A past relationship (e.g., ex-lover).
(d) A loss that does not generate spontaneity in social support. (e.g., suicide).

Additionally, a grieving style that defies gender norms (e.g., male grieving as a female or female grieving as a male) could go unrecognized.

In disenfranchised grief, the grief is denied *publicly*. Yet the grief remains private to the survivor. According to philosopher Thomas Attig (2004), in disenfranchised grief, the bereaved is denied the "right" to grief that is granted to everyone else. Yet the survivor can exercise the right to grieve among like-minded people who validate their loss (e.g., people who have experienced a similar loss in pregnancy).

Parental identity is a challenge that parents face after the loss of a child. The issue of parental identity impacts on coping with bereavement. Some parents want to keep alive their deceased children's memory. Yet such a behavior may not receive the validation of others, including family members and friends (Toller, 2008). Researcher Paige Toller (2008) studied 53 bereaved parents who experienced the death of a child. Prior to start of the study, the period of child's death ranged from 6 months to 29 years, with an average of 9.7 years. At death the children's ages ranged from 0 years to 42 years, with an average of 7.7 years. The parents in Toller's (2008) study wanted to maintain their parental identity by tending to their deceased children's grave, regularly. They saw this action as furthering their parental nurturing role. In response to disapproving family members and friends, the bereaved parents adopted the following approaches: (a) limit their interactions with non-supportive family and friends; (b) interact mostly with bereaved individuals with similar experience; and (c) counterbalance non-supportive persons with supportive individuals.

In Toller's (2008) study the bereaved parents are disenfranchised grievers, *if* they aligned their behavior to those of disapproving family members and friends. Instead they chose an environment that approved of their grief. In other words, humans can exercise *agency* even when their grief is disenfranchised (Eyetsemitan, 2022).

In exercise of human agency, however, cultural values could have an intermediary role. Funerals provide context for both expression of and acknowledgment of grief. As noted by sociologist Tony Walter and colleague (Walter & Bailey, 2020) in funerals, the *family* as opposed to personal relationships to the deceased can define grieving rules. Tony Walter and colleague (2020) reviewed accounts of funeral attendees in England and noted the central role of family in funerals. Funerals are occasions for grief expression not just by family members but also friends, neighbors, or coworkers of the deceased. Yet during funerals family members have reserved seating closer to the decedent's casket than nonfamily members. Compared to family members, nonfamily members' grief appeared to be disenfranchised. Tony Walter and colleague (2018) note that nonfamily members never complained about this arrangement, and, therefore, their grief cannot be pathologized. Instead, with preferential treatment given to family members, nonfamily members acknowledged that family members, especially children and grandchildren with biological ties to the deceased, helped to concretize the symbolic immortality of the deceased (Walter & Bailey, 2020). Similarly, in the first 3 days following a death, in orthodox Jewish tradition the family members' grief is expected to be more intense than that of non-family members (Kalish, 1980).

Thus, disenfranchised grief may have a subjective component at odds with objective evaluations. Also, cultural context provides a relative understanding to the construct.

Researcher Tony Walter (2010) proposes a checklist of questions (and answers) that takes into consideration the cultural background of the survivor. A question raised is whether a society's dominant belief system can marginalize the grieving rules of minority group members in that society? For example, in the United States, where the dominant belief system is to approach life with optimism and to consider death as a loss, would the grief of minority groups such as African Americans and Native Americans who dwell on loss be pathologized or be disenfranchised (e.g., Doka, 1987)? Tony Walter (2010) sounds a note of caution that within each society, there are heterogenous belief systems (some major and others minor) that affect grief rules.

The Disruption of Daily Functioning Scale in Bereavement

A complicated grief is persistent and prolonged and has the bereaved person's daily functioning compromised as a result (Shear, 2012). Psychiatrist Katherine Shear (2012) identifies the following characteristics that are associated with complicated grief:

- Continuous rumination about the circumstance of the death.
- Continuous worrying about what the future holds in the absence of the deceased.
- Inability to find meaning to the loss.
- Excessive avoidance of reminders of the loss.

Complicated grief occurs when neither cognitive nor affective aspect of grief is helpful in coping with bereavement. It reflects the inability to cognitively regulate the emotion of pain (Burton et al., 2012; Golden & Dalgleish, 2012).

Certain predispositional factors contribute to complicated grief including personality type, genetic makeup, age, cultural factors, or spirituality. Older adults, especially older women, are more prone to complicated grief than younger adults, due to experience with multiple losses and spousal loss (Kersting et al., 2011).

In coping with complicated grief, psychiatrist Katherine Shear (2012) recommends the redirecting of cognitive thoughts. However, for a grief to be described as complicated, there should be a violation of cultural norms. Therefore, diagnostic tools used for complicated grief should be culturally sensitive (Prigerson et al., 2009).

Based on John Bowlby's (1980) attachment theory, death causes a severance of attachment between the living and the dead. The depth of attachment to the deceased could predict the depth of loss experienced by the bereaved. Consequently, the depth of loss experienced could impact on the survivor's daily functioning. Yet each survivor's daily functioning is unique. The disruption of daily functioning pertaining to one individual may not be similar for another. For example, to one individual, the disruption of daily functioning may pertain to having daily meals with the deceased which will no longer obtain. To another person, it may be watching a particular TV program with the deceased which has now ceased. In coping with a loss, therefore, a "disruption of daily functioning scale in bereavement" could help to provide insight into the following:

(a) Depth of the loss.
(b) Progress made in coping with a loss.

There are five levels to the disruption of daily functioning scale proposed in bereavement:

Level 1: No disruption to daily functioning.
At level 1, there is no disruption to daily functioning because the deceased was not a part of the daily life of the survivor. Attachment to the deceased is at 0%. For example, prior to death, a severance of attachment to a dying loved one could occur, with the survivor's daily functioning having been adjusted beforehand, in post-loss.

Level 2: Weak disruption of daily functioning.
At level 2, there is a weak disruption to the daily functioning of the survivor. When alive, the deceased featured in the survivor's daily functioning at about 25%. With the balance of 75%, in daily functioning the survivor devotes relatively less time to the pain of the loss but more time on moving forward with their life (e.g., Stroebe & Schut, 1999).

Level 3: Moderate disruption of daily functioning.
At level 3, there is a moderate disruption to the daily functioning of the survivor. It is at about 50%. The deceased constitutes an important element in the daily life of the survivor, yet the survivor is able to balance the amount of time attending to the pain of the loss and moving forward with her life (e.g., Stroebe & Schut, 1999).

Level 4: Significant disruption of daily functioning.
At level 4, a significant interruption to the daily life of the survivor occurs. Prior to death, the deceased had a remarkable impact on the survivor's daily functioning. Therefore, the survivor devotes 75% of his/her time to experiencing the pain of the loss with only one-quarter of his/her time devoted to moving forward with his/her life.

Level 5: Very significant disruption of daily functioning.
At level 5, the loss has quite a profound impact on the daily functioning of the deceased. The deceased devotes his/her entire time to experiencing the pain of the loss, with symptoms reminiscent of complicated grief or prolonged grief disorder. As earlier noted, psychiatrist Katherine Shear (2012) describes these symptoms to include (a) continuous rumination about what caused the death, (b) continuous concerns about life without the deceased, (c) excessive avoidance of reminders of the deceased, and (4) inability to find meaning or explanation to the loss.

Of pertinent importance in complicated grief or prolonged grief disorder is the *disruption of daily functioning* of the bereaved. Thus, the "disruption of daily functioning scale in bereavement" is useful in monitoring the progress being made by the bereaved with complicated grief or prolonged grief (from level 5 to level 1). An approach proposed in therapy for complicated grief or prolonged grief disorder is to change cognitive functioning first with behavior to follow (e.g., Shear, 2012). However, with the disruption of daily functioning scale, a survivor with the help of a bereavement counselor could recover his or her daily functioning first, with cognitive functioning to follow. Yet behaving one way and thinking another way could result in cognitive dissonance. Psychologist Leon Festinger (1957) however suggests that to reduce the distress caused by cognitive dissonance, a person can change the way they think to align with their behavior.

Key Takeaways

1. The grief pattern for each survivor is unique. Each model or a combination of grief models could help with understanding the grief trajectory of a survivor. However, a model that is helpful to one survivor may not be helpful to another. For example, as important as exploring the meaning for a loss, this may not be helpful to every survivor.
2. Not every bereaved person whose grief is disenfranchised may perceive it the same way.
3. In coping with a loss, cultural values and beliefs could influence personal values and beliefs.

Critical Cultural Thinking

1. If you have experienced a death or know of someone who has, which coping model or combination of bereavement models would help with explaining your or that person's situation?
2. John lost his son and keeps his room intact because John wants to hold on to reminders of his son. However, Peter who lost his son moved out of their home and does not want any reminders of the deceased. Who is coping better with their loss?

References

Attig, T. (2004). Disenfranchised grief revisited: Discounting hope and love. *OMEGA-Journal of Death and Dying, 49*(3), 197–215.

Baker, J. E. (2001). Mourning and the transformation of object relationships: Evidence for the persistence of internal attachments. *Psychoanalytic Psychology, 18*(1), 55.

Baloyi, L. (2019): *The African conception of death: A cultural implication*. Accessed May 17, 2023, from www.iaccp.org/wp-content/uploads/2019/04/Baloyi.pdf

Bandura, A. (1977). Self-efficacy: Toward a unifying theory of behavioral change. *Psychological Review, 84*(2), 191.

Bowlby, J. (1980). *Attachment and loss* (Loss, sadness and depression) (Vol. 3). Basic Books.

Burton, C. L., Yan, O. H., Pat-Horenczyk, R., Chan, I. S., Ho, S., & Bonanno, G. A. (2012). Coping flexibility and complicated grief: A comparison of American and Chinese samples. *Depression and Anxiety, 29*(1), 16–22.

Calhoun, L. G., Cann, A., & Tedeschi, R. G. (2010). The posttraumatic growth model: Sociocultural considerations. In T. Weiss & R. Berger (Eds.), *Posttraumatic growth and culturally competent practice: Lessons learned from around the globe* (pp. 1–14). Wiley.

Doka, K. J. (1987). Silent sorrow: Grief and the loss of significant others. *Death Studies, 11*(6), 455–469.

Doka, K. J. (2002). *Disenfranchised grief: New directions, challenges, and strategies for practice*. Research Press Publication.

Doka, K. J. (2008). Disenfranchised grief in historical and cultural perspective. In M. S. Stroebe, R. O. Hansson, H. Schut, & W. Stroebe (Eds.), *Handbook of bereavement research and practice: Advances in theory and intervention* (pp. 223–240). American Psychological Association.

Doka, K. J., & Martin, T. L. (2011). *Grieving beyond gender: Understanding the ways men and women mourn*. Routledge.

Dutton, Y. C., & Zisook, S. (2005). Adaptation to bereavement. *Death Studies, 29*(10), 877–903.

Eyetsemitan, F. (1998). Stifled grief in the workplace. *Death Studies, 22*(5), 469–479.

Eyetsemitan, F. E. (2021). *Death, dying, and bereavement around the world: Theories, varied views and customs*. Charles C Thomas Publisher.

Eyetsemitan, F. E. (2022). Bereavement theories and models. In *The deceased-focused approach to grief: An alternative model* (pp. 59–76). Springer Nature.

Festinger, L. (1957). *A theory of cognitive dissonance*. Stanford University Press.

Folkman, S., & Moskowitz, J. T. (2007). Positive affect and meaning-focused coping during significant psychological stress. *The Scope of Social Psychology: Theory and Applications, 10*, 193–208.

Foster, T. L., Dietrich, M. S., Friedman, D. L., Gordon, J. E., & Gilmer, M. J. (2012). National survey of children's hospitals on legacy-making activities. *Journal of Palliative Medicine, 15*(5), 573–578.

Freud, A. (1960). Discussion of Dr. John Bowlby's paper. *The Psychoanalytic Study of the Child, 15*(1), 53–62.

Freud, E. L. (1992). *Letters of Sigmund Freud*. Courier Corporation.

Freud, S. (1917). Mourning and melancholia. *The Standard Edition of the Complete Psychological Works of Sigmund Freud, 14*(1914–1916), 237–258.

Gillies, J., & Neimeyer, R. A. (2006). Loss, grief, and the search for significance: Toward a model of meaning reconstruction in bereavement. *Journal of Constructivist Psychology, 19*(1), 31–65.

Golden, A. J., & Dalgleish, T. (2012). Facets of pejorative self-processing in complicated grief. *Journal of Consulting and Clinical Psychology, 80*(3), 512.

Hofmann, S. G., & Hay, A. C. (2018). Rethinking avoidance: Toward a balanced approach to avoidance in treating anxiety disorders. *Journal of Anxiety Disorders, 55*, 14–21.

Jones, K. (2015). *It is normal to remember: Death and grief in Australia* (pp. 243–263). Cultural Perspectives on Death in Families.

Kalish, R. (1980). *Death and dying: Views from many cultures*. Routledge.

Kersting, A., Brähler, E., Glaesmer, H., & Wagner, B. (2011). Prevalence of complicated grief in a representative population-based sample. *Journal of Affective Disorders, 131*(1–3), 339–343.

Klass, D., Silverman, P., & Nickman, S. (1996). *Continuing bonds: New understandings of grief*. Taylor & Francis.

Lamm, M. (1969). *The Jewish way in death and mourning*. Jonathan David Publishers.
Lazarus, R. S., & Folkman, S. (1984). *Stress, appraisal, and coping*. Springer Publishing Company.
Maboea, S. I. (2002). *The influence of life-giving power in the African traditional religion and the zionist churches in Soweto: A comparative study*. University of South Africa Press.
McManus, R., Walter, T., & Claridge, L. (2018). Restoration and loss after disaster: Applying the dual process model of coping in bereavement. *Death Studies, 42*, 405–414.
Neimeyer, R. A., Klass, D., & Dennis, M. K. (2014). A social constructionist account of grief: Loss and the narration of meaning. *Death Studies, 0*, 1–14.
Petit, S. (2018, January 24). *Katie Couric remembers late husband Jay Monahan on 20th Anniversary of his death: 'We miss you'*. www.people.com/tv/katie-couric-remembers-late-husband-jay-monahan/).
Prigerson, H. G., Horowitz, M. J., Jacobs, S. C., Parkes, C. M., Aslan, M., Goodkin, K., et al. (2009). Prolonged grief disorder: Psychometric validation of criteria proposed for DSM-V and ICD-11. *PLoS Medicine, 6*(8), e1000121.
Schoenmakers, E. C., van Tilburg, T. G., & Fokkema, T. (2015). Problem-focused and emotion-focused coping options and loneliness: How are they related? *European Journal of Ageing, 12*, 153–161.
Schram, R. (2007). Sit, cook, eat, full stop: Religion and the rejection of ritual in auhelawa (Papua New Guinea). *Oceania, 77*(2), 172–190.
Shear, M. K. (2012). Getting straight about grief. *Depression and Anxiety, 29*(6), 461–464.
Simmons, S. (2018, June 5). *Kate Spade's family just released a heartbreaking statement about her death*. www.bustle.com/p/kate-spades-family-statement-about-her-death-asks-for-privacy-during-grief-9299806
Stroebe, M., & Schut, H. (1999). The dual process model of coping with bereavement: Rationale and description. *Death Studies, 23*(3), 197–224.
Toller, P. W. (2008). Bereaved parents' negotiation of identity following the death of a child. *Communication Studies, 59*(4), 306–321.
Triplett, K. N., Tedeschi, R. G., Cann, A., Calhoun, L. G., & Reeve, C. L. (2012). Posttraumatic growth, meaning in life, and life satisfaction in response to trauma. *Psychological Trauma: Theory, Research, Practice, and Policy, 4*(4), 400.
Walter, T. (2010). Grief and culture. *Bereavement Care, 29*(2), 5–9.
Walter, T., & Bailey, T. (2020). How funerals accomplish family: Findings from a mass-observation study. *OMEGA - Journal of Death and Dying, 82*(2), 175–195.
Windfuhr, K., & Kapur, N. (2011). Suicide and mental illness: A clinical review of 15 years findings from the UK National Confidential Inquiry into suicide. *British Medical Bulletin, 100*(1), 101–121.
Worden, J. W. (2018). *Grief counseling and grief therapy: A handbook for the mental health practitioner*. Springer Publishing Company.
Xiurong, Z. (2020). An analysis of suicide in the Chinese and English cultural contexts in the early modern period. *Social Sciences in China, 41*(2), 183–204.

Chapter 3
Cultural Elements in Death, Dying, and Bereavement

Culture is both objective and subjective; that is, we can point to it (e.g., food, language, clothing), yet it can be internalized in our thoughts, emotions, and behaviors.

Culture, Social Norms, and Beliefs

Over the years *culture* has been defined differently. Researcher Geert Hofstede (1994) defines culture as the collective programming of the mind that distinguishes membership in one group from another. Psychologist David Matsumoto (1996) describes culture as the shared values, attitudes, beliefs, and behaviors of a particular group of people, although with individual variations, that is communicated from one generation to another. While not codified as law, shared values, attitudes, beliefs, and behaviors become *social norms.*

Social norms are not legally enforced but are values, attitudes, beliefs, and behaviors that are typically expected as standards and are socially sanctioned, if need be. Social norms originate to either solve a problem or meet a need in society. Generally, social norms help a society to run smoothly (Brittanica.com, n.d.). Social norms can be learned by observing others, especially significant individuals in a person's life (Bandura, 1977), through reward or punishment (Skinner, 1948), or by observing the relationship between events that occur almost simultaneously (Pavlov, 1997).

Beliefs

As part of a society's social norms are *beliefs* that may originate from any of the learning methods earlier described.

F. E. Eyetsemitan, *Cultural Influences in Coping with Grief*,
https://doi.org/10.1007/978-3-031-86817-7_3

From different cultures around the world, beliefs form part of the social norm that help to regulate behaviors regarding death, dying, and bereavement. Of particular importance are beliefs about death causation as these can affect grief outcomes. In an autopsy report, a medical officer determines the cause of death which is included in a death certificate. Yet *beliefs* about the cause of death are equally important, even if contrary to a medical report. Although some beliefs may seem irrational, they nonetheless require the attention of bereavement counselors and healthcare practitioners. For example, the belief in evil forces, witchcraft, or evil acts as cause of death may seem irrational. Yet in Africa such beliefs can lead to the excuse of a medical malpractice in death causation (Baloyi, 2019). Researcher Schmidt-Leukel (2006) notes that "Evil spirits or witches may also cause death against God's intentions. Especially people who die at a young age or under strange circumstances are considered to be killed by evil forces (p. 41)."

A belief in "evil eye" (the belief that certain people can put a spell on others to cause them harm or death) as cause of death is commonplace in several central American countries including Panama, Dominican Republic, Honduras, and El Salvador where over 50% of Catholics hold such beliefs (Pew Research Center, November 13, 2014).

Cultural Value Systems

As earlier noted, researcher Geert Hofstede (1980) characterizes in most societies two broad value systems: *individualism* embraced mostly by Westerners and *collectivism* as practiced mostly by non-Westerners. Individualists have a tendency towards independence, self-containment, and autonomy. They also value equality, freedom, and an exciting lifestyle (Caffaro et al., 2014; Finkelstein, 2012). Collectivists however value social order, honoring of parents/elders and self-discipline. They also value relatedness, interdependence, and social obligation (Schwartz & Bilsky, 1990).

Social psychologist Harry Triandis (1995) provides the following broad dimensions to the individualism-collectivism construct:

1. *Definition of self*: In cultures that embrace individualism, the self is defined as autonomous, whereas in cultures with a tendency toward collectivism, the self is relational.
2. *Personal beliefs versus emphasis on norms*: In individualist cultures people are guided by personal beliefs and perceived rights, whereas in collectivist cultures norms, duties, and obligations help to guide behaviors.
3. *Structure of goals*: In individualist cultures the individual's goals and ambitions take precedence over those of others, whereas in collectivist cultures the individual ensures that his or her goals and ambitions are in harmony with those of others (e.g., tribe, kin, race, religion).

4. *Emphasis on rationality versus relatedness*: In individualist cultures, emphasis is on what is rational even when it hurts relationships, whereas in collectivist cultures attention is given to relatedness even when it is irrational.

Therefore, in coping with a loss, a bereaved person with individualist values may not abide by cultural norms. For example, he or she may decide to get into a new relationship at a time of his or her own choosing than a collectivist who may prefer to follow a culturally prescribed period of mourning.

The *individualist* culture influences bereavement practices in the following ways:

- Advance directive/living will that enables the deceased prior to death to make his or her choice known, regarding how they want to be treated if unable to make that decision in the future. With the knowledge of the decedent's choice, the bereaved is better able to cope with their loss.
- The death industry allows the bereaved to exercise choice in the services and products provided by casket manufacturers, morticians, funeral directors, funeral homes, and grief counselors. The exercise of choice aligns with individualist value system.
- The option to have physician-assisted suicide/euthanasia for the mentally competent but terminally ill person is provided and so is hospice as an alternative. Also, the bereaved is better able to cope with their loss knowing the choice of the deceased. Physician-assisted suicide or euthanasia is legalized in several countries (Table 3.1).

In these selected countries, mostly Western, an individualist value system seemed to be reflected in the legalization of physician-assisted suicide or euthanasia. Also, physician-assisted suicide is legal in the United States in several states and in the District of Columbia.

The *collectivist* culture however influences bereavement practices in the following ways:

Table 3.1 Selected countries where physician-assisted suicide or euthanasia is legalized

Country	Physician-assisted suicide	Euthanasia
Belgium	Legal	Legal
Canada	Legal	Legal
Columbia	Legal	Legal
Luxembourg	Legal	Legal
Netherlands	Legal	Legal
Switzerland	Legal	Illegal

Source: Davis, N. (2019): Euthanasia and physician-assisted suicide rates are soaring. But where are they legal? (https://www.theguardian.com/news/2019/jul/15/euthanasia-and-assisted-dying-rates-are-soaring-but-where-are-they-legal)

1. Elaborate funerals that include friends, family, and well-wishers with participation open to all. This aligns with the collectivist value of relatedness that makes bereavement a shared experience.
2. Limited choice in funeral and in burial practices to allow for norms and traditions to be affirmed in burials and funerals. Although limited in choice of funeral and burial practice, the bereaved is better able to cope with their loss knowing that norms and traditions were followed.
3. Rather than being an individual decision in advance directives, physician-assisted suicide or euthanasia, a group decision would have to prevail. In India (a collectivist culture), studies show that a physician respects the wishes of the family over the individual's. In Germany (an individualist society) where individual rights take precedence, the opposite is the case (Chattopadhyay & Simon, 2008). End-of-life decisions for the seriously ill among Latinos (with collectivist culture) are made by family members with little or no input from the patient (e.g., Kelley et al., 2010).

Cultural Values

Cross-cultural psychologist Shalom Schwartz (2012) notes that cultural values determine our attitudes, which could be positive or negative. Values point to what are important to us and form the basis by which we judge the actions of others. Through the value lens we can evaluate death as well. For example, a person with a high value for risk-taking behavior may better cope with a death that results from skydiving. This would be contrary to another individual who values safety, if a loved one's death resulted from skydiving. This individual may not cope well with such a death.

Values also occur in hierarchical order. The same value may have a high importance for one person yet a low value for another. For example, an individual high on patriotism may cope better with a loved one's death resulting from service to their country than another person with a low value for patriotism. Values provoke emotions (and actions), especially during the *acute stage* of grief. The acute stage of grief is the period immediately following a loss. It is characterized by extreme sadness, crying, and disinterest in normal daily activities (Zisook & Shear, 2009). After a period of 6 months, however, most people are able to make a transition from the acute stage of grief to the *integrated* phase of grief where emotional reactions become less intense and the bereaved is able to integrate the grief into their normal daily functioning. The period of time it takes to make the transition from acute grief to integrated grief may be determined by values. A death that aligns with the values of the survivor would take a relatively shorter time than a death that does not align with the values of the bereaved.

In the United States, between 7% and 10% of bereaved individuals fail to make the transition from acute grief to integrated grief, resulting in complicated grief or prolonged grief disorder (Shear, 2012).

Shalom Schwartz (2007) notes that in the midst of social and political transitions, cultural values hardly change. For example, the value of conformity is higher among Nigerians and Indonesians than among Germans and Swedes (Schwartz, 1994). A study by Scwartz (2007) of 80 countries identifies three polar opposite dimensions to values:

Autonomy vs. Embeddedness: In cultures that place emphasis on autonomy, people freely express their thoughts and are encouraged to do so. Autonomy is exercised both cognitively and emotionally, and it is expressed independently of others. For example, people can independently decide on how to grieve a loss, irrespective of cultural norms. In cultures that embrace embeddedness, however, independent cognitive and emotional expressions are discouraged. Thus, coping with a loss is reflective of cultural norms. In other words, burials and funerals for the deceased would be in conformity to cultural practices and expectations. A burial that aligns with cultural norms and expectations would help the bereaved to better adjust to their loss.

Egalitarianism vs. Hierarchy: In cultures that value egalitarianism, people are treated as equals, whereas in cultures that value hierarchy, the opposite is the case. In hierarchical cultures respect is given based on a person's age or gender. Older persons command more respect than younger individuals and males more than females. For example, in India the tradition of *sati (meaning virtuous woman)* demonstrates a cultural value based on gender. In this tradition, a widow accompanies her husband in death and is applauded as being virtuous. She jumps into her late husband's funeral pyre to be cremated alongside her husband. The husband however is exempt from this cultural practice. Although banned by the Indian government, this practice continues to be perpetuated in the rural areas because it validates the people's values of male superiority over females (Mukerjee, December 26, 1999).

Mastery vs. Harmony: In mastery cultures changes are made to the natural world to suit people's needs. In harmony cultures, however, the people align their needs to the natural world and hardly make changes to their natural world (Table 3.2).

Within each society, cultural values are not homogenous, and as noted by researcher Tony Walter (2010) in chapter 2, grief patterns of minority group members need to be acknowledged, as their cultural values may not align with that of the dominant culture. Also, cultural values over time are subject to changes due to modernization influences (Windfuhr & Kapur, 2011) and based on the convenience of group members (e.g., Schram, 2007). As a society modernizes with more demands on people's time (e.g., work), less time may be spent on loss orientation than on restoration orientation. Also, to meet the common good of all instead of the individual's may become a priority. For example, a disaster that affects the day-to-day functioning of community members makes restoration orientation become the focus of attention instead of loss orientation (McManus et al., 2018; Schram, 2007).

Table 3.2 Factors that influence coping with death and dying in individualist and collectivist cultures

Individualist culture	Collectivist culture
Funeral and mourning are personalized and aligned with the values of the deceased	Funeral and mourning are subject to collective norms
Belief in medical science as cause of death, e.g., autopsy reports	Belief in cause of death other than medical science (e.g., witchcraft, evil eye, sorcery)
Maintaining a continuing bond with the deceased is a personal choice, e.g., letter writing	Maintaining a continuing bond with the deceased is based on the cost/benefit of not doing so
A belief that life is linear and not circular	A belief that life is circular and not linear, e.g., reincarnation
Social support in grief is based on personal choice	Social support in grief is provided, irrespective of the survivor's choice
Decision of death by physician-assisted suicide or euthanasia is a personal choice	Decision of death by physician-assisted suicide or euthanasia requires the prevailing input of family members and friends
In bereavement, the survivor's needs are *more* important for attention	In bereavement, the decedent's needs are *more* important to avoid the perceived negative consequences for lack of attention

Source: Author's creation

Acculturation

With acculturation a person embraces another culture, which could lead to changes in cognition, emotion, and behavior (Berry, 2003; Tadmor et al., 2009). The initial focus of acculturation studies was on immigrants in a new culture (Berry, 2003), but it pertains also to international students, refugees, asylum seekers, and migrant workers (Berry, 2006). Acculturation could occur as well when a person is not a migrant but a resident in his or her home country. At the heart of acculturation is the influence of a dominant culture over a minority culture, which can occur among citizens in the same society. Yet, as humans, we can exercise agency in choosing our environment. John Berry's (2006) acculturation model has the following outcomes:

Assimilation: This occurs when a person adopts a foreign culture's norms and practices in replacement of their heritage culture. In coping with a loss, a bereaved person who has assimilated a foreign culture's norms and practices may reflect the value system of that foreign culture.

Integration: This happens when a person adopts a foreign culture's norms and practices but maintains his or her heritage culture as well. In coping with a loss, a bereaved individual integrates the norms and practices of both foreign culture and heritage culture.

Separation: This occurs when a person maintains his or her indigenous culture and rejects a foreign culture. In coping with a loss, a bereaved person with separation experience adheres to the values of their heritage culture.

Marginalization: This happens when a person rejects the norms and practices of both foreign and indigenous cultures. In coping with a loss, a bereaved person who is marginalized is guided by neither the values of the foreign culture nor those of their heritage culture. However, this acculturation outcome has come under scrutiny because it is almost impossible for an individual to lack a cultural sense of self (Del Pilar & Udasco, 2004). Yet it may apply to an individual who feels rejected by both the foreign culture and their heritage culture (Berry, 2006).

John Berry's (2006) acculturation model has been validated among Hispanic young adults in Miami, USA. This especially true for integration, separation, and assimilation outcomes (Schwartz & Zamboanga, 2008). However, Berry's (2006) acculturation model is limited to national origin. Within each nation, however, immigrants or foreign students come from different ethnic groups. Therefore, to lump them up may confound results in acculturation studies (Rudmin, 2003). Also, while it is a foreign student or migrant's choice on how to acculturate, contextual imperatives as well have consequential impact on acculturation outcomes. For example, an English-speaking migrant can easily adopt an assimilation strategy where English language is also spoken by the host country. Values of individualism and collectivism do influence acculturation outcomes as well. An individualist might assimilate better in a host country that values individualism than would a collectivist and vice versa.

Key Takeaways

1. A medical report for cause of death may not align with the *beliefs* people hold about death causation. Yet beliefs could be more influential in grief outcomes than medical reports.
2. People could hold dual beliefs, e.g., A Catholic may believe that God is sovereign yet may have beliefs in evil eye (non-Catholic belief) as cause of death as well.
3. Death is evaluated through the lens of personal and cultural values. A death that aligns with the personal and cultural values of the bereaved will be easier to cope with than a death that does not. It would be helpful to explore the survivor's personal and cultural values.
4. Migrants, international students, asylum seekers, and similar others in a host country experience different acculturation outcomes—assimilation, integration, separation, and marginalization.
5. Within a society, cultural values may differ. For example, in the United States African Americans, Whites, American Indians, Hispanics, and Asian Americans have different cultural values. Cultural values of ethnic minority group members should be acknowledged and not be supplanted by the values of the dominant cultural group.
6. Cultural values could change over time due to modernization influences and the convenience of group members.

Critical Cultural Thinking

Jonathan lost his daughter unexpectedly but refused to accept a medical autopsy report on the cause of his daughter's death as a congestive heart failure. Due to his cultural values, Jonathan instead believed in the divination of a witch doctor that said his daughter's death was caused by the evil eye of a jealous aunt, who had no child of her own to look after her in old age. Is Jonathan's belief irrational? Would it be helpful to change Jonathan's beliefs to help him better cope with his loss?

References

Baloyi, L. (2019). *The African conception of death: A cultural implication*. Accessed May 17, 2023, from www.iaccp.org/wp-content/uploads/2019/04/Baloyi.pdf

Bandura, A. (1977). Self-efficacy: Toward a unifying theory of behavioral change. *Psychological Review, 84*(2), 191.

Berry, J. W. (2003). *Conceptual approaches to acculturation*. American Psychological Association.

Berry, J. W. (2006). Contexts of acculturation. *The Cambridge Handbook of Acculturation Psychology, 27*(42), 328–336.

Britannica.com. (n.d.) *Norm*. www.britannica.com/topic/norm-society

Caffaro, F., Ferraris, F., & Schmidt, S. (2014). Gender differences in the perception of honour killing in individualist versus collectivistic cultures: Comparison between Italy and Turkey. *Sex Roles, 71*(9), 296–318.

Chattopadhyay, S., & Simon, A. (2008). East meets west: Cross-cultural perspective in end-of-life decision making from Indian and German viewpoints. *Medicine, Health Care and Philosophy, 11*(2), 165–174.

Del Pilar, J. A., & Udasco, J. O. (2004). Marginality theory: The lack of construct validity. *Hispanic Journal of Behavioral Sciences, 26*(1), 3–15.

Finkelstein, M. A. (2012). Individualism/collectivism and organizational citizenship behavior: An integrative framework. *Social Behavior and Personality: An International Journal, 40*(10), 1633–1643.

Hofstede, G. (1994). The business of international business is culture. *International Business Review, 3*(1), 1–14.

Kelley, A. S., Wenger, N. S., & Sarkisian, C. A. (2010). Opiniones: End-of-life care preferences and planning of older Latinos. *Journal of the American Geriatrics Society, 58*(6), 1109–1116.

Matsumoto, D. R. (1996). *Unmasking Japan: Myths and realities about the emotions of the Japanese*. Stanford University Press.

McManus, R., Walter, T., & Claridge, L. (2018). Restoration and loss after disaster: Applying the dual process model of coping in bereavement. *Death Studies, 42*, 405–414.

Mukerjee, S. (1999, December 26). *Woman's death on husband's pyre inspires Hundus*. Accessed May 17, 2023, from www.latimes.com/archives/la-xpm-1999-dec-26-mn-47664-story.html

Pavlov, I. P. (1997). Excerpts from the work of the digestive glands (W. H. Thompson, Trans.). *American Psychologist, 52*(9), 936–940.

Pew Research Center. (2014, November 13). *Religion in Latin America*. www.pewresearch.org/religion/2014/11/13/religion-in-latin-america/

Rudmin, F. W. (2003). Critical history of the acculturation psychology of assimilation, separation, integration, and marginalization. *Review of General Psychology, 7*(1), 3–37.

Schmidt-Leukel, P. (2006). *Buddhism, Christianity and the question of creation: Karmic or divine?* Ashgate Publishing.

Schram, R. (2007). Sit, cook, eat, full stop: Religion and the rejection of ritual in auhelawa (Papua New Guinea). *Oceania, 77*(2), 172–190.

Schwartz, S. H. (1994). Are there universal aspects in the structure and contents of human values? *Journal of Social Issues, 50*(4), 19–45.

Schwartz, S. H. (2007). Basic human values: Theory, measurement, and applications. *Revue Française de Sociologie, 47*(4), 929.

Schwartz, S. H. (2012). An overview of the Schwartz theory of basic values. *Online Readings in Psychology and Culture, 2*(1) 2307-0919.1116.

Schwartz, S. H., & Bilsky, W. (1990). Toward a theory of the universal content and structure of values: Extensions and cross-cultural replications. *Journal of Personality and Social Psychology, 58*(5), 878.

Schwartz, S. J., & Zamboanga, B. L. (2008). Testing berry's model of acculturation: A confirmatory latent class approach. *Cultural Diversity and Ethnic Minority Psychology, 14*(4), 275.

Shear, M. K. (2012). Getting straight about grief. *Depression and Anxiety, 29*(6), 461–464.

Skinner, B. F. (1948). 'Superstition' in the pigeon. *Journal of Experimental Psychology, 38*(2), 168.

Tadmor, C. T., Tetlock, P. E., & Peng, K. (2009). Acculturation strategies and integrative complexity: The cognitive implications of biculturalism. *Journal of Cross-Cultural Psychology, 40*(1), 105–139.

Triandis, H. C. (1995). A theoretical framework for the study of diversity. In M. M. Chemers, S. Oskamp, & M. A. Costanzo (Eds.), *Diversity in organizations: New perspectives for a changing workplace* (pp. 11–36). Sage Publications.

Walter, T. (2010). Grief and culture. *Bereavement Care, 29*(2), 5–9.

Windfuhr, K., & Kapur, N. (2011). Suicide and mental illness: A clinical review of 15 years findings from the UK National Confidential Inquiry into suicide. *British Medical Bulletin, 100*(1), 101–121.

Zisook, S., & Shear, K. (2009). Grief and bereavement: What psychiatrists need to know. *World Psychiatry, 8*(2), 67.

Chapter 4
Culture and the Dying Experience

Usually, the stage of *dying* is a medical condition that is determined by a trained medical doctor. The stage of dying can take the following approaches:

Dying with Hope

In dying with hope, a medical intervention is deployed to redress a patient's failing health. Researcher Jessica Muller and colleague (Muller and Koenig, 1988) note that medical intervention could continue even when the outcome is known to be futile. The reasons for this include advances in biomedical technology, a physician's fear of failure in having their patient die, and a physician's fear of malpractice suit from the dying patient's loved ones. Given these scenarios, therefore, it becomes fluid to determine when a patient is determined as dying. Furthermore, while some patients may welcome medical interventions, others may reject them. Thus, the patient becomes the determiner of when dying occurs.

Dying Without Hope

In this situation, palliative care to keep the dying person as comfortable as possible becomes the approach. Unlike dying with hope, there is no curative approach in dying without hope, and the dying patient could resort to physician-assisted suicide or euthanasia to speed up death. In dying without hope, medical intervention becomes "futile," "hopeless," or "impossible." Medical intervention could become "non-beneficial" or "inappropriate" (Truog et al., 1992). Yet medical intervention can be declared as "futile" because the dying person wishes to stop treatment in order to spend quality time with family members. This is dissimilar to

F. E. Eyetsemitan, *Cultural Influences in Coping with Grief*,
https://doi.org/10.1007/978-3-031-86817-7_4

physician-assisted suicide or euthanasia (Lesage and Portenoy, 2001). However, when a dying patient is unable to decide on the futility of a medical intervention, a third party such as a court of law could make that decision, based on the principle of "beneficence." The court of law could decide that to withhold or to withdraw medical intervention would be to the patient's benefit. For example, in certain medical conditions, artificial hydration or nutrition could lead to edema (retention), to ascites (buildup of fluid in the abdomen), or to shortness of breath (Zerwekh, 1997). Yet to withhold water or nutrition from a patient is a culturally sensitive issue. Some cultural groups perceive this action as a form of physician-assisted suicide or euthanasia, even if the intent was different. Among non-Whites, physician-assisted suicide or euthanasia is unpopular, based on cultural and religious beliefs (MacDonald, 1998; Braun et al., 2001). In the United States, almost 20 years after the enactment of laws that made physician-assisted suicide legal in the state of Oregon, only 3% of patients who died after receiving aid-in-dying drugs identified as racial or ethnic minorities (Oregon Government Health Authority, 2022).

Cultural Factors and Elisabeth Kubler-Ross's Five-Stage Model of Dying

Psychiatrist Elisabeth Kubler-Ross's (1969) work on dying cancer patients in the Chicago area of the United States highlights five stages that a dying person goes through. Elisabeth Kubler-Ross's model remains the most popular model on dying (see Corr, 2019 for details in sampling recent textbooks published in ten countries outside of the United States). Elisabeth Kubler-Ross's (1969) five stages of dying are highlighted below, with discussions on the impact of cultural factors.

Denial: A way to understanding denial is "disbelief" or "rejection," which follows the bad news of dying from a trained medical doctor. The patient could contest the physician's verdict of dying by seeking further opinions and/or solutions from both orthodox and unorthodox sources. The duration of the denial stage could vary from one individual to another or from one cultural group to another.

In the United States Black people mostly prefer to die in the hospital by seeking conventional Western medical treatment. Researcher Nan Tracy Zheng and colleagues (Zheng et al., 2011), from reviewing 49,048 long-term care residents in New York state nursing homes, report that Blacks are almost twice (40.33%) as Whites (24.07%) to die in the hospital. Blacks refuse to go into hospice or go home to die either.

Complementary and alternative medicine (CAM) are unorthodox approaches to illness. Whereas *complementary* medicine is used to augment Western conventional medicine, *alternative* medicine is used as replacement for Western conventional medicine (United States National Cancer Institute, n.d.). Usually, in pursuit of *denial*, people resort to CAM when Western conventional medicine fails. Researcher Ralph Muecke and colleagues (Muecke et al., 2016) note that 40% of cancer patients in Germany use CAM. Also, in Germany, about 60–90% of women with breast cancer and gynecological problems use CAM (e.g., Molassiotis et al., 2006). However, in the case of advance cancer, alternative medicine is used (Micke et al., 2009).

Traditional medicine is considered complimentary or alternative medicine. Researcher Lichtenstein and colleagues (Lichtenstein et al., 2017) suggest that traditional medical practice around the world is an admixture of cultural, psychological, social, and spiritual elements. There is a strong belief in the supernatural, and through oral tradition this knowledge is passed on from one generation to another. In non-Western societies, due to limited availability and access to Western medical care, traditional medicine is popular. Besides, there is strong belief in the efficacy of traditional medicine. In India, for example, there is a form of traditional medicine called *Ayurveda*, which means knowledge of life and longevity (Dwarakanath, 1970). Native Indians believe that sweating brings about healing by purifying the body, soul, and mind. People therefore engage in sweating ceremonies (e.g., Garrett et al., 2011). In Africa, there is a strong belief in sorcery, witchcraft, or evil eye as cause for illness that is remedied through appeasement of ancestral spirits (Essien, 2013). In Mexico and in Latin American cultures, the origin of diseases is believed to be supernatural, and a priest (curandero) is approached because he is believed to have supernatural abilities to heal and cure illnesses (Padilla et al., 2001).

The Chinese use herbs for treatment of illness, and through a process called *moxibustion*, these herbs are sometimes burned to produce heat and applied close to the body to distribute body energy (Dong and Zhang, 2001).

Anger: When denial efforts fail, anger becomes the next stage of dying. Anger is a biologically wired universal emotion. It occurs when someone believes that they have been unfairly treated or prevented from achieving their goal. In this case, the goal is to live and not die. Yet how anger is expressed or its depth is influenced by culture (Matsumoto et al., 2010). Anger could lead to self-blame or blame of others. In Western culture, people have a strong motive for self-fulfillment and for the pursuit of one's goals. Anger and frustration could result from a negative experience that stifles or prevents such from happening. Anger can be directed toward others if there is a perception of unfairness (Kitayama et al., 1995). In non-Western cultures where there is a high value for interconnectedness, people are more likely to understand their frustration beyond a perpetrator. Also, people tend to be fatalistic (Norenzayan and Lee, 2010) and believe in the inevitability of negative events in their lives (Choi and Nisbett, 1998). Thus, anger may be muted and accompanied by sadness (e.g., Smith and Ellsworth, 1985).

In the Middle Eastern region, breast cancer is a common killer among the 13 million females who lack health education (e.g., Kristiansen and Sheikh, 2012). When faced with a health crisis such as breast cancer, women hold on to their Islamic belief that Allah (God) is the sole determiner of the timing of one's death. They are also comforted by the Islamic teaching that disease comes with suffering and that Allah (God) rewards those who are patient (Tayeb et al., 2010).

Although Middle Easterners are united by Islam, they have diverse cultures (e.g., Kristiansen and Sheikh, 2012). In both Western and non-Western societies, heterogenous cultures with subcultures do exist (Walter, 2010).

Also, anger could be directed at someone unintentionally. Psychoanalyst Sigmund Freud refers to this as *displacement* behavior (see a review in Samuel and Akhtar (2009) for details). For example, an unintentional anger can occur when an instructor, annoyed by a work situation, directs his anger at his spouse back home by being rude to her. An intentional anger is different, however. During the HIV/AIDS epidemic, there was a willful spreading of the disease by some individuals who had the disease. This was intentional anger directed at others. Some HIV/AIDS-infected individuals felt that life had been unfair to them in contracting the deadly disease and wanted others to join them in dying. A study of AIDS patients in the state of Minnesota, USA, reported that 13% of study participants admitted to knowingly infect others, postdiagnosis (Rosser et al., 1999). In response to the willful spreading of AIDS (through anger), many countries enacted laws that make it a crime to willfully expose or transmit HIV to another person (Worth et al., 2005).

Bargaining: In bargaining the behavior of anger gives way to rational cognitive thought. To save their life, the dying person thinks of trade-offs. Bargaining is made with someone the dying person perceives to have extraordinary abilities (e.g., God, medical doctor, or spiritualist). This takes the form of a future promise for a current relief. Bargaining could be private (between the dying person and God only), or it could be public (between the dying person and a medical doctor known to family members and friends). Bargaining with a medical doctor may include acceptance of a risky medical procedure previously rejected with the hope of a favorable outcome.

In non-Western cultures, in exchange for life, bargaining with ancestors and making sacrifices to appease ancestors are common. In Haiti *vodou* practice (an admixture of African and Catholic practices) is common, and vodou practitioners bargain with ancestors (lesser gods/spirits) because they believe that God is too busy (e.g., Rey and Stepick, 2013). In Puerto Rican and Cuban communities, *Espiritismo* (Portuguese and Spanish word for spiritism) is practiced, and bargaining involves ancestor worship and communion with dead loved ones (e.g., Anderson, 2015). Also, ancestor worship and bargaining with ancestors are common across Africa, South America, and Asia (e.g., Hsu et al., 2009) and among Indigenous people of Australia. In New Zealand, the Maoris believe in maintaining harmony between the physical world and the spiritual world (Ngata, 2005), and ancestors, if not appeased, are believed to have extraordinary powers to influence the living. Therefore, a dying person's illness may be attributed to the wrath of an ancestor (e.g., van der Pijl, 2016).

Depression: This stage is marked by sadness that is profound. Sadness is common in grief and is a universally shared emotion (Bonanno et al., 2008). The depression stage is twofold: (1) sadness over a past robbed by an impending death that includes friends, family members, and possessions and (2) sadness over a future robbed by an impending death that includes unfinished businesses and an afterlife that for some people is not comprehended. Generally, afterlife thoughts are influenced by belief in *body* and *self* separation in death (e.g., Copp, 1997). The dying person may keep their thoughts private if culturally expected to look strong and not weak in all circumstances. Many cultures have this expectation of men. In the Kenneth Doka and Terry Martin (2011) model of bereavement, the *instrumental* griever is less likely to express emotions.

Acceptance: During this stage the dying person awaits death, after expending all resources in preventing it from happening. The dying person's response could be active (take actions to end their life as in euthanasia) or passive (await death to occur as in hospice).

Active (Take Actions to End Life): The dying person could take advantage of physician-assisted suicide or euthanasia, which is more common in Western societies. Physician-assisted suicide or euthanasia validates the values of individualism. In the United States, on November 1, 2014, Brittany Maynard, a lady with a brain tumor, decided she could no longer endure the pain caused by her disease. She then took advantage of the nation's first Death with Dignity Act passed by the state of Oregon and ended her life through physician-assisted suicide (Deathwithdignity.org, 2019). The Oregon Death with Dignity Act, the nation's first, was passed into law in 1997. In 2019, over 20 years after, the people who took advantage of the law provided as primary reasons for their action the following: decreased inability to participate in enjoyable activities (90%), loss of autonomy (87%), and loss of dignity (72%) (Oregon Government Health Authority, 2022). A dying patient in making a request for physician-assisted suicide or euthanasia is screened for mental health problems including depression (Emanuel et al., 2016).

Passive (Await Death to Occur): When passively awaiting death, the waiting period may develop into hope due to a discovery of an experimental treatment procedure for the disease that is ailing the dying person. Yet hope does not remove the preparation for an afterlife. In Chinese Buddhism, a combination of Chinese traditional values of filial piety and ancestor worship, there is the belief on the importance of the dying person's last thoughts to influence either a good rebirth or a bad rebirth. To keep the dying person's mind in focus for an afterlife, therefore, the Sutra (statement of belief) is recited (e.g., Hsieh, 2002; Hsu et al., 2009). Hinduism, another religion with a large following in Southeast Asia, also believes that death should be faced with clear conscious and any mind-altering medication should be avoided (Sharma et al., 2013). Hinduism is the major religion in Nepal (81%), in India (80%), and in Mauritius (56%) (Pew Research Center, 2012).

However, while awaiting death, some dying persons may choose to travel the world. They may however face challenges of fitness to travel, loneliness, immunization, and medical emergencies in a foreign country (e.g., Willson et al., 2018). Other dying individuals may spend time mending fences with loved ones and friends while awaiting death. They may seek forgiveness and/or extend forgiveness to and from others and pursue unfinished businesses. In Hindu belief system, unfinished businesses not completed prior to death would lead to bad karma, and to undo this would take another lifetime (Firth, 2005).

Limitations of Kubler-Ross's Five-Stage Model of Dying

Elisabeth Kubler-Ross's (1969) five stages of dying appear to be intuitive. Obviously, the shock of bad news would lead to a denial. The frustration of a life with an unplanned ending could elicit anger; the desperation to delay death could lead to bargaining; and if all efforts fail, depression could follow, and the dying individual ultimately comes to terms with his or her situation in acceptance. However, not everyone goes through these stages and in the order prescribed. A dying individual who opts for physician-assisted suicide or euthanasia may do so with the belief that death is more welcoming than living (e.g., Oregon Government Health Authority, 2022). Also, a dying person may go back and forth these stages, given changes to their circumstance and expectation. For example, after bargaining fails, the dying person could return to anger, out of frustration from hopes not met. The sociocultural context of dying is important as well. A dying person and loved ones may exchange farewells and make peace with each other. There are anecdotes of dying persons who slip into death after receiving their loved ones' assurances that they would be reuniting with family members and friends who had gone before them and that they too would be joining the dying person later. Such assurances may change the dying person's perception of an afterlife as a lonely existence. Also, a dying individual may slip into death in the absence of loved ones, out of protection for their feelings. Paula Spencer Scott (n.d.) shares the following dying experience that is narrated by writer Lise Funderbeurg:

> *The hospice people had told me that sometimes people won't die when their loved ones are in the room, especially if the person has played a protective role in their lives. Or that they hang on if they feel you can't let them go. So, before I stepped out to get something to eat, I told my Dad that if he had to go it was okay, that he had done everything he could to raise us and we could raise ourselves now. Not seven minutes later, a nurse met me in the hall and said he was gone. I guess I felt a bit cheated because I wanted to witness this crossing over.*

Verbal instructions from the dying person to loved ones are part of the sociocultural context of dying. In societies with low rates of literacy, such as in many non-Western societies, verbal instructions by the dying person to loved ones are commonplace. However, the United States with a high rate of literacy acknowledges *oral will* (a nuncupative will) under certain conditions. The state of North Carolina prescribes oral will as legal under the following conditions (North Carolina General Assembly, n.d.):

> *[The will has been made] orally by a person who is [in his or her]last [stages of] sickness or in imminent peril of death, and who does not survive such illness or imminent peril, and [The will is] declared to be that person's will before two competent witnesses simultaneously present at the making thereof and specially requested by the persons to bear witness thereto.* (North Carolina General Assembly; 31–3.5)

Physician-assisted suicide or euthanasia is the equivalence of Kubler-Ross's stage of acceptance. This act demonstrates a value for autonomy that is associated with individualistic cultures. A dying person who opts for physician-assisted suicide (or euthanasia) does not want to become a burden on others (e.g., Oregon.gov,

2022). As much as it is about them, this decision is also made out of consideration for loved ones. However, in cultures with values high for interdependence (mostly non-Western), dependence on loved ones would not be a basis to end one's life (Eyetsemitan and Gire, 2003).

A Task-Based Model of Coping with Dying

Another model on dying is task based. Researcher Charles Corr (1992) notes that a stage-based model lacks individuality, with the erroneous assumption that a dying person has to be guided through a particular sequence by a professional helper. Corr (1992) believes that dying humans can exercise agency and that this agency extends to loved ones and helpers as well. In coping with dying, Corr (1992) describes this human agency as *tasks* to be done in physical, psychological, social, and spiritual areas. The dying person can carry out these tasks in a discretionary way. For example, the dying person may choose to sleep, to write, or to spend time with others. In the physical arena, the task is to satisfy bodily needs and to minimize suffering; the psychological task is to have a sense of autonomy or richness in living, and the social task is to have a sense of connectedness to others. In the spiritual arena, the task is to have hope in various respects that includes a cure. This hope extends to loved ones being left behind to do well or to celebrate a milestone event. Corr's (1992) model brings other players into the dying process that include loved ones and professional helpers. In a culture that values individualism, the dying person is empowered through a task-based approach. In a culture that values collectivism, however, the dying person's family takes the lead in a task-based approach. The family makes decisions on tasks deemed as appropriate or salient, e.g., physical versus psychological. For example, as earlier discussed, in the Hindu tradition death before an unfinished business would lead to bad karma (Firth, 2005). Therefore, irrespective of the dying person's task preference, family members may prevail on their task priority, based on normative beliefs.

In individualist cultures, the dying person may decide on physician-assisted suicide or euthanasia as a psychological task. In physician-assisted suicide or euthanasia, self-esteem needs are fulfilled (Allen et al., 2006). The following are statements that relate to people who seek physician-assisted or euthanasia: "I don't want to depend on others," "I don't want to become a vegetable," "I don't want to go into a nursing home," or "I don't want to live like this" (Eyetsemitan, 2020; p. 111). A study finds that 67% of Americans support physician-assisted suicide (Dugan, 2017). In collectivist cultures, however, a dying person's options are limited in this regard. As a psychological task, physician-assisted suicide or euthanasia is not a decision the dying person can solely exercise. In Malaysia (a collectivist culture), researcher Mohammed Rathor and others (Rathor et al., 2014) note that 91.2% of patients and 87% of physicians believe that patients have no right to take their life, regardless of their illness or disease, and, also, irrespective of the patient's suffering, physicians should not help a patient to die.

Death Communication and the Dying Experience

Communication is an important aspect in the dying experience. This starts with the medical doctor. Usually, when and to whom the communication is made are the issue. Studies show that medical doctors hold off on communication of bad news while they explore other cure options, because the communication of bad news is not a triumphant experience. Rather, it is perceived as a sign of professional failure (e.g., Bates and Kearney, 2015). Therefore, a patient receives the bad news with relatively little time to live. In an interview of parents whose children died of cancer, researcher Joan Wolfe and colleagues (Wolfe et al., 2000) report that parents did not receive the bad news prior to their children's death, on an average of 103 days.

To whom should the communication be made? The following are some considerations: The individual who is the recipient of the bad news, is he or she of age? Also, should the recipient of the bad news hear directly from the doctor or from family members? While the case could be made for parents to receive the bad news on behalf of their children, it becomes a different issue when an adolescent is involved. The case of the "mature minor" provides a different outlook. The "mature minor," a legal principle, recognizes that teenagers can make decisions about their own health and welfare. The Canada Supreme Court ruled that "young people under 16 will have the right to demonstrate mature medical decisional capacity" (Supreme Court of Canada; A.C. Vs. Manitoba, 2009). In Belgium, Geert Pousset and others (Pousset et al., 2010) note that adolescents are in position to make decisions about assisted death. Therefore, in the sharing of bad news, Western cultures emphasize that honesty and truth be made available to the critically ill person (Wiener et al., 2013). In non-Western cultures, however, honesty and truth are also valued, but this should not be communicated to the critically ill patient directly. Family members believe that bad news shared directly to the critically ill could hasten their death (Wiener et al., 2013).

In sharing of bad news, the physician may be honest and truthful with family members. Yet family members may not be truthful and honest with the dying person with the bad news. In certain instances, both physician and family members may *collude* to not share bad news with the dying person. Collusion is common in non-Western cultures, including in the Middle East, in Asia (e.g., Yamaguchi et al., 2021), and in Africa (e.g., Kpanake et al., 2016). In the Middle east, family members feel an obligation to protect loved ones from bad news (Silbermann et al., 2011). In Turkey, family members believe that the disclosure of bad news could cause psychological distress to the dying patient (Öksüzoğrlu et al., 2006). In Europe, though mostly individualistic in outlook, collusion has been reported among parents and doctors as well, due to a strong parental instinct to protect an adolescent child (Lyon et al., 2013).

Thus, the sharing of bad news to the adolescent/adult directly or to family members first has cross-cultural benefits; see Table 4.1.

Table 4.1 Cross-cultural advantages to sharing of bad news in individualistic and collectivistic cultures

Advantages of sharing bad news to a dying person directly in individualistic cultures	Advantages to sharing bad news to a dying person's family first in collectivistic cultures
Respect for the dying person's autonomy	Assume that family members know the dying person's personality and how they would react to the bad news
Assumes that the dying person knows what is best for them and not others, in making end-of-life decisions	Family members are able to explore other options on behalf of the dying person, including complementary and alternative medicine
Provides opportunity for the dying person to take care of unfinished businesses and legacy issues	Respect cultural norms regarding how the bad news should be shared, based on hierarchy

Source: Adapted from advantages and disadvantages of sharing bad news directly with adolescent instead of with parents and/or family and advantages and disadvantages of sharing bad news with parent and/or family instead of with adolescent. In Eyetsemitan, F.E. (2020): *Understanding death and dying: Encountering, death, dying, and the afterlife*: Sage Publication

Key Takeaways

1. Dying could occur with *hope* or *without hope*. In dying with hope, medical intervention is used, but in dying without hope, palliative care becomes an option after medical intervention is deemed as futile.
2. Elisabeth Kubler-Ross proposes a five-stage model of dying. A dying person may go back and forth these stages. Thus, these stages should not be understood as progressive nor as required to be. The emotions of anger and sadness are universal, yet they are influenced by cultural values.
3. The sociocultural context of dying includes farewells and verbal instructions.
4. Charles Corr's (1992) task-based model recognizes input from the dying person, family members, and professional helpers in the dying process through agency. The dying person can exercise agency in physical, psychological, social, and spiritual areas. In individualist cultures the dying person exercises agency, but in collectivist cultures family members exercise agency on behalf of the dying person.
5. Communication by a medical doctor in sharing of bad news about dying is important. Equally important is *how* and *to whom* the bad news is shared. There are cross-cultural benefits to sharing of bad news with the dying adolescent/adult directly and sharing the bad news with the dying person's family members first. Generally, communication of bad news with the dying patient directly is more valued in individualist cultures, whereas communication of bad news with family members first is preferred in collectivist cultures.

Critical Cultural Thinking

John was both angry and scared when he learned that he had a terminal illness. Are there cross-cultural benefits if John's doctor has to tell him the bad news directly or tell his parents first? John is 16 years old.

References

Allen, J., Chavez, S., DeSimone, S., & Howard, D. (2006). Americans' attitudes toward euthanasia and physician-assisted suicide, 1936–2002. *The Journal of Sociology & Social Welfare, 33*, 5.

Anderson, J. E. (2015). *The voodoo encyclopedia: Magic, ritual, and religion: Magic, ritual, and religion*. ABC-CLIO.

Bates, A. T., & Kearney, J. A. (2015). Understanding death with limited experience in life: Dying children's and adolescents' understanding of their own terminal illness and death. *Current Opinion in Supportive and Palliative Care, 9*(1), 40.

Bonanno, G. A., Goorin, L., & Coifman, K. G. (2008). Sadness and grief. In M. Lewis, J. M. Haviland-Jones, & L. F. Barrett (Eds.), *Handbook of emotions* (pp. 797–810). The Guilford Press.

Braun, K. L., Tanji, V. M., & Heck, R. (2001). Support for physician-assisted suicide: Exploring the impact of ethnicity and attitudes toward planning for death. *The Gerontologist, 41*(1), 51–60.

Choi, I., & Nisbett, R. E. (1998). Situational salience and cultural differences in the correspondence bias and actor-observer bias. *Personality and Social Psychology Bulletin, 24*(9), 949–960.

Copp, D. (1997). Belief, reason, and motivation: Michael smith's "the moral problem". *Ethics, 108*(1), 33–54.

Corr, C. A. (1992). A task-based approach to coping with dying. *OMEGA-Journal of Death and Dying, 24*(2), 81–94.

Corr, C. A. (2019). The 'five stages' in coping with dying and bereavement: Strengths, weaknesses and some alternatives. *Mortality, 24*(4), 405–417.

Deathwithdignity.org. (2019, November 1). *Brittany Maynard's legacy, five years on*. www.deathwithdignity.org/news/2019/11/brittany-maynards-legacy-five-years-on/

Doka, K. J., & Martin, T. L. (2011). *Grieving beyond gender: Understanding the ways men and women mourn*. Routledge.

Dong, H., & Zhang, X. (2001). An overview of traditional Chinese medicine. *Traditional Medicine in Asia*, 17–29.

Dugan, A. (2017). *In US, support up for doctor-assisted suicide. 2015*. https://news.gallup.com/poll/183425/support-doctor-assisted-suicide.aspx

Dwarakanath, C. (1970). Some significant aspects of the origin and development of medicine in ancient India. [abridged]. *Indian Journal of History of Science, 5*, 1–12.

Emanuel, E. J., Onwuteaka-Philipsen, B. D., Urwin, J. W., & Cohen, J. (2016). Attitudes and practices of euthanasia and physician-assisted suicide in the United States, Canada, and Europe. *JAMA, 316*(1), 79–90.

Essien, E. D. (2013). Notions of healing and transcendence in the trajectory of African traditional religion: Paradigm and strategies. *International Review of Mission, 102*(2), 236–248.

Eyetsemitan, F. E. (2020). *Understanding death and dying: Encountering death, dying, and the afterlife*. Sage.

Eyetsemitan, F. E., & Gire, J. T. (2003). *Aging and adult development in the developing world: Applying western theories and concepts*. Greenwood Publishing Group.

Firth, S. (2005). End-of-life: A Hindu view. *The Lancet, 366*(9486), 682–686.

Garrett, M. T., Torres-Rivera, E., Brubaker, M., Portman, T. A. A., Brotherton, D., West-Olatunji, C., et al. (2011). Crying for a vision: The Native American sweat lodge ceremony as therapeutic intervention. *Journal of Counseling & Development, 89*(3), 318–325.

Hsieh, D. H. (2002). Buddhism: China. *Encyclopedia of Modern Asia, 1*, 337–341.
Hsu, C., O'Connor, M., & Lee, S. (2009). Understandings of death and dying for people of Chinese origin. *Death Studies, 33*(2), 153–174.
Kitayama, S., Takagi, H., & Matsumoto, H. (1995). Causal attribution of success and failure: Cultural psychology of the Japanese self. *Japanese Psychological Review, 38*(2), 247–280.
Kpanake, L., Gossou, K., Sorum, P. C., & Mullet, E. (2016). Misconceptions about ebola virus disease among lay people in Guinea: Lessons for community education. *Journal of Public Health Policy, 37*, 160–172.
Kristiansen, M., & Sheikh, A. (2012). Understanding faith considerations when caring for bereaved Muslims. *Journal of the Royal Society of Medicine, 105*(12), 513–517.
Kubler-Ross, E. (1969). *On death and dying*. Macmillan.
Lesage, P., & Portenoy, R. K. (2001). Ethical challenges in the care of patients with serious illness. *Pain Medicine, 2*(2), 121–130.
Lichtenstein, A. H., Berger, A., & Cheng, M. J. (2017). Definitions of healing and healing interventions across different cultures. *Annals of Palliative Medicine, 6*(3), 248–252.
Lyon, M. E., Jacobs, S., Briggs, L., Cheng, Y. I., & Wang, J. (2013). Family-centered advance care planning for teens with cancer. *JAMA Pediatrics, 167*(5), 460–467.
MacDonald, W. L. (1998). The difference between blacks' and whites' attitudes toward voluntary euthanasia. *Journal for the Scientific Study of Religion, 37*, 411–426.
Matsumoto, D., Yoo, S. H., & Chung, J. (2010). The expression of anger across cultures. In *International handbook of anger: Constituent and concomitant biological, psychological, and social processes* (pp. 125–137).
Micke, O., Bruns, F., Glatzel, M., Schönekaes, K., Micke, P., Mücke, R., & Büntzel, J. (2009). Predictive factors for the use of complementary and alternative medicine (CAM) in radiation oncology. *European Journal of Integrative Medicine, 1*(1), 19–25.
Molassiotis, A., Scott, J. A., Kearney, N., Pud, D., Magri, M., Selvekerova, S., et al. (2006). Complementary and alternative medicine use in breast cancer patients in Europe. *Supportive Care in Cancer, 14*, 260–267.
Muecke, R., Paul, M., Conrad, C., Stoll, C., Muenstedt, K., Micke, O., et al. (2016). Complementary and alternative medicine in palliative care: A comparison of data from surveys among patients and professionals. *Integrative Cancer Therapies, 15*(1), 10–16.
Muller, J. H., & Koenig, B. A. (1988). *On the boundary of life and death: The definition of dying by medical residents*. Springer.
Ngata, P. (2005). Death, dying, and grief: A Maori perspective. *Death and Bereavement Around the World, 4*, 29–38.
Norenzayan, A., & Lee, A. (2010). It was meant to happen: Explaining cultural variations in fate attributions. *Journal of Personality and Social Psychology, 98*(5), 702.
North Carolina General Assembly. (n.d.). *Nuncupative will*. www.ncleg.gov/EnactedLegislation/Statutes/
Öksüzoğrlu, B., Abalı, H., Bakar, M., Yıldıırıim, N., & Zengin, N. (2006). Disclosure of cancer diagnosis to patients and their relatives in Turkey: Views of accompanying persons and influential factors in reaching those views. *Tumori Journal, 92*(1), 62–66.
Oregon.gov. (2022). *Oregon death with dignity act: Annual reports*. www.oregon.gov/oha/ph/providerpartnerresources/evaluationresearch/deathwithdignityact/pages/ar-index.aspx
Padilla, R., Gomez, V., Biggerstaff, S. L., & Mehler, P. S. (2001). Use of curanderismo in a public health care system. *Archives of Internal Medicine, 161*(10), 1336–1340.
Pew Research Center. (2012, December 18). *The global religious landscape*. www.pewresearch.org/religion/2012/12/18/global-religious-landscape-exec/
Pousset, G., Bilsen, J., Cohen, J., Chambaere, K., Deliens, L., & Mortier, F. (2010). Medical end-of-life decisions in children in Flanders, Belgium: A population-based postmortem survey. *Archives of Pediatrics & Adolescent Medicine, 164*(6), 547–553.
Rathor, M. Y., Rani, M. F. A., Shahar, M. A., Jamalludin, A. R., Abdullah, S. T. B. C., Omar, A. M. B., & Shah, A. S. B. M. (2014). Attitudes toward euthanasia and related issues among physicians and patients in a multi-cultural society of Malaysia. *Journal of Family Medicine and Primary Care, 3*(3), 230.

Rey, T., & Stepick, A. (2013). *Crossing the water and keeping the faith: Haitian religion in Miami*. NYU Press.
Rosser, B. S., Gobby, J. M., & Carr, W. P. (1999). The unsafe sexual behavior of persons living with HIV/AIDS: An empirical approach to developing new HIV prevention interventions targeting HIV-positive persons. *Journal of Sex Education and Therapy, 24*(1–2), 18–28.
Samuel, S., & Akhtar, S. (2009). The identity consolidation inventory (ICI): Development and application of a questionnaire for assessing the structuralization of individual identity. *The American Journal of Psychoanalysis, 69*, 53–61.
Scott, P. S. (n.d.). *The passing: What to expect when witnessing a loved one's death*. www.maggiecallanan.com/pdf/201107_WitnessingaLovedOnesDeath.pdf
Sharma, H., Jagdish, V., Anusha, P., & Bharti, S. (2013). End-of-life care: Indian perspective. *Indian Journal of Psychiatry, 55*(Suppl 2), S293.
Silbermann, M., Khleif, A., Tuncer, M., Pitsillides, B., Shad, A., Oberman, A., et al. (2011). Can we overcome the effect of conflicts in rendering palliative care? An introduction to the middle eastern cancer consortium (MECC). *Current Oncology Reports, 13*, 302–307.
Smith, C. A., & Ellsworth, P. C. (1985). Patterns of cognitive appraisal in emotion. *Journal of Personality and Social Psychology, 48*(4), 813.
Supreme Court of Canada. (2009). *AC v. Manitoba (Director of Child and Family Services)*. www.scc-csc.lexum.com/scc-csc/scc-csc/en/item/7795/index.do
Tayeb, M. A., Al-Zamel, E., Fareed, M. M., & Abouellail, H. A. (2010). A "good death": Perspectives of Muslim patients and health care providers. *Annals of Saudi Medicine, 30*(3), 215–221.
Truog, R. D., Brett, A. S., & Frader, J. (1992). The problem with futility. *New England Journal of Medicine, 326*(23), 1560–1564.
United States National Cancer Institute. (n.d.). *Complementary and Alternative medicine*. https://www.cancer.gov/about-cancer/treatment/cam
Van der Pijl, Y. (2016). Death in the family revisited: Ritual expression and controversy in a creole transnational mortuary sphere. *Ethnography, 17*(2), 147–167.
Walter, T. (2010). Grief and culture. *Bereavement Care, 29*(2), 5–9.
Wiener, L., McConnell, D. G., Latella, L., & Ludi, E. (2013). Cultural and religious considerations in pediatric palliative care. *Palliative & Supportive Care, 11*(1), 47–67.
Willson, G., McIntosh, A. J., Morgan, A., & Sanders, D. (2018). Terminal illness and tourism: A review of current literature and directions for future research. *Tourism Recreation Research, 43*(2), 268–272.
Wolfe, J., Grier, H. E., Klar, N., Levin, S. B., Ellenbogen, J. M., Salem-Schatz, S., et al. (2000). Symptoms and suffering at the end of life in children with cancer. *New England Journal of Medicine, 342*(5), 326–333.
Worth, H., Patton, C., & McGehee, M. T. (2005). Legislating the pandemic: A global survey of HIV/AIDS in criminal law. *Sexuality Research & Social Policy, 2*, 15–22.
Yamaguchi, T., Maeda, I., Hatano, Y., Suh, S., Cheng, S., Kim, S. H., et al. (2021). Communication and behavior of palliative care physicians of patients with cancer near end of life in three east Asian countries. *Journal of Pain and Symptom Management, 61*(2), 315–322.e1.
Zerwekh, J. V. (1997). Do dying patients really need IV fluids? *AJN the American Journal of Nursing, 97*(3), 26–30.
Zheng, N. T., Mukamel, D. B., Caprio, T., Cai, S., & Temkin-Greener, H. (2011). Racial disparities in in-hospital death and hospice use among nursing home residents at the end-of-life. *Medical Care, 49*(11), 992.

Chapter 5
Culture, Widowhood, and Bereavement

To lose a spouse is a very traumatic experience. Its impact is probably next to that of losing a child (Bennett et al., 2005). Widowhood is more common in later life. In the United States, within the preceding year, 71% of men and 69% of women at ages 65 and older are widowers and widows, respectively. Yet this age group makes up only 19% of people ages 15 and over. From ages 75 years and over, however, compared to 20% of men, 54% of women experience spousal loss within the previous 12 months. Over the life course, there are more widows than widowers. Reasons adduced for this include differences in life expectancy with women living longer than men and the tendency for women to marry men older than them (United States Census. Gov, April 22, 2021).

For most people, marriage is a transformative experience; it leads to new identities that include spouse, parent, and/or grandparent. With most spousal losses in later life, spousal identity persists the longest. Therefore, after a spousal loss, the survivor spouse would grieve for both the deceased spouse and himself/herself.

Grief Reactions for the Deceased Spouse by the Survivor Spouse

The following factors would influence grief reactions for the deceased spouse by the survivor spouse:

- *How he or she died*: Grief reaction for the deceased spouse would be influenced by how he or she died. Was it peaceful or traumatic? Was the death expected or not? A peaceful or an expected death (e.g., death during hospice care) may not elicit a strong grief reaction as a traumatic or an unexpected death (e.g., death from a fall, a drug overdose, or a vehicular accident). Aside medical autopsy report, the *belief* about death causation is equally important. Was the deceased a

F. E. Eyetsemitan, *Cultural Influences in Coping with Grief*,
https://doi.org/10.1007/978-3-031-86817-7_5

victim of sorcery, witchcraft, or evil eye? Belief in sorcery or evil eye as cause of death is commonplace in Africa, South America, and Central America.

- *What/who he or she left behind*: The bereaved spouse would grieve for the people (and valuable possessions) the deceased spouse left behind. For example, the thought of the deceased spouse not being part of important milestones in his or her child's life (e.g., college graduation or marriage) would influence grief reactions. This is reflected in the survivor spouse's statement to the child that your dad or mom would have loved to be at your graduation or marriage ceremony today.
- *Unfinished business*: The survivor spouse would grieve for the deceased spouse's unfinished businesses. These might include an uncompleted book project or an unfulfilled promise to go on a religious pilgrimage (e.g., a visit to Mecca or Jerusalem for a Muslim or Christian).
- *Afterlife worries*: Most world religions believe in an afterlife. These include Christianity, Islam, Hinduism, and Buddhism. Christians believe in heaven and hell, Muslims believe in paradise and eternal damnation, and practitioners of both Hinduism and Buddhism believe in reincarnation. These religions profess an afterlife in which the deceased is either *rewarded* or *punished*, based on adhering to the teachings or precepts of his or her religion, prior to death. For example, in Christianity, the deceased is rewarded with heaven as destination, if he or she asks for forgiveness of their sins and accepted Christ (the son of God) as redeemer and savior, prior to death. Generally, eulogies about the deceased tend to be positive and are publicly made to portray heaven (and not hell) as the decedent's afterlife destination. Besides, the precept is not to say negative things about a dead person who cannot defend himself or herself.

Yet, given his or her intimate knowledge of the deceased spouse, the survivor spouse may privately hold a contrary opinion about the deceased spouse's afterlife destination. For example, while public statements may eulogize the deceased spouse as a good Christian who is heavenly bound, the survivor spouse may have a different opinion, based on his or her intimate knowledge about the decedent's lifestyle. In private, therefore, the survivor spouse may believe that heaven is not the afterlife destination of the deceased spouse but hell. Also, survivors look forward to a reunion with their deceased loved ones in the afterlife. With concerns about a deceased spouse's afterlife destination, the survivor spouse's grief would be exacerbated.

Grief Reactions by a Survivor Spouse for Himself or Herself

The following factors would influence grief reactions by a survivor spouse for himself or herself:

Confronting a new identity: Following a spousal loss, the official nomenclature of the survivor spouse changes from *married* to *widow (or widower)*. Yet the bereaved spouse may choose to remain married to his or her decedent spouse. Some widows retain their marital title of "Mrs." Psychologist John Bowlby (1980) acknowledges that for attachment to the deceased spouse to subsist, some widows or widowers decide to not remarry, as this would change their identity. However, widows or widowers who chose to remarry would have to confront a new identity.

The issue of whether to hold on to an old identity or to embrace a new identity could create a crisis in self-grief. This is further compounded by the expectations of others, including family members and friends, who may have contrary opinions on a new direction the survivor spouse may choose to embrace. For example, family members and friends may not want the survivor spouse to remarry or to have a new identity. Furthermore, a lack of an available partner may limit the survivor spouse's identity choice. Researcher William Worden's (2018) last task of coping with bereavement is to memorialize the deceased and move on with one's life, including forming new relationships. In coping with grief, psychologist Margaret Stroebe and colleague's (Stroebe & Schut, 1999) dual process model of grief suggests that the survivor oscillates between *loss orientation* (or looking backward to the loss) and *restoration orientation* (or looking forward to life after the loss). Yet, based on a combination of factors, the survivor spouse could be hindered from exploring a new identity or moving forward with a new relationship. India, for example, has about 33 million widows who make up 54% of women age 60 and over (Kapur, 2018), and remarriage poses a challenge because a woman's social status (or identity) is tied to her husband's. A survivor spouse's identity is tied to her deceased husband's, and this is reflected in the traditional practice of *sati* whereby a survivor spouse throws herself into her deceased husband's funeral pyre to be cremated along with him. Also, following a spousal loss, there is the belief that the survivor spouse might have been the cause of her husband's death through an "evil eye" which she could bring into a new relationship. Also, in remarriage, the survivor spouse could be concerned about the loss of her children's custody to her deceased husband's kin (UN Division for the Advancement of Women, n.d.).

Adjusting to a new family configuration: Gender role socialization is common in cultures around the world. The traditional roles of males are different from those of females. Traditionally, men go outside the home to work, while women take care of the home and the children (However, as more women participate in the workforce, traditional roles between men and women become blurred). In spousal death, traditional roles are lost as well. For example, if the deceased husband was the main "breadwinner" (which is usually the case), the survivor spouse could experience financial hardship. Studies show that in spousal loss, widows experience more economic hardship than widowers (e.g., Fasoranti & Aruna, 2007). In grief, therefore, the female survivor spouse could be forced to prioritize restoration orientation over loss orientation, in seeking paid employment (e.g., McManus et al., 2018).

In acculturation experiences, people can choose on to interact with their environment, based on human agency (e.g., Berry, 2006). After a spousal loss, a woman can take on a man's customary role and vice versa. However, when culturally sanctioned, a strict adherence to traditional gender roles may inhibit readjustments to role loss due to spousal death (e.g., Doka, 1999).

Adjusting to loneliness: In the loss of a companion spouse, widowhood could lead to loneliness (Vedder et al., 2021). This is particularly true among elderly couples who have been married over a long period of time (Utz et al., 2014).

Loneliness could lead to self-grief. This could be manifested in depression (Fried et al., 2015), in post-traumatic stress disorder and other mental health, or in physical health disturbances (Erzen & Çikrikci, 2018). Psychiatrist Katherine Shear and colleagues (Shear et al., 2011) suggest that loneliness is a symptom of complicated grief disorder.

After spousal loss family members and friends may provide social support, through their presence. Such social support is no substitute for *companionship*, however. With regard to loneliness, researchers Nicole Valtorta and Barbara Hanratty (2012) note that "One of the most widely-used definitions has loneliness as a subjective negative feeling associated with a perceived lack of a wider social network (social loneliness) or the absence of a specific desired companion (emotional loneliness)" (p. 518).

In the course of a marital relationship, a person's self-concept could be derived from a companion spouse. Self-concept is how you perceive yourself and includes characteristics, abilities, and actions (Baumeister, 1999; Woolfolk, 2001). Self-concept is learned from interacting with your environment (Bharathi & Sreedevi, 2016). In the context of marriage, a spouse's self-concept could derive from their marital status and roles, and, therefore, in spousal loss, a widow or widower's self-concept may face challenges. As noted by psychiatrist Katherine Shear (2012), in prolonged grief disorder or complicated grief, there is a constant rumination about the loss and an inability to contemplate a future without the deceased by the survivor. Although self-concept is learned, it however could be modified or changed (Franken, 1994). This would require the motivation to acquire a new self-concept or a new identity. It might also include a desire to explore who one *truly* is, in beliefs and in actions (Schlegel et al., 2009). In the absence of the deceased spouse, this self-discovery could lead to a post-bereavement growth or decline. In growth, the survivor spouse discovers his or her interests and pursues them, in the absence of a possible constraint from the deceased spouse (e.g., travel the world). However, in decline, the survivor spouse pursues interests that are negative (e.g., experimentation with hard drugs), without guardrails from a deceased spouse.

Self-concept is defined as the value that an individual places on his or her own characteristics, qualities, abilities, and actions (Woolfolk, 2001). Self-concept is not innate, but is developed or constructed by the individual through interaction with the environment and reflecting on that interaction. This aspect of self-concept is important because it indicates that it can be modified or changed.

Reminders of the departed spouse: For some widows or widowers, a reminder of the departed spouse (e.g., birthday or anniversary dates) could trigger off self-grief. Reminders include personal belongings of the deceased spouse. A constant reminder (either conscious or unconscious) of the deceased spouse could stand in the way of grief integration or in moving forward with life. Over time, however, the bereaved spouse could become *habituated* to reminders of the departed spouse and have a decremental behavioral response (e.g., Rankin et al., 2009). At the initial period of grief, however, reminders could be difficult, but a perpetual avoidance of reminders could indicate a lack of grief integration into daily functioning, which could pass as sign of complicated grief or prolonged grief disorder (Shear, 2012).

Some cultures discourage reminders of the deceased. Among Australia's Indigenous people, any reminder of the deceased is avoided. The survivor relocates from the home where the death occurred and disposes of any personal belongings of the deceased (Jones, 2015). Culturally, reminders are perceived as causes for pain to the bereaved. Yet the pain experience should be part of coping with grief (Worden, 2018; Stroebe & Schut, 1999).

Whereas avoidance of reminders of the deceased may be based on cultural practices, the survivor spouse may have a personal reason for doing so. Aside from cultural prescriptions, some survivors might find reminders of loved ones difficult to handle, whose deaths were due to violence or were unexpected. Grief researchers note maintaining a continuing bond with a deceased loved is a personal choice (e.g., Stroebe & Schut, 2005). From their qualitative study of 49 bereaved individuals in Ecuador, researcher Terrah Foster et al. (2012) noted that participants who lost loved ones from accidents or drug overdose did not find comfort in maintaining continuing bonds with the deceased. Yet each person's grief is different, and based on personal or cultural proclivities, there is a wide spectrum of grief reactions (Zisook & Shear, 2009). Some people cope better through avoidance of reminders of the deceased, yet others do so by embracing reminders of the deceased and maintaining continuing bonds with departed loved ones (Klass et al., 1996).

Widowhood Effect

Widowhood effect occurs when a bereaved spouse dies soon after his or her spouse's death (e.g., Schaefer et al., 1995). This is one of the consequences of spousal bereavement which, as discussed earlier, is very painful and distressful. Spousal death is a risk factor for diseases including cardiovascular problems, diabetes, and arthritis (Einiö & Martikainen, 2019). It is also a risk factor for mental health problems including depression and anxiety (Kristiansen et al., 2019). Therefore, widowhood is a risk factor for mortality (Moon et al., 2011; Shor et al., 2012). Researchers Felix Elwert and Nicholas Christakis (2008) reviewed a national data of 373,189 married couples and found widowhood effect of the survivor spouse, for both men and women, was implicated by the precedent spouse's causes of death. These included various cancers, infections, and heart diseases. However, the survivor spouse was at greater risk of dying from certain causes than others. For elderly persons, a spousal death from cancer (especially colon and lung cancers) had a significant effect on widowhood mortality. Also, a spousal death from vascular diseases (including ischemic heart disease, congestive heart failure, cerebral vascular accident, or stroke) had a significant impact on widowhood mortality. However, a spousal death from Alzheimer's disease or Parkinson's disease had lesser impact on widowhood mortality. This perhaps is due to anticipatory or preparatory grief.

Death causations that are acute or unexpected (infections, accidents) or that are chronic but require treatment or prevention (e.g., diabetes, cancer) are particularly impactful on widowhood deaths. The knowledge of death causation type that could trigger widowhood death is helpful in planning support structures for the survivor spouse. However, as discussed earlier, a compromised self-concept or loneliness in the aftermath of spousal loss may not be adequately redressed by social support structures.

Across cultures, widowhood effect is reported in different age groups for men and women (Parkes et al., 1969; Helsing et al., 1982; Hu & Goldman, 1990). However, among elderly people, widowhood effect increases at between 30 and 90% in the first 3 months of spousal loss. But in subsequent months this percentage falls to around 15% (Schaefer et al., 1995; Martikainen & Valkonen, 1996; Johnson et al., 2000; Elwert & Christakis, 2008). Thus, the period immediately following a spousal loss may be consequential in widowhood effect.

With chronic illnesses being common among elderly people, there is the tendency to undermine the effect of bereavement on mortality (Jaul & Barron, 2017). Although chronic illnesses are reported in both married people and widowed individuals of the same age (Blanner et al., 2020), widowhood effect is of concern with the widowed elderly. Preventive measures for widowhood effect should include coping strategies (Carr et al., 2018), approaches to mitigating financial strain (DiGiacomo et al., 2015), and family support (Zhou & Hearst, 2016). The effectiveness of these intervention measures are still unknown (Stroebe et al., 2017). However, grief should not be considered a disease before the introduction of professional interventions. Rather, it should be allowed to take its normal course (Zisook & Shear, 2009). Preventive measures should be geared toward improvements of mental health and physical well-being of people most likely to be at risk of widowhood effect (Nseir & Larkey, 2013; Stroebe & Schut, 2005).

Although health issues are implicated in widowhood, there are cultural practices that encourage widowhood effect. Studies from both married and widowed individuals of the same age suggest that widowhood effect is not a function of health problems alone (Blanner et al., 2020; Einiö & Martikainen, 2019). While some cultural practices discourage widowhood effect, others encourage it.

Cultural Practices That Discourage Widowhood Effect

The following cultural factors help to minimize widowhood effect:

Social support: Social support could act as a distraction or temporarily fill in the void created by a loved one's absence. Social support structures include family and friends, members of sociocultural or religious groups, coworkers, or neighbors. Community groups such as Widows Connection (https://widowsconnection.org) also provide social support. Social support does the following: reassures the bereaved that he or she is not alone, provides strength in numbers even in a loss, and gives the feeling of shared grief.

Values of individualism: Values associated with individualism may help to reduce the occurrence of widowhood effect. With individualism, the *self* is perceived as separate from others. In contrast, in collectivism, the self is perceived as shared with others. In India, the cultural practice of *sati* earlier mentioned is an example. In delineating between individualist and collectivist value systems, social psychologist Harry Triandis (1995) notes that individualists value a self that is autonomous, whereas collectivists value a self that is relational.

Life insurance policy: Studies from both developed and developing societies suggest that in the death of a spouse, widows are more affected than widowers financially (Fadlon et al., 2020). With spousal loss, financial burden is an additional stress element that could result in widowhood effect. One of the characteristics of complicated grief or prolonged grief disorder is the inability to contemplate a life without the deceased (Shear, 2012). If the decedent spouse was the breadwinner, a financial burden on a survivor spouse with an existing chronic illness could trigger distress with mortality as a possible outcome. However, a life insurance policy that has the survivor spouse as a beneficiary would provide the following benefits (Eyetsemitan, 2020):

(a) A tax-free lump sum death payment. This amount could be used in a variety of ways including paying off debts, mortgages, and funeral costs.
(b) Payment is immediate. This would preclude delays that may involve settling of an estate, including court cases.
(c) Payout is not subject to a creditor's claims, probate, or legal and executor's fees.

Social security survivors benefit: In the United States, the Social Security survivors' benefits program helps the survivor spouse, mostly female, to make up for shortfalls in the decedent partner's income. The eligibility age is 60 years; however, it would be helpful if smaller benefits become available to widows who are not yet 60 years old (Fadlon et al., 2020). As early as age 50, however, a disabled widow or widower could receive benefits, and he or she could start receiving benefits if they had been disabled before or within 7 years prior to the spouse's death (SSA.gov, n.d.)

According to the United States Bureau of Labor Statistics (September, 2021), between the ages 55 and 64 years, women on average earn three-quarters of what men make in the workforce. Therefore, the Social Security survivors' benefits would help to maintain financial solvency for widows.

Cultural Practices That Encourage Widowhood Effect

Cultural practices that subject a survivor spouse to abuse and guilt could encourage widowhood effect. In Nigeria, among the Ibos, following a spousal loss, the survivor spouse would have to prove that she was not the cause of her husband's death. This practice is done before an oracle and includes being made to drink the water used to bath her deceased husband (Ajayi et al., 2019). The widow is first declared guilty and then asked to prove her innocence before an inanimate oracle whose veracity is questionable. Yet the oracle's verdict as interpreted by a priest is final. If the verdict comes in as guilty, the widow is stigmatized, ostracized, and put to shame. In a period of intense distress, this act constitutes an additional burden on the survivor spouse. Even with government laws and international treaties that the Nigerian government is signatory to that protect the widow from human rights abuses, this cultural practice continues to be popular in rural areas (Ajayi et al., 2019).

Long-Term Living Arrangement After Spousal Loss

Spousal death raises the issue of long-term living arrangement for the survivor spouse. The cultural values of individualism (independence) versus collectivism (interdependence) become important consideration. Consequent upon a spousal loss, living alone could be lonely for the survivor spouse. Therefore, the living arrangement of the survivor spouse becomes an important issue, especially for elderly people who do not have young children living with them. However, the following factors could influence a future living arrangement of a survivor spouse:

Current accommodation: Prior to spousal loss the accommodation size might have been adequate, but after spousal loss, the house could become oversized for the survivor spouse alone. Therefore, the pressure to downsize and move into a smaller accommodation might come from family members. However, to relocate might be problematic given that people are attached to their homes, based on length of occupancy, familiarity with their neighborhood, and memories created with the deceased spouse.

Another consideration against a relocation is "aging in place," a concept which the United States Center for Disease Control and Prevention defines as "the ability to live in one's own home and community safely, independently, and comfortably, regardless of age, income, or ability level" (CDC.gov, n.d.).

Relocation: Even when a relocation is considered (including moving in with an adult child), maintaining one's *independence*, an important cultural value for individualists, is important (Hofstede, 1980). Relocation with an adult child could occur if the deceased spouse provided care for the survivor spouse, and if the survivor spouse's health demands it, a relocation to an assisted living facility or a skilled care facility becomes an option.

In some cultures, a spousal death provides with the survivor spouse an opportunity to relocate and experience the care of one's own children. This aligns with collectivism or *interdependence*, a cultural value held mostly by non-Westerners. The Indigenous Australians provide another cultural reason for relocation. After a death, reminders of the deceased are avoided. These include removing and destroying personal belongings of the deceased and relocating from the home where the death occurred (Jones, 2015). These cultural measures are intended to help the bereaved to cope with the pain of their loss.

Living space with social support: Following a spousal loss, social support is greatly affected within the home if no children or loved ones are co-dwellers.

Therefore, social support within the home could influence a future living arrangement. This includes children or relatives moving in with the survivor spouse, the survivor spouse moving in with children or relatives, or a co-residency arrangement between survivor spouse and other bereaved family members or friends. Social support within the home could be beneficial in the following ways: (a) have someone to talk to; (b) hear another live voice in the house, (c) feel safe with the presence of others, (d) financial savings in shared living expenses, and (e) complement or compensate for each other's physical, mental, or emotional deficits. A study of participants who lived alone after spousal loss reported significant increase in the proportion of depression, when compared to the period prior to spousal death (Hung et al., 2021).

Key Takeaways

1. Spousal loss has a significant impact on the survivor spouse. Grief outcomes are related to the cause of death, and the precedent spouse's death could provide an insight into the survivor spouse's grief trajectory. In spousal death the impact of some health issues (e.g., cancer) is more salient than others (e.g., Alzheimer's disease) in effecting widowhood effect.
2. Cultural beliefs (e.g., evil eye, witchcraft, or sorcery) regarding death causation are important as they impact on grief outcomes.
3. There are two types of spousal grief: (1) grief for the deceased spouse and (2) grief by the survivor spouse for himself or herself.
4. Some cultural factors discourage widowhood effect, while others encourage widowhood effect.
5. Following a spousal death, loneliness could influence future living arrangement by the survivor spouse. The reasons to remain in a current accommodation are different from those for relocation. Furthermore, cultural or personal reasons (e.g., to avoid reminders of the deceased) could be influential in relocation.

Critical Cultural Thinking

1. In coping with her loss, Jessica made the following statement about her late husband: "John died doing what he loved." What cultural value is reflected in this statement, and how is this likely to affect Jessica's grief trajectory?
2. After David's death, his survivor spouse, Jane, is not sure whether to relocate or not. What options does Jane have, and what issues should she consider in relocating or not relocating?

References

Ajayi, L. A., Olanrewaju, F. O., Olanrewaju, A., & Nwannebuife, O. (2019). Gendered violence and human rights: An evaluation of widowhood rites in nigeria. *Cogent Arts & Humanities, 6*(1), 1676569.

Baumeister, R. F. (1999). Self-concept, self-esteem, and identity. In V. J. Derlega, B. A. Winstead, & W. H. Jones (Eds.), *Personality: Contemporary theory and research* (pp. 339–375). Nelson-Hall Publishers.

Bennett, K. M., Smith, P. T., & Hughes, G. M. (2005). Coping, depressive feelings and gender differences in late life widowhood. *Aging & Mental Health, 9*(4), 348–353.

Berry, J. W. (2006). Contexts of acculturation. In *The Cambridge handbook of acculturation psychology* (Vol. 27, No. 42, pp. 328–336).

Bharathi, T. A., & Sreedevi, P. (2016). A study on the self-concept of adolescents. *International Journal of Science and Research, 5*(10), 512–516.

Blanner, C., Mejldal, A., Prina, A. M., Munk-Jørgensen, P., Ersbøll, A. K., & Andersen, K. (2020). Widowhood and mortality: A Danish nationwide register-based cohort study. *Epidemiology and Psychiatric Sciences, 29*, e149.

Bowlby, J. (1980). *Attachment and loss. Vol. 3: Loss, sadness and depression*. Basic Books.

Carr, D. C., Ureña, S., & Taylor, M. G. (2018). Adjustment to widowhood and loneliness among older men: The influence of military service. *The Gerontologist, 58*(6), 1085–1095.

CDC.gov. (n.d.). *Aging in place*. www.cdc.gov/healthyplaces/terminology

DiGiacomo, M., Lewis, J., Phillips, J., Nolan, M., & Davidson, P. M. (2015). The business of death: A qualitative study of financial concerns of widowed older women. *BMC Women's Health, 15*, 1–10.

Doka, K. J. (1999). Disenfranchised grief. *Bereavement Care, 18*(3), 37–39.

Einiö, E., & Martikainen, P. (2019). Risk of hospitalization for cancer, musculoskeletal disorders, injuries, or poisonings surrounding widowhood. *American Journal of Epidemiology, 188*(1), 110–118.

Elwert, F., & Christakis, N. A. (2008). The effect of widowhood on mortality by the causes of death of both spouses. *American Journal of Public Health, 98*(11), 2092–2098.

Erzen, E., & Çikrikci, Ö. (2018). The effect of loneliness on depression: A meta-analysis. *International Journal of Social Psychiatry, 64*(5), 427–435.

Eyetsemitan, F. E. (2020). *Understanding death and dying: Encountering death, dying, and the afterlife*. Sage.

Fadlon, I., Ramnath, S., Tong, P. K., & MacKay, L. C. (2020, May). Financial life after the death of a spouse; Federal Reserve Bank of Chicago. *Chicago Fed Letter*, No. 438.

Fasoranti, O. O., & Aruna, J. O. (2007). A cross-cultural comparison of practices relating to widowhood and widow-inheritance among the Igbo and Yoruba in Nigeria. *Journal of World Anthropology: Occasional Papers, 3*(1), 53–73.

Foster, T. L., Roth, M., Contreras, R., Jo Gilmer, M., & Gordon, J. E. (2012). Continuing bonds reported by bereaved individuals in Ecuador. *Bereavement Care, 31*(3), 120–128.

Franken, R. (1994). *Human motivation*. Brooks.

Fried, E. I., Bockting, C., Arjadi, R., Borsboom, D., Amshoff, M., Cramer, A. O., et al. (2015). From loss to loneliness: The relationship between bereavement and depressive symptoms. *Journal of Abnormal Psychology, 124*(2), 256.

Helsing, K. J., Comstock, G. W., & Szklo, M. (1982). Causes of death in a widowed population. *American Journal of Epidemiology, 116*(3), 524–532.

Hofstede, G. (1980). Culture and organizations. *International Studies of Management & Organization, 10*(4), 15–41.

Hu, Y., & Goldman, N. (1990). Mortality differentials by marital status: An international comparison. *Demography, 27*, 233–250.

Hung, Y., Chen, Y., Lee, M., & Yeh, C. (2021). Effect of spousal loss on depression in older adults: Impacts of time passing, living arrangement, and spouse's health status before death. *International Journal of Environmental Research and Public Health, 18*(24), 13032.

Jaul, E., & Barron, J. (2017). Age-related diseases and clinical and public health implications for the 85 years old and over population. *Frontiers in Public Health, 5*, 335.

Johnson, N. J., Backlund, E., Sorlie, P. D., & Loveless, C. A. (2000). Marital status and mortality: The national longitudinal mortality study. *Annals of Epidemiology, 10*(4), 224–238.

Jones, K. (2015). It is normal to remember: Death and grief in Australia. In *The world of bereavement: Cultural perspectives on death in families* (pp. 243–263).

Kapur, R. (2018). Problems of the aged people in India. *On May, 15*, 2018.

Klass, D., Silverman, P., & Nickman, S. (1996). *Continuing bonds: New understandings of grief.* Taylor & Francis.

Kristiansen, C. B., Kjær, J. N., Hjorth, P., Andersen, K., & Prina, A. M. (2019). Prevalence of common mental disorders in widowhood: A systematic review and meta-analysis. *Journal of Affective Disorders, 245*, 1016–1023.

Martikainen, P., & Valkonen, T. (1996). Mortality after the death of a spouse: Rates and causes of death in a large Finnish cohort. *American Journal of Public Health, 86*(8_Pt_1), 1087–1093.

McManus, R., Walter, T., & Claridge, L. (2018). Restoration and loss after disaster: Applying the dual process model of coping in bereavement. *Death Studies, 42*, 405–414.

Moon, J. R., Kondo, N., Glymour, M. M., & Subramanian, S. V. (2011). Widowhood and mortality: A meta-analysis. *PLoS One, 6*(8), e23465.

Nseir, S., & Larkey, L. K. (2013). Interventions for spousal bereavement in the older adult: An evidence review. *Death Studies, 37*(6), 495–512.

Parkes, C. M., Benjamin, B., & Fitzgerald, R. G. (1969). Broken heart: A statistical study of increased mortality among widowers. *British Medical Journal, 1*(5646), 740–743.

Rankin, C. H., Abrams, T., Barry, R. J., Bhatnagar, S., Clayton, D. F., Colombo, J., et al. (2009). Habituation revisited: An updated and revised description of the behavioral characteristics of habituation. *Neurobiology of Learning and Memory, 92*(2), 135–138.

Schaefer, C., Quesenberry, C. P., Jr., & Wi, S. (1995). Mortality following conjugal bereavement and the effects of a shared environment. *American Journal of Epidemiology, 141*(12), 1142–1152.

Schlegel, R. J., Hicks, J. A., Arndt, J., & King, L. A. (2009). Thine own self: True self-concept accessibility and meaning in life. *Journal of Personality and Social Psychology, 96*(2), 473.

Shear, M. K. (2012). Getting straight about grief. *Depression and Anxiety, 29*(6), 461–464.

Shear, M. K., Simon, N., Wall, M., Zisook, S., Neimeyer, R., Duan, N., et al. (2011). Complicated grief and related bereavement issues for DSM-5. *Depression and Anxiety, 28*(2), 103–117.

Shor, E., Roelfs, D. J., Bugyi, P., & Schwartz, J. E. (2012). Meta-analysis of marital dissolution and mortality: Reevaluating the intersection of gender and age. *Social Science & Medicine, 75*(1), 46–59.

SSA.gov. (n.d.). *Planning for your survivors.* https://www.ssa.gov/benefits/survivors/onyourown.html

Stroebe, M., & Schut, H. (1999). The dual process model of coping with bereavement: Rationale and description. *Death Studies, 23*(3), 197–224.

Stroebe, M., & Schut, H. (2005). To continue or relinquish bonds: A review of consequences for the bereaved. *Death Studies, 29*(6), 477–494.

Stroebe, M., Schut, H., & Boerner, K. (2017). Cautioning health-care professionals: Bereaved persons are misguided through the stages of grief. *OMEGA-Journal of Death and Dying, 74*(4), 455–473.

Triandis, H. C. (1995). A theoretical framework for the study of diversity. In M. M. Chemers, S. Oskamp, & M. A. Costanzo (Eds.), *Diversity in organizations: New perspectives for a changing workplace* (pp. 11–36). Sage.

UN.org. (n.d.). *Committee on the elimination of discrimination against women*. Retrieved May 17, 2023, from www.un.org/womenwatch/daw/cedaw/cdrom_cedaw/EN/files/cedaw25years/content/english/about_daw.html

United States Bureau of Labor Statistics. (2021, September). *Highlights of women's earnings in 2020*. https://www.bls.gov/opub/reports/womens-earnings/2020/home.htm

Utz, R. L., Swenson, K. L., Caserta, M., Lund, D., & DeVries, B. (2014). Feeling lonely versus being alone: Loneliness and social support among recently bereaved persons. *Journals of Gerontology Series B: Psychological Sciences and Social Sciences, 69*(1), 85–94.

Valtorta, N., & Hanratty, B. (2012). Loneliness, isolation and the health of older adults: Do we need a new research agenda? *Journal of the Royal Society of Medicine, 105*(12), 518–522.

Vedder, A., Stroebe, M. S., Schut, H. A., Boerner, K., Stokes, J. E., & Boelen, P. A. (2021). Loneliness in bereavement: Measurement matters. *Frontiers in Psychology, 12*, 741762.

Woolfolk, R. L. (2001). The concept of mental illness: An analysis of four pivotal issues. *The Journal of Mind and Behavior*, 161–178.

Worden, J. W. (2018). *Grief counseling and grief therapy: A handbook for the mental health practitioner*. Springer Publishing Company.

Zhou, J., & Hearst, N. (2016). Health-related quality of life of among elders in rural China: The effect of widowhood. *Quality of Life Research, 25*, 3087–3095.

Zisook, S., & Shear, K. (2009). Grief and bereavement: What psychiatrists need to know. *World Psychiatry, 8*(2), 67.

Chapter 6
Culture, Abortion, and Bereavement

Abortion is the *voluntary* termination of a pregnancy, different from an involuntary termination due to a miscarriage. According to Harvard Health Publishing (2019), other terms for abortion include *elective abortion, induced abortion, termination of pregnancy, and therapeutic abortion*. There are varied factors that could influence the voluntary termination of a pregnancy. They include an unplanned pregnancy due to unprotected consensual sex, rape, or incest. Also, an abortion decision could be due to competing demands including the pressure to complete an educational program, especially for young school-age persons. Also, another contributory factor is the perceived lack of social support from family members and friends, both during and after a pregnancy. In some cultures, in adolescence motherhood is perceived as not age appropriate which could lead to pregnancy termination. A partner's lack of commitment to a future that includes the child and the child's mother could lead to the pregnancy termination as well (e.g., Shain, 1986). However, across cultures, the prevalent factors that contribute to an abortion include a mother's unmarried status, a mother's poor health, adultery, rape, incest, or illegal union (Shain, 1986).

Trends in Abortion

Around the world, from 1990 to 1994, 51% of abortion cases was due to unintended pregnancies. From 2015 to 2019, abortion cases rose to 61% because abortion is in demand in countries where it is both legal and illegal (Guttmacher.org, March, 2022). However, an induced abortion when not carried out by someone with the necessary skills (e.g., a trained medical personnel) could become unsafe. Globally, 45% of all abortions are unsafe with almost all of them (97%) occurring in developing societies, where access to good healthcare remains a challenge, especially in rural areas. For example, in Latin America and in Africa, an estimated three out of four abortions are unsafe (Ganatra et al., 2017). In developed societies, however, an

F. E. Eyetsemitan, *Cultural Influences in Coping with Grief*,
https://doi.org/10.1007/978-3-031-86817-7_6

estimated 30 out of 100,000 women die from unsafe abortion. But with developing societies, this number increases to 220 per 100,000 women. Each year, unsafe abortion accounts for 4.7–13.2% of all maternal deaths (Say et al., 2014).

In the United States, in most states abortion is legal and is relatively safe. However, in the United States abortion takes on a different perspective: the mother's rights versus the fetus' rights. A Pew Research Center (May 6, 2022) survey found that in the United States 61% of adults think that abortion should be legal at most or all the time, whereas 37% of the people think that abortion should be illegal at most or all of the time. Approximately 56% of the people who believe that abortion should be legal also believe that how far along a pregnancy has come should be given consideration.

In 1973 the United States Supreme Court in its *Roe v. Wade* decision confers on the woman the right to have an abortion. This annuls state laws on abortion. In 1969, "Jane Roe" (or Norma McCorvey) was pregnant and wanted an abortion but lived in the state of Texas where abortion was illegal. She filed a lawsuit against the Texas district attorney alleging that Texas' laws on abortion were unconstitutional. Both the United States District Court for the Northern District of Texas and the United States Supreme Court ruled in Roe's favor. In its judgment delivered on January 22, 1973, the United States Supreme Court notes that under the 14th Amendment of the US Constitution, the "right to privacy" extends to abortion. However, on June 24, 2022, the United States Supreme Court reversed itself. Now states could make their own decision on abortion. Consequent upon the United State Supreme Court's decision of June 24, 2022, abortion became illegal in some states (Axios.com, June 24, 2022).

Culturally, the United States (as well as other Western societies) has high values for *individual rights*. With abortion, this cultural value for individual rights could impact on grief outcomes differently, as some people perceive the individual rights to extend to both the woman and the fetus *equally*. Proabortion advocates, however, believe that both the mother's rights and the fetus' rights should be vested in the pregnant woman, who knows what is best for her and the fetus in her womb. Therefore, a third party such as the courts or the government should not be making decisions on abortion. Thus, a pregnant woman who exercises her right to an abortion would have a different grief trajectory than a pregnant woman who had a third party's decision on abortion imposed on her. Also, family members or friends who believe that an abortion decision is the pregnant woman's right to exercise would have a different grief outcome than those who do not share a similar belief.

On the contrary, individuals who believe that the fetus' rights are superior to the pregnant woman's rights are more likely to welcome a third party's (e.g., the courts or government) intervention in abortion. The Christian religion takes the side of the fetus in individual rights and not the pregnant woman's (Shain, 1986). The Catholic Church has a tradition against abortion because it ascribes the right to life to God, which includes the fetus. The Catholic Church has several followers around the world, who based on the church's doctrine believe in the rights of the fetus. According to the Pew Research Center (February 13, 2013), Catholics make up about 50% of Christians and about 16% of the world's population.

Models of Disenfranchised Grief

According to researcher Kenneth Doka (2002, 2008), and as highlighted by Eyetsemitan (2022), the following scenarios exemplify *disenfranchised* grief (a grief not publicly shared or sanctioned) in loss:

(a) A relationship that is not socially approved (e.g., an extramarital affair)
(b) A relationship not based on recognizable kin ties (e.g., a neighbor or a companion animal)
(c) A relationship from the past (e.g., an ex-lover)
(d) A death that limits the support of others (e.g., suicide)
(e) A grieving style that is not culturally approved (e.g., a male grieving as a female or vice versa)

Abortion can lead to disenfranchised grief, based on the following cultural or religious orientation:

Individualism versus collectivism: In an individualist value system, an abortion decision would be the pregnant woman's. However, in a collectivist value system, an abortion decision is viewed differently; it has to be approved by others (e.g., family and friends).

Egalitarianism versus hierarchy: In cultures that value egalitarianism, people expect to be treated as equals, whereas in cultures that value hierarchy, older persons command more respect than younger individuals and males more than females (Schwartz, 2007). Within an egalitarian value system, abortion rights should be extended to all. However, in cultures that value hierarchy, individual abortion rights should be subjugated to group approval.

Healthcare providers: In individualist cultures individual rights and egalitarianism impact on healthcare decisions. However, in a collectivist value system, a physician (or a healthcare provider) would respect the family's wishes over that of the individual's in healthcare decisions that pertain to a patient (e.g., Shain, 1986). Studies suggest this to be the case in India (a collectivist culture) in contrast to Germany (individualist society) (Chattopadhyay & Simon, 2008). In Latino culture (also a collectivist culture), end-of-life decisions are made by family members with little or no input from the patient (e.g., Kelley et al., 2010). In collectivist cultures, an individual seeking an abortion in the absence of family members and friends is less likely to receive the willing support of professional healthcare practitioners. This makes abortion to be popular among untrained medical practitioners, which is unsafe. As earlier mentioned, in Latin America and in Africa, an estimated three out of four abortions are unsafe (Ganatra et al., 2017).

Infertility tied to a previous abortion act: When infertility is perceived as punishment from a previous abortion act, this could lead to disenfranchised grief. In the Hindu religion, karma is the belief that a person's good or bad act is repaid in kind in the future (e.g., Sharma et al., 2013). Suffering is believed to relate to karma (Thrane, 2010). In India, the dominant religion is Hinduism, which has a worldwide following of about 1 billion people (Pew Research Center, 2012).

An abortion act that does not align with religious or cultural norms could lead to disenfranchised grief. However, researcher Tony Walter (2010) cautions that there are heterogenous cultures within each society, and, therefore, it would be wrong to assume that the grief outcomes of minority group members are influenced by the dominant religions or cultural groups. For example, the dominant normative behavior in the United States is to approach life with optimism and to consider death as a loss. Yet, as minority groups, African Americans and Native Americans dwell on loss as part of their historical and cultural fabric.

Cross-Cultural Socialization Patterns

Within each society, the socialization experience of individuals is different due to reasons including interracial marriage, immigration, and globalization influences. As earlier discussed in Chap. 4, cross-cultural psychologist John Berry (2006) notes that people may choose the values of their indigenous culture over a foreign culture; they may value a foreign culture over their native culture; they may hold on to both indigenous and foreign cultures; or they may reject both indigenous and foreign cultures. Therefore, within a society with a dominant value for individualism, a healthcare practitioner may work with a bereaved person who does not subscribe to the values of individualism. The same applies to a healthcare practitioner who operates in a culture where collectivism is dominant. Therefore, due to acculturative influences, each bereaved person's values have to be acknowledged by a healthcare practitioner (e.g., Berry, 2006). Absent this would be disenfranchised grief.

Intervention for Disenfranchised Grief

A "culture of support" is helpful for women who have experienced an abortion (Littman et al., 2009). In the United States, researcher Lisa Littman et al. (2009) report on positive feedback of 20 women who received information about services and groups that provide support that validate a woman's right to reproduction. All of the study participants find their intervention experience personally helpful in reducing any possible stigma attached to their abortion. Other studies show that abortion stigma could negatively impact on a woman's well-being (Hanschmidt et al., 2016). From reviewing seven quantitative and seven qualitative studies of women who had had an abortion, researcher Franz Hanschmidt et al. (2016) noted that majority of their study participants experienced fear of judgment by others. They also experienced self-judgment and a need for secrecy. The study participants were drawn from both collectivist cultures (Ghana, Mexico, Nigeria, Pakistan, Peru, and Zambia) and individualist cultures (the United States and the United Kingdom).

Abortion and Maternal-Fetal Attachment

In interaction between an infant and its mother, psychologist John Bowlby (1980) proposes an attachment model that provides the infant with emotional comfort and security. Attachment behavior has been reported in adult romantic relationships as well (e.g., Cassidy et al., 2013) and documented in cross-cultural studies (Grossmann et al., 1985; Nakagawa et al., 1989; Sagi et al., 1985). The original concept of attachment (Bowlby, 1980) pertains to a postnatal relationship between the infant and its mother (or a care provider) that is predicated on the following:

- The child is at the receiving end of the relationship. However, attachment relationship between mother and infant could be *reciprocal* (Eyetsemitan, 2022).
- The attachment relationship is throughout the life course, and as John Bowlby notes attachment behavior extends "from the cradle to the grave" (Bowlby, 1979; p. 129).
- Maternal and fetal attachment (MFA) occurs as well (Mehran et al., 2013). In pregnancy, the woman is at the receiving end of this attachment, and it influences her identity as mother-to-be or not-mother-to-be. Whereas in *postnatal* death a de-attachment occurs between the woman and the child (Eyetsemitan, 2022), in *prenatal* loss a de-attachment occurs between the woman and the fetus. In a perinatal loss, the *de-attachment* types that occur between the woman and the fetus include the following:

  Physical: After an abortion, the physical presence of the fetus (which is more pronounced in advanced pregnancy) will be no more. This physical change becomes an important marker to the woman's identity. Her identity changes from mother-to-be to not-mother-to-be. Yet this physical change and identity may be welcome or not, depending on the circumstances that lead to the abortion.

  Cognitive: Cognitively, there would be a readjustment from being pregnant to *not being pregnant*. A change in the woman's cognitive schema and perceptual set to *accommodate* her new identity would be required (e.g., Piaget, 1952). This change would lead to a new way of thinking, believing, and acting. Inability to accommodate a new way of thinking, believing, and acting may negatively impact on her grief outcome.

  Emotional/Affective: There would be a need to detach from the fetus, emotionally. However, this would depend on factors that led to the abortion. A decision freely made by the woman would have a different grief outcome than a decision made by factors outside of her control or forced on her.

Pre-abortion and Postabortion Meanings

The meaning ascribed to an abortion would impact on the individual, her friends/family, and people that facilitated the procedure. Abortion meaning would help with sensemaking, with benefit making, and with identity changing (e.g., Gillies & Neimeyer, 2006). Abortion meaning could fit into the following categories:

Pre-abortion meaning: The *pre-abortion meaning* precedes an abortion decision. It is based on one's worldview and is influenced by factors that include religious beliefs on the sanctity of life and on cultural values such as individualism and collectivism. It is also influenced by the perceived stereotypes about abortion. If a pre-abortion meaning adequately makes sense to ending a fetus, any accompanying distress would be minimized (e.g., Gillies & Neimeyer, 2006). Examples of pre-abortion meaning include exercising one's right to terminating a pregnancy due to incest. However, if an abortion act is in conflict with a pre-abortion meaning (e.g., religious beliefs on the sanctity of life), this could lead to distress.

Postabortion meaning: When a pre-abortion meaning is not helpful with sense-making or is in conflict with an abortion act, a postabortion meaning reconstruction may be required to reducing any distress. However, it would be helpful if a postabortion meaning reconstruction reflects elements of the pre-abortion meaning. For example, if the pre-abortion meaning is based on religious beliefs, a postabortion meaning reconstruction should also be made within a religious framework. A pre-abortion meaning may be based on the Christian belief that only God can give or take a life, which would be in conflict with an abortion act. However, a postabortion meaning reconstruction could be based on another Christian precept that says God forgives a sinner who confesses and turns away from their sin. The Catholic Church has embraced a similar postabortion meaning reconstruction, as discussed in Chap. 10.

Dual Religious Beliefs and Acculturation Outcomes

Religious beliefs can be helpful in reducing grief that accompanies an abortion act, at the stage of either pre-abortion meaning or postabortion meaning reconstruction. Yet some individuals have dual but conflicting religious beliefs. For example, among non-Westerners it is common practice to hold on to both Christian beliefs and African traditional religious beliefs (e.g., Eyetsemitan, 2021). In many Central American countries where Catholicism is the dominant religion, Afro-Caribbean or Indigenous religion is common as well (Pew Research Center, 2014). Similar dual religious practices are common in Panama, in Dominican Republic, in Honduras, in Nicaragua, in El Salvador, and in Costa Rica. Also, dual religious beliefs are found in Mexico, in Guatemala, and in Puerto Rico. In Afro-Caribbean or Indigenous religion, practitioners believe in reincarnation, evil eye, witchcraft, or sorcery, and they communicate with spirits and offer food or flowers to spirits. They also participate in spiritual cleansing ceremonies and in consulting with spiritual healers (Pew Research Center, 2014). Brazil is a society where dual religious practices is common. The *Umbanda* religion (belief in spirit, in reincarnation, and in use of intermediary mediums to contact the spirit of the dead) is practiced alongside Catholicism. Based on an interview of 17 Brazilian families from diverse religious backgrounds who had been bereaved, researcher Regina Bousso et al. (2011) reported that a family said neither Catholicism nor Protestantism could help with *meaning* to their loss, but Spiritism did instead. Therefore, at the pre-abortion meaning stage, it is important to explore which of the conflicting beliefs is salient to the individual.

In some cultures, based on socialization practices, a woman's gender identity and gender roles (as a nurturer or mother) could be salient in pre-abortion meaning. In Korean society, for example, traditional gender roles are given great importance (Sung, 2018). Therefore, following an abortion there is shame and guilt. This is similar to the bereaved parent who refuses to make sense of her child's death because it would justify her loss. Yet the bereaved parent is subject to intense grief (Keesee et al., 2008). Therefore, in the bereavement process social support is important (Lee et al., 2022). Also, in postabortion meaning reconstruction, rituals are helpful in restoring the woman's gender identity. In Japan, the practice of *mizuko kuyo* is the cultural-religious ritual which focuses on the "unseen" child or fetus, who is no more because of an abortion or a miscarriage. This also applies to a stillbirth child (Yamada & Shupe, 2013). In this ritual of *mizuko kuyo,* known also as "water-child," which is a representation of the mother's amniotic fluid and the purifying nature of water in the Buddhist-Shinto beliefs, the child's pain is taken away in the same manner that the mother's pain is resolved. Thus, the deceased is in harmony with the living mother (Klass & Heath, 1997). With this ritual, the cultural identity of the woman as a *nurturant* mother becomes restored. In a Swedish study, women also feel the need to mark their abortion experience with rituals. This helps to bring about some closure to their situation. These rituals are not normative but are personally constructed (Stålhandske et al., 2012). They could be before or after an abortion and in symbolic form (Stålhandske et al., 2012). Thus, in death meaning, rituals are important, and they also provide a sense of continuing bond with the deceased (Neimeyer & Harris, 2023).

Self-Concept and Abortion

Self-concept is a person's understanding of who they think they are, based on their attributes (e.g., Baumeister, 1999). As authors Sean Laurent and Michael Myers (2011) also put it, self-concept is a response to the question: "Who am I?" The answer to the question of who am I is derived from others and includes the individual's socialization experiences. In other words, the self is anchored within a social system. Thus, a person's self-concept could provide an insight into their pre-abortion meaning or postabortion meaning reconstruction. For example, an abortion stigma is derived from a violation of the assumptive world of a *female* in these three areas: motherhood, breeding, and nurturing (Kumar et al., 2009). Also, an abortion stigma is contextualized within a cultural framework (e.g., race, ethnicity, age, socioeconomic class) and the location of the abortion act (Norris et al., 2011; Steinberg et al., 2016; Moreno López et al., 2019). In the United States, there is racial disparity in abortion stigma. When compared to African-American/Black women, White women have relatively higher perception scores on abortion sigma by the general public. However, when compared to both African American/Black women and White women, Latino women have relatively higher perception scores on abortion stigma from family members/friends (but not the general public) (Shellenberg & Tsui, 2012). The internalization of an abortion stigma could lead to shame in family planning (Gelman et al., 2017). In other words, in family planning, should a good mother place quality over quantity or base their abortion decision on financial exigencies? In South Korea, however, an abortion act is accompanied by shame and guilt, irrespective of the circumstance (Lee et al., 2022).

In the United States, almost two-thirds of over 4000 abortion patients from a national study, reported that they would be scorned if people knew they had committed an abortion (Shellenberg & Tsui, 2012). Abortion stigma could affect a woman's psychological well-being (Steinberg et al., 2016). Yet abortion stigma could occur at two levels: the cultural level (enacted stigma) and the societal level (structural stigma) from government policies that limit abortion (Pescosolido & Martin, 2015).

At the societal level (structural stigma), abortion stigma may be perceived as infringing on individual rights. This could lead to a pushback from the individual and their loved ones. Yet at the cultural level (enacted abortion) of family, friends, and community, abortion stigma may not face a pushback as it is not legal. Abortion stigma extends to abortion providers and to abortion supporters including advocates, family, partners, and friends (Norris et al., 2011). Each individual would have to evaluate the relative impact of both societal and cultural dimensions of abortion stigma on them (Beynon-Jones, 2017).

In coping with abortion stigma, abortion becomes a "concealable" act that is revealed to others, only as needed (Quinn & Chaudoir, 2009). In the United Kingdom, studies demonstrate that *secrecy* is used as a coping mechanism for abortion (Astbury-Ward et al., 2012). Yet secrecy only reinforces abortion stigma (Kumar et al., 2009; Major & Gramzow, 1999).

The Quality of an Abortion Decision on Grief

Abortion decision may be made based on either short-term thinking or long-term thinking. In *short-term thinking*, an abortion decision is influenced by current circumstances including financial problems, the need to get even with a male partner, or the relative importance of completing an education program. An abortion decision that is based on short-term thinking could bring about a temporary relief. Yet it could lead to future regrets and delayed grief, if the circumstance that prompted the abortion act changes in the future, e.g., improvements in finances or a change in the male partner's behavior. In South Africa, for example, teenagers who committed abortion expressed regrets afterwards (Sebola, 2021).

An abortion decision that is based on *long-term* thinking would take into consideration various options, including anticipated future changes to current circumstances. To be perceived as a wife in good standing with the husband's family, as well as progenitor of the husband's family name, *female selective abortion* (FSA) is a practice that opts for a female over a male in an abortion act. Researcher Maya Unnithan-Kumar (2010) notes that in several Asian countries, this practice is commonplace and is a reflection of long-term thinking rather than short-term thinking.

Conflicts and Coping with an Abortion Decision

For some individuals, an abortion decision is not clear-cut and could be stressful. There could be conflicts on whether to keep a pregnancy or not. According to psychologist Kurt Lewin (1948), conflicts could arise from any of the following scenarios:

Approach-approach conflict: In this conflict situation, the individual has two positives: there are good reasons to aborting a pregnancy, and there are also good reasons to keeping a pregnancy. For example, a person's life circumstance (e.g., poor finances) may justify an abortion, yet the person's self-concept as a nurturant woman may instigate the need to keeping the pregnancy. If both reasons have *equal* saliency, the individual has difficulty in choosing one option over the other. She cannot commit an abortion yet be a nurturant mother at the same time. This could lead to distress.

Avoidance-avoidance conflict: With the avoidance-avoidance conflict, the individual has to choose between two negatives: having an abortion is wrong, yet keeping the pregnancy is also wrong. For example, abortion is wrong based on the person's moral judgment, yet keeping the pregnancy is also wrong, based on the circumstance that led to the pregnancy (e.g., an incest). With equal saliency, this situation could cause distress.

Approach-avoidance conflict: In this conflict situation, the individual can identify both positive and negative reasons for having an abortion or keeping the pregnancy. It would have been helpful, however, if all the positives are on one side of the argument and all the negatives are on the other side of the argument. For example, on one side of the argument, abortion is morally wrong, but you have the resources to take care of the child; on another side of the argument, you can keep the pregnancy but do not have the resources to take care of the child. Unfortunately, a forced choice would have to be made which could cause distress as well.

Cognitive Dissonance and Postabortion Meaning Reconstruction

Pre-abortion meaning relates to Jean Piaget's (1952) *assimilation* concept. As earlier discussed, assimilation is when a person applies their existing cognitive framework to comprehend a new information. If this framework is successfully applied, the new information becomes assimilated. However, if it does not, the individual would have to expand on their existing framework to *accommodate* the new information. Accommodation might be required in postabortion meaning reconstruction. With an unfamiliar information as reflected in the spiritual struggles that attend to a loss, a shift from assimilation to accommodation is required in postabortion meaning reconstruction. Absent this shift, the individual may experience *cognitive dissonance*, which occurs when one's behavior and cognition are in conflict with each other (Festinger, 1962). For example, why behave like a Christian if you believe that God does not love you in your loss? Cognitive dissonance creates distress, and, therefore, a person's cognition has to align with their actions or vice versa, in order to reduce the distress. Postabortion meaning reconstruction would require a shift in cognition in order to justify an abortion act. Yet, as Festinger (1962) would suggest, the individual may not necessarily have to change their original cognition (e.g., that abortion is wrong) but could instead take on a new cognition (e.g., that everybody does an abortion, hidden or not, or that times have changed).

Key Takeaways

1. Across all cultures, the prevalent factors that contribute to abortion include a mother's unmarried status, a mother's poor health, adultery, rape, incest, and illegal union (Shain, 1986).
2. An abortion act comes with a stigma. There are two types of stigma: stigma from society and stigma from friends/family members. Abortion stigma at the societal level originates from government policies that limit abortion. Based on cultural orientation, however, each individual would be affected differently by abortion stigma from society (and not friends and family), from friends and family (and not society), or from both society and friends/family.
3. Cultural values do influence attitude toward an abortion, including *individualism* that allows for personal responsibility in an abortion act and *collectivism* that encourages the input of others in an abortion decision. Also important are the cultural values of *egalitarianism* (equal treatment for everyone) and *hierarchy* (treatment of people based on age, gender, or importance in society).
4. Within each society there are heterogenous cultural values—dominant and minority—that affect grief outcomes.
5. To cope with the shame and guilt of abortion, *concealment* from others (or disenfranchised grief) could occur.

6. Both *pre-abortion meaning* and *postabortion meaning reconstruction* are important in coping with abortion grief. Culturally, a woman's gender identity and gender roles (e.g., a nurturer or mother) could influence pre-abortion meaning or postabortion meaning reconstruction.
7. An abortion decision may not be clear-cut; it could lead to distress and be burdened by conflicts including approach-approach, avoidance-avoidance, and approach-avoidance conflicts.
8. After an abortion, the woman is de-attached from the fetus. This has implications at the physical, cognitive, and affective levels.

   Physical: The physical presence of the fetus (which is more pronounced in advanced pregnancy) will be no more.
   Cognitive: A readjustment is required from being pregnant to *not being pregnant* and from being mother-to-be to being *not-mother-to-be.*
   Affective: Emotionally, a decision on abortion that is freely made would have a different grief outcome than one that is influenced by others.

9. Grief outcomes of an abortion decision that is based on *short-term* thinking would be different than one that is based on *long-term* thinking.

Critical Cultural Thinking

Victoria had an abortion but now regrets her action and is experiencing a belated grief. What cultural factors might have contributed to her abortion decision?

References

Astbury-Ward, E., Parry, O., & Carnwell, R. (2012). Stigma, abortion, and disclosure—Findings from a qualitative study. *The Journal of Sexual Medicine, 9*(12), 3137–3147.

Axios.com. (2022, June 24). *US joins only 3 other countries that have rolled back abortion rights since 1994.* www.axios.com/2022/05/05/only-3-countries-have-rolled-back-abortion-rights-since-1994

Baumeister, R. F. (1999). Self-concept, self-esteem, and identity. In V. J. Derlega, B. A. Winstead, & W. H. Jones (Eds.), *Personality: Contemporary theory and research* (pp. 339–375). Nelson-Hall Publishers.

Berry, J. W. (2006). Contexts of acculturation. In *The Cambridge handbook of acculturation psychology* (Vol. 27, No. 42, pp. 328–336).

Beynon-Jones, S. M. (2017). Untroubling abortion: A discourse analysis of women's accounts. *Feminism & Psychology, 27*(2), 225–242.

Bousso, R. S., Poles, K., de Souza Serafim, T., & de Miranda, M. G. (2011). Religious beliefs, illness and death: Family's perspectives in illness experience. *Revista da Escola de Enfermagem da USP, 45*, 397–403.

Bowlby, J. (1979). The Bowlby-Ainsworth attachment theory. *Behavioral and Brain Sciences, 2*(4), 637–638.

Bowlby, J. (1980). *Attachment and loss. Vol. 3: Loss, sadness and depression.* Basic Books.

Cassidy, J., Jones, J. D., & Shaver, P. R. (2013). Contributions of attachment theory and research: A framework for future research, translation, and policy. *Development and Psychopathology, 25*(4pt2), 1415–1434.
Chattopadhyay, S., & Simon, A. (2008). East meets west: Cross-cultural perspective in end-of-life decision making from Indian and German viewpoints. *Medicine, Health Care and Philosophy, 11*(2), 165–174.
Doka, K. J. (2002). *Disenfranchised grief: New directions, challenges, and strategies for practice*. Research Press Pub.
Doka, K. J. (2008). Disenfranchised grief in historical and cultural perspective. In M. S. Stroebe, R. O. Hansson, H. Schut, & W. Stroebe (Eds.), *Handbook of bereavement research and practice: Advances in theory and intervention* (pp. 223–240). American Psychological Association.
Eyetsemitan, F. E. (2021). *Death, dying, and bereavement around the world: Theories, varied views and customs*. Charles C Thomas Publisher.
Eyetsemitan, F. E. (2022). Bereavement theories and models. In *The deceased-focused approach to grief: An alternative model* (pp. 59–76).
Festinger, L. (1962). Cognitive dissonance. *Scientific American, 207*(4), 93–106.
Ganatra, B., Gerdts, C., Rossier, C., Johnson, B. R., Tunçalp, Ö., Assifi, A., et al. (2017). Global, regional, and subregional classification of abortions by safety, 2010–14: Estimates from a bayesian hierarchical model. *The Lancet, 390*(10110), 2372–2381.
Gelman, A., Rosenfeld, E. A., Nikolajski, C., Freedman, L. R., Steinberg, J. R., & Borrero, S. (2017). Abortion stigma among Low-Income women obtaining abortions in western Pennsylvania: A qualitative assessment. *Perspectives on Sexual and Reproductive Health, 49*(1), 29–36.
Gillies, J., & Neimeyer, R. A. (2006). Loss, grief, and the search for significance: Toward a model of meaning reconstruction in bereavement. *Journal of Constructivist Psychology, 19*(1), 31–65.
Grossmann, K., Grossmann, K. E., Spangler, G., Suess, G., & Unzner, L. (1985). Maternal sensitivity and newborns' orientation responses as related to quality of attachment in northern Germany. *Monographs of the Society for Research in Child Development, 50*, 233–256.
Guttmacher.org. (2022, March). *Unintended pregnancy and abortion worldwide*. www.guttmacher.org/fact-sheet/induced-abortion-worldwide
Hanschmidt, F., Linde, K., Hilbert, A., Riedel-Heller, S. G., & Kersting, A. (2016). Abortion stigma: A systematic review. *Perspectives on Sexual and Reproductive Health, 48*(4), 169–177.
Harvard Health Publishing. (2019). *Abortion (termination of pregnancy)*. www.health.harvard.edu/medical-tests-and-procedures/abortion-termination-of-pregnancy-a-to-z
Keesee, N. J., Currier, J. M., & Neimeyer, R. A. (2008). Predictors of grief following the death of one's child: The contribution of finding meaning. *Journal of Clinical Psychology, 64*(10), 1145–1163.
Kelley, A. S., Wenger, N. S., & Sarkisian, C. A. (2010). Opiniones: End-of-life care preferences and planning of older Latinos. *Journal of the American Geriatrics Society, 58*(6), 1109–1116.
Klass, D., & Heath, A. O. (1997). Grief and abortion: Mizuko kuyo, the Japanese ritual resolution. *OMEGA-Journal of Death and Dying, 34*(1), 1–14.
Kumar, A., Hessini, L., & Mitchell, E. M. (2009). Conceptualising abortion stigma. *Culture, Health & Sexuality, 11*(6), 625–639.
Laurent, S. M., & Myers, M. W. (2011). I know you're me, but who am I? Perspective taking and seeing the other in the self. *Journal of Experimental Social Psychology, 47*(6), 1316–1319.
Lee, S., Jeon, Y., & Yoon, M. (2022). Dual mediating effects of changes in daily life and anxiety on the relationship between occupation and depression in Korea during the COVID-19 pandemic. *BMC Public Health, 22*(1), 1492.
Lewin, K. (1948). *Resolving social conflicts; selected papers on group dynamics*. Harper.
Littman, L. L., Zarcadoolas, C., & Jacobs, A. R. (2009). Introducing abortion patients to a culture of support: A pilot study. *Archives of Women's Mental Health, 12*(6), 419–431.
Major, B., & Gramzow, R. H. (1999). Abortion as stigma: Cognitive and emotional implications of concealment. *Journal of Personality and Social Psychology, 77*(4), 735.

Mehran, P., Simbar, M., Shams, J., Ramezani-Tehrani, F., & Nasiri, N. (2013). History of perinatal loss and maternal–fetal attachment behaviors. *Women and Birth, 26*(3), 185–189.

Moreno López, M., Flores Celis, K., González-Forteza, C., Saltijeral, M. T., Schiavon, R., Collado, M. E., et al. (2019). Relationship between perceived stigma and depressive symptomatology in women who legally interrupt pregnancy in Mexico city. *Salud Mental, 42*(1), 25–32.

Nakagawa, M., Lamb, M. E., & Miyake, K. (1989). Psychological experiences of Japanese infants in the strange situation. 乳幼児発達臨床センター年報*, 11*, 13–24.

Neimeyer, R. A., & Harris, D. L. (2023). Bereavement and grief. In H. S. Friedman & C. H. Markey (Eds.), *Encyclopedia of mental health* (Vol. 1, pp. 204–211). Elsevier, Academic Press.

Norris, A., Bessett, D., Steinberg, J. R., Kavanaugh, M. L., De Zordo, S., & Becker, D. (2011). Abortion stigma: A reconceptualization of constituents, causes, and consequences. *Women's Health Issues, 21*(3), S49–S54.

Pescosolido, B. A., & Martin, J. K. (2015). The stigma complex. *Annual Review of Sociology, 41*, 87–116.

Pew Research Center. (2012, December 18). *The global religious landscape*. www.pewresearch.org/religion/2012/12/18/global-religious-landscape-exec/

Pew Research Center. (2013). *The global Catholic population*. www.pewresearch.org/religion/2013/02/13/the-global-catholic-population/

Pew Research Center. (2014, November 13). *Religion in Latin America*. www.pewresearch.org/religion/2014/11/13/religion-in-latin-america/

Pew Research Center. (2022, May 6). *America's abortion quandary*. www.pewresearch.org/religion/2022/05/06/americas-abortion-quandary/

Piaget, J. (1952). Introduction: The biological problem of intelligence (J. Piaget & M. Cook, Trans.). In *The origins of intelligence in children* (pp. 1–20). W. W. Norton & Co.

Quinn, D. M., & Chaudoir, S. R. (2009). Living with a concealable stigmatized identity: The impact of anticipated stigma, centrality, salience, and cultural stigma on psychological distress and health. *Journal of Personality and Social Psychology, 97*(4), 634.

Sagi, A., Lamb, M. E., Lewkowicz, K. S., Shoham, R., Dvir, R., & Estes, D. (1985). Security of infant-mother,-father, and-metapelet attachments among kibbutz-reared Israeli children. *Monographs of the Society for Research in Child Development, 50*, 257–275.

Say, L., Chou, D., Gemmill, A., Tunçalp, Ö., Moller, A., Daniels, J., et al. (2014). Global causes of maternal death: A WHO systematic analysis. *The Lancet Global Health, 2*(6), e323–e333.

Schwartz, S. H. (2007). Universalism values and the inclusiveness of our moral universe. *Journal of Cross-Cultural Psychology, 38*(6), 711–728.

Sebola, B. R. (2021). Interaction of culture and grief amongst women who terminated a pregnancy in adolescence: A narrative approach. *CURATIONIS Journal of the Democratic Nursing Organisation of South Africa, 44*(1), 2247.

Shain, R. N. (1986). A cross-cultural history of abortion. *Clinics in Obstetrics and Gynaecology, 13*(1), 1–17.

Sharma, I., Pandit, B., Pathak, A., & Sharma, R. (2013). Hinduism, marriage and mental illness. *Indian Journal of Psychiatry, 55*(Suppl 2), S243.

Shellenberg, K. M., & Tsui, A. O. (2012). Correlates of perceived and internalized stigma among abortion patients in the USA: An exploration by race and Hispanic ethnicity. *International Journal of Gynecology & Obstetrics, 118*, S152–S159.

Stålhandske, M. L., Makenzius, M., Tydén, T., & Larsson, M. (2012). Existential experiences and needs related to induced abortion in a group of Swedish women: A quantitative investigation. *Journal of Psychosomatic Obstetrics & Gynecology, 33*(2), 53–61.

Steinberg, J. R., Tschann, J. M., Furgerson, D., & Harper, C. C. (2016). Psychosocial factors and pre-abortion psychological health: The significance of stigma. *Social Science & Medicine, 150*, 67–75.

Sung, S. (2018). Women's experiences of balancing work and family in South Korea: Continuity and change. In *Women of Asia* (pp. 98–110). Routledge.

Thrane, S. (2010). Hindu end of life: Death, dying, suffering, and karma. *Journal of Hospice & Palliative Nursing, 12*(6), 337–342.
Unnithan-Kumar, M. (2010). Female selective abortion–beyond 'culture': Family making and gender inequality in a globalising India. *Culture, Health & Sexuality, 12*(2), 153–166.
Walter, T. (2010). Grief and culture. *Bereavement Care, 29*(2), 5–9.
Yamada, M., & Shupe, A. (2013). Internet accessibility of the mizuko kuyo (water-child ritual) in modern Japan: A case study in weberian rationality. *Sociological Focus, 46*(3), 229–240.

Chapter 7
Culture and Workplace Bereavement

Most adults spend a good amount of time in the workplace. Therefore, the loss of a child, a spouse, a parent, a grandparent, a companion animal, or a friend would likely involve a worker (Gibson et al., 2010; Wilcox et al., 2015).

Some workers, during COVID-19 pandemic, experienced multiple deaths of loved ones in close succession. In the United States, in 2021, about 3.4 million deaths were recorded (Ahmad et al., 2022). Older workers are more likely to experience multiple losses over time. A survey of 1200 working age adults in Canada found that 96% of the respondents experienced at least one bereavement. Another 20% described their grief as either severe or extreme (Wilson et al., 2018). Bereavement, besides the emotional aspect, does take a toll on cognition. Bereavement could lead to lapses in judgment and forgetting, and it could cause confusion, disorientation, as well as detachment from others (Shulman, 2020). Thus, workplace bereavement could have adverse effect on an employee's performance. The cost of death-related grief to organizations is said to approximate $45 billion, annually (James et al., 2003). Organizations pay the price of bereavement in forms of lower productivity, stress-related absenteeism, and medical and health insurance costs (Sunoo & Sunoo, 2002). Not long ago, bereavement leave was excluded from a literature review of United States employer-provided benefits programs (Dulebohn et al., 2009). Yet workplace bereavement requires both formal and informal responses.

Formal Workplace Response to Bereavement

Organizations have formal workplace policies that govern their response to bereavement. Usually, these policies are meant to address cultural aspects of bereavement such as giving an employee paid time off to attend funerals. The number of paid days off allowed for bereavement is based on the employer's cultural construction

F. E. Eyetsemitan, *Cultural Influences in Coping with Grief*,
https://doi.org/10.1007/978-3-031-86817-7_7

of emotional closeness of the bereaved to the deceased. Therefore, the loss of certain individuals attracts more days off for funerals than others. For example, a study of 145 working adults who had experienced bereavement in the state of Illinois, USA, showed a disparity in the average number of days they were allowed for bereavement: parent, 4.08; relative, 2.58; friend, 2.00; and pet, 1.0 (Eyetsemitan, 1998). Based on cultural constructions, organizations believe that attachment to a parent should be stronger than attachment to a pet. Yet attachments are personal constructions; some people may be more attached to their pets than parents (Eyetsemitan, 1998).

The United States Fair Labor Standards Act (FLSA) does not require employers to provide their employees with paid time off for funerals. Rather, this should be an agreement reached between an employer and an employee (US Department of Labor, n.d.). While no formal laws govern bereavement policy in the workplace, in the United States 88% of companies do offer some form of paid bereavement leave, according to the Society for Human Resource Management (SHRM, n.d.). The United Kingdom also allows employers to make the decision to grant a "compassionate leave" to a bereaved employee, based on the worker's contract, which could be paid or unpaid (Gov.uk, n.d.-b).

In Australia, based on the 2009 Fair Work Act, 2 days of bereavement leave, which could be consecutive or not, is granted for an *immediate family* member for all workers, full-time or part-time (Gov.au, 2021). The paid leave policy identifies immediate family members, based on cultural constructions of human attachment, as earlier discussed. A casual (or temporary) employee, however, is granted bereavement or compassionate leave but without pay (Gov.au, 2021). Given this situation, casual or temporary employees are forced to make the choice between attending a funeral without pay or not attending a funeral with pay, even for an *immediate family* member. While government legislating brings to the fore the issue of workplace grief, it also points to an organization's discretionary role in granting paid leave for funeral to a bereaved casual (or temporary) worker. In Oceania, the government of New Zealand grants paid bereavement leave to an employee for a minimum of 3 days, if someone close to them dies, such as a parent, a child, a partner/spouse, a grandparent, a grandchild, a brother, a sister, or a parent-in-law. This also applies to a miscarriage or a stillbirth. However, the employer grants a minimum of 1 day, if there is proven reason to believe that the employee has experienced the loss of someone close to them or has cultural responsibilities relating to the funeral of the deceased (Gov.nz, n.d.). Thus, the government of New Zealand allows an employer some flexibility to extend bereavement leave to a worker who may have cultural obligations at a funeral, even if the loss is not personal.

China, under its 2008 Employment Contract Law Provisions, grants 3 days off in the loss of a spouse or a child and 1 day off for the loss of a sibling or a parent (Russell et al., 2008). Unlike China, however, New Zealand in approving the number of paid bereavement days does not consider differences in "closeness" among spouse, child, sibling, or parent. However, in each of these cases the number of work period allowed for bereavement does not extend beyond 5 days.

Informal Workplace Response to Bereavement

According to researchers Alexis Stein and Robin Winokuer (1989), "Three to five days of funeral leave cannot begin to address the grieving individual's needs" (p. 98). Thus, a worker's grief may continue after the period of a formal bereavement leave. Studies conducted in the United States and in Canada report on work-related changes that include resignation from work or escaping grief through overwork (Gilmer et al., 2012). In the Netherlands, a study reported that 50% of the people whose loved ones died in intensive care units had problems returning to work and resuming full-blown responsibilities (van der Klink et al., 2010). Also, in Sweden, a large population-based study found that among parents who lost their children, there was sickness-related absenteeism compared to other working parents (Wilcox et al., 2015).

Yet, due to other reasons, a bereaved employee may be keen to resume work at the expiration of their bereavement leave. Margaret Stroebe and Henk Schut's (1999) dual process model of bereavement helps with an explanation. In this model, the bereaved person oscillates between coping with the pain of the loss (loss orientation) and moving forward with their life (restoration orientation). In post-loss adjustments, the bereaved is assumed to make good progress if more time is spent on restoration orientation such as returning to work (e.g., Bennett et al., 2010). Also, the disruption of daily functioning scale in bereavement discussed earlier in Chap. 2 may help to explain this situation, whereby levels 1, 2, and 3, respectively, indicate no disruption, weak disruption, and moderate disruption in daily functioning.

In most cultures, men grieve differently than women. Unlike females, males are encouraged to not openly express their emotions, which aligns with workplace culture that discourages emotional display. Researchers Jannell Bauer and Margaret Murray (2018) alluded to this in an article they entitled *"Leave your emotions at home": bereavement, organizational space, and professional identity* published in the journal *Women's Studies in Communication*. However, for a female worker to assume a stoic countenance in returning to work from a short bereavement leave is to go against cultural expectations in the society.

Psychiatrist Colin Murray Parkes (1985) views certain individuals as "grief prone," and such a trait could be acquired through cultural socialization. Research conducted by Paul Rosenblatt (2008) in Bali and in Egypt among two Muslim communities demonstrated that whereas the Bali Muslims were more restoration oriented (or moving on with their lives after a loss), the Egyptian Muslims were more loss oriented (or focused more on the deceased and openly expressed their grief in feelings and thoughts). In other words, the latter were more grief prone in socialization.

Researchers Kenneth Doka and Terry Martin (2011) also suggest two types of grievers: the *instrumental* griever and the *intuitive* griever. The instrumental griever is the cognitive griever who tries to master the loss, whereas the intuitive griever is the griever that allows their emotions to take a better part of them. While not suggesting gender differences, culturally men are generally encouraged to be the cognitive griever or are thrust into that situation. They become the "man of the house" who has to be strong for others. Studies have shown that people with Type C personality hold off on the expression of their emotion (Eysenck, 1994). The origin of Type C personality came about from the study of women with breast cancer when researchers found a co-occurrence of behavior patterns in their abnormal expression of emotion (Greer & Morris, 1975). The primary mission of a work organization is to produce goods or services. Anything that disrupts this mission (including emotional display of grief) could become a distraction. Yet a workplace could become a breeding ground for acquiring a Type C personality trait by discouraging the healthy expression of grief emotions. In other words, to focus on work rather than the *worker* could become a disadvantage to organizations. As earlier mentioned, annually, organizations lose approximately $45 billion due to workplace bereavement (James et al., 2003). Additionally, the bereaved worker is exposed to stress-related illnesses (Sunoo & Sunoo, 2002), leading to ancillary downsides that include absenteeism and increased healthcare cost to the organization.

Workplace Grief: Diversity, Equity, and Inclusion (DEI)

Increasingly, diversity, equity, and inclusion (DEI) is becoming a discussed topic in the workplace. In the United States, based on federal law enforceable by the Equal Employment Opportunity Commission (EEOC), "it is illegal to discriminate against someone (applicant or employee) because of that person's race, color, religion, sex (including gender identity, sexual orientation, and pregnancy), national origin, age (40 or older) disability or genetic information" (EEOC.gov, n.d.) Similarly, in the United Kingdom, the 2010 Equality Act legally protects people against workplace discrimination (Gov.uk, n.d.-a). Also, the Australian Human Rights Commission Act of 1986 protects people against workplace discrimination based on religion, national extraction, and social origin, among others (Gov.au, 2019).

While culture is a topic for academic discourse, humans do embody culture also. Humans are both biological and cultural beings. The culture that resides inside of a person is referred to as "personal culture," but the culture that is outside of the individual is known as "public culture" (Cerulo & Ruane, 2021). There are two ways to the understanding of personal culture, however: the *declarative* aspect which is verbalized and the *non-declarative* aspect that is not verbalized and includes habits (Lizardo, 2017).

Thus, in the workplace to discriminate against someone is to also discriminate against the culture they embody. This includes their culturally sanctioned ways of grieving. Researcher Kenneth Doka (2002) suggests that *every* culture has social rules and norms that govern its grieving styles and includes how to grieve, for whom, and for how long. Therefore, a worker socialized to express his or her emotions should not have their grief "stifled" in the workplace (e.g., Eyetsemitan, 1998). Organizations should be able to acknowledge different grieving styles. In the United States where the dominant culture is death denying, however, it becomes a challenge to affirm different workplace grieving styles. Yet, in a dominant culture, minorities should have their grieving style affirmed (e.g., Walter, 2010).

Culturally Diverse Groups and Workplace Response to Bereavement

As earlier discussed, culture exists at both public and personal levels. Whereas the public aspect is that which is exterior of the person, the personal culture resides within the individual (Cerulo & Ruane, 2021). Within the personal culture, however, are the expressive and non-expressive parts (Lizardo, 2017).

Both public culture and personal culture are influential of each other. Public culture could be subject to stereotypes (either positive or negative), and the internalization of these stereotypes could influence the expression or lack of expression of personal culture. As described by researchers Claude Steele and Joshua Aronson (Steele & Aronson, 1995), *stereotype threat* is the fear of being negatively judged, based on a preconceived notion that others have of a group to which an individual belongs (e.g., Roberson & Kulik, 2007). When public culture is negatively stereotyped, personal culture could be negatively impacted, both in expression and in non-expression.

The concept of stereotype threat was initially studied in the context of educational settings and why minority groups underperformed relative to their White counterparts. Expanded studies have found that stereotype threat also occurs in other settings, including safe driving (Yeung & von Hippel, 2008) and memory performance among older adults (Mazerolle et al., 2021). Usually, stereotype threat is triggered by a *cue* that pertains to a negative stereotype of a group to which an individual belongs. For example, in mathematics, based on negative stereotype about females underperforming relative to males, a mathematics question becomes a cue to trigger stereotype threat in females (Davies et al., 2002, 2005). A cue that triggers stereotype threat does not have to be blatant; it could be less blatant due to a high level of sensitivity among the group members being stereotyped. In other words, the person being stereotyped has developed a relatively low threshold to react to such a cue. Therefore, blatant or no-so-blatant cues can elicit similar reactions (McGlone & Aronson, 2006).

Stereotype Threat, Minoritized Groups, and Workplace Bereavement

Stereotype threat can have negative effect on a person's identity and influence how they feel or react in a given situation (Spencer et al., 2016). Pregnancy loss in the workplace, for example, could become a cue that triggers stereotype threat among certain individuals. One such group is the LGBTQ+ community. Usually, pregnancy is associated with heterosexual people. Among nonheterosexual individuals, therefore, pregnancy loss becomes a cue that triggers stereotype threat. This cue could be blatant when in alignment with the general society, an organization fails to recognize pregnancy loss among lesbians in its bereavement policy (Cacciatore & Raffo, 2011). The experience of some lesbians has been described as "double jeopardy" because they not only have to openly admit to a pregnancy loss, but they have to also "come out" as lesbians. Discrimination in both formal workplace policy (and its interpretations) and informal daily interactions with colleagues can add to the burdens of bereaved LGBTQ+ individuals in the workplace (McNutt & Yakushko, 2013). Even when an organization has anti-discriminatory policies, such policies hardly change coworkers' behavior toward their LGBTQ+ colleagues (Priola et al., 2014). Thus, due to stereotype threat, pregnancy loss may not be disclosed in the workplace by LGBTQ+ members (e.g., Capell et al., 2018).

Unlike LGBTQ+ individuals, however, stereotype threat may elicit a different type of response from minority group members who are heterosexuals. In the *Annual Review of Psychology*, researcher Steven Spencer and colleagues (Spencer et al., 2016) narrated how during a college visit by one of the researchers stereotype threat was observed in two Black men. One of the Black men said out of fear of being misjudged based on his race, he spends several hours studying in his chemistry class. Also, his self-doubt on whether he belongs to the prestigious college keeps him from asking his professors for help. The second Black man, an administrator, feels the pressure to succeed, and to not confirm stereotypes, he decides to skip an important day-long event to avoid a workload pile in his absence. Likewise, a minority group member may feel the pressure to forego a bereavement leave even when offered or, if they do, to immediately return to work and resume full-blown responsibilities, to not confirm stereotypes of incompetence. The minority group member being stereotyped may also be less likely to accept workplace help or support, even if available to them. Furthermore, in a workplace dominated by men, women may be less expressive of their emotions in bereavement to not validate stereotypes.

The need to return to work soon after a loss could be tied to an employee's *perception* of their job status prior to bereavement. An employee who perceives that they are easily replaceable, even when offered paid bereavement leave, is less likely to accept it. For example, in sports, a bereaved player who perceives that they risk losing their roster spot to another player is less likely to miss a game by taking a bereavement leave.

Cultural Sensitivity Toward Bereaved Individuals

In the workplace, a supervisor or a colleague may want to be supportive to a bereaved coworker but lacks cultural competence. Social support is not about number; it is about knowing at least one individual that the bereaved person perceives to demonstrate an understanding of their situation. Such a person may be culturally different, yet he or she could bring comfort to the grieving individual.

A common question often asked the bereaved regarding the deceased is "what caused his/her death?" In Western societies, the usual response to this question is provided in medical terms or based on what is identified as cause of death in the death certificate of the deceased. For example, he or she died of cancer. Among non-Westerners, however, the belief in nonmedical cause of death is common. Therefore, "what caused his/her death?" may not be culturally sensitive to ask in a diverse workplace. For example, researcher Lesiba Baloyi (2008) raised the alarm that Africans are likely to excuse a medical malpractice in deaths, because of strong beliefs in evil forces, witchcraft, or evil acts as cause of death. In Christian teachings, God is the giver and taker of life. Yet many non-Westerners who profess Christianity also believe in the forces of evil eye or witchcraft as cause of death (Schmidt-Leukel, 2006). Evil eye is a curse or a malevolent glare believed to cause injury or destruction (e.g., Ross, 2010). A Pew research survey (2014) of some non-Western societies notes a high percentage of people who both profess Christianity and believe in "evil eye" (see Table 7.1). This is known as "accommodation" behavior (e.g., Eyetsemitan, 2021).

Due to immigration factors, Western societies have a diverse workforce of people with non-Western cultural background who believe in evil eye or sorcery as cause of death. Therefore, supervisors and coworkers need to be culturally sensitive in relating to a bereaved colleague of non-Western background, regarding death causation. Thus, the bereaved person of non-Western background should be allowed to voluntarily share information on cause of death, without expecting a medical explanation. Yet John Berry's (2006) acculturation model notes that a worker of non-Western background could acculturate to their host culture in the following ways:

1. *Assimilation*: Foreigner adopts the norms and practices of the host culture.
2. *Integration*: Foreigner maintains their indigenous culture and assimilates the norms and practices of the host culture at the same time (accommodation behavior).
3. *Separation*: Foreigner keeps his or her indigenous culture and rejects the norms and practices of the host culture.

Table 7.1 Percentage of Catholics and Protestants that believe in evil eye

Country	Percentage (%) of Catholics who believe in evil eye	Percentage (%) of Protestants who believe in evil eye
Panama	69	49
Dominican Republic	58	47
Honduras	55	55
Nicaragua	46	51
El Salvador	53	40

Source: Pewforun.org (2014); https://www.pewforum.org/2014/11/13/religion-in-latin-america/

4. *Marginalization*. Foreigner embraces neither his indigenous culture nor the host culture.

In further analysis, Berry's (2006) *separation* outcome reflects a "native self," whereas *assimilation* an "acquired self" (Eyetsemitan, 2020). A person with a *native-self* orientation is less likely to accept nor is willing to provide as death causation a Western explanation, because this calls into question an identity that is deeply rooted in their indigenous cultural belief system. Generally, such an individual is very passionate about matters that involves his or her native culture, relative to the host culture. The native culture reinforces their identity. Unlike the native-self individual, the *acquired-self* person has an outlook that embraces the host culture's norms and practices. Through interactions, however, an observant supervisor or a coworker can learn the proclivities of their non-Western colleague and engage them accordingly.

Also, in the expression of condolence to the bereaved, the terms "death" and "loss" are often used. Yet these words may have cultural implications. For example, among the Chinese, death is often associated with bad luck, and therefore the word death should be avoided (e.g., Chan & Chow, 2006). Also, for people who maintain continuing bond with the deceased (e.g., ancestor worshippers), the word loss is not appropriate either. Rather, a more suitable word is "departed," as this indicates that the deceased may be departed from this world but is believed to be somewhere else. Personally, some bereaved individuals maintain continuing bonds with their deceased loved ones through letter writing.

Some organizations make available professional counselors to their bereaved employees. Researchers Ann Laurie and Robert Neimeyer (2008) however note that African Americans, compared to Whites, are less likely to speak about their grief experience to professional counselors. Instead, they are more likely to approach a clergy. Also, African Americans (and people of African descent in general) have "fictive" kins who are not blood relatives. Yet they relate to these fictive kins as blood relatives because of their collectivist values. The fictive kin could be called a "brother" or a "sister," and their death could elicit as intense emotion as a blood relative. An organization's bereavement policy may not recognize the death of a fictive kin. On the need for a flexible bereavement policy, researcher Diane Bergeron (2023) suggests that organizations should be elastic in interpreting the term "immediate" family member, as some individuals are raised by their grandparents. Common among African Americans is the *skip generation* family, a situation whereby grandparents raise grandchildren full-time in the absence of parents (Fields, 2003).

Also, an organization that understands cultural differences in funeral arrangements may be flexible in its bereavement policy. In Western societies, funerals are held soon after a death; in the United Kingdom funerals occur on average within a week, in Scandinavian countries it takes place within several days, and in New Zealand it happens within 3 days (e.g., Raudon, 2011). Funerals could be expensive. In Western societies, funerals take place within a relatively short period of time after a death because third-party insurance, and financing options offered by funeral homes are available to those who want to take advantage of them. In the United States, about one-third of all funerals are paid for in advance (Dugas, 2003). Furthermore, people who are unable to attend funerals due to distance or short notice could participate through technology including webcasting and livestreaming (Eyetsemitan, 2020). Generally, in Western Europe, the United States, and Australia, funerals are not elaborate and could be considered private, based on individualistic values (Sunoo & Sunoo, 2002). However, in non-Western cultures, usually funerals are elaborate and are communal affairs, reflecting collectivist values (Parkes et al., 2015). Thus, funerals are not held soon after a death (except for religious reasons, e.g., Islam), as more time is needed for consultations with people both far and near and for funds to be raised. Generally, third-party payment through insurance or other financing sources is not available, and therefore a funeral can be delayed for a relatively long period of time to raise funds. A supervisor or a coworker, without a non-Western cultural background, may wonder why a bereavement leave request is made long after the news of a death is shared. Therefore, a bereavement leave policy that is time sensitive may not be appropriate.

Key Takeaways

1. Grief is common in the workplace, as most adults spend a good amount of time at work. Workers experience a variety of loss. This includes the death of a child, a parent, a grandparent, a companion animal, or a friend.
2. An organization's formal response is to allow for paid days off to a bereaved employee to attend a funeral. The number of paid days off depends on the bereaved employee's "closeness" or "attachment" to the deceased, as determined by the organization.
3. Yet a bereaved employee's closeness or attachment to the deceased should not be based on the organization's social construction. Rather, it is personal to the bereaved.
4. A formal bereavement leave policy that is made to apply to every bereaved worker may miss out on each bereaved worker's personal attachment experience to the deceased.
5. After a funeral, grief continues in the workplace.
6. There are bereaved individuals with "hidden" grief and organizations may be unaware of their loss.
7. Hidden grief could arise when a bereaved employee believes that he or she does not fit into the organization's formal bereavement leave policy. Thus, these workers are reticent about their grief and keep it to themselves.
8. A common question asked of the bereaved of the deceased is "what caused his/her death?" The expected response is a medical term for cause of death or what is recorded on the death certificate. In a multicultural workforce, bereaved individuals may believe in nonmedical cause of death (e.g., "evil eye" or witchcraft) as well. Therefore, cultural sensitivity is required with this question.

9. Also, commonly used terms to describe a bereaved person's experience are "loss" and "death." Some individuals do not believe in loss as they maintain continuing bond with the deceased. The word "departed" would be appropriate instead of death. The implication is that, though departed from this world, the deceased is located somewhere else and still relatable.

Critical Cultural Thinking

Jessica was bereaved and informed her supervisor and human resources director, accordingly. The organization needs proof of her loss (e.g., a published obituary notice) to determine her eligibility for paid bereavement leave (and number of paid days off). What suggestions would be appropriate to Jessica's supervisor and human resource director in a culturally diverse workforce?

References

Ahmad, F. B., Cisewski, J. A., & Anderson, R. N. (2022). Provisional mortality data—United States, 2021. *Morbidity and Mortality Weekly Report, 71*(17), 597.

Baloyi, L. (2008). *Psychology and psychotherapy redefined from the view point of the African experience*. https://uir.unisa.ac.za/handle/10500/1346

Bauer, J. C., & Murray, M. A. (2018). "Leave your emotions at home": Bereavement, organizational space, and professional identity. *Women's Studies in Communication, 41*(1), 60–81.

Bennett, K. M., Gibbons, K., & Mackenzie-Smith, S. (2010). Loss and restoration in later life: An examination of dual process model of coping with bereavement. *OMEGA-Journal of Death and Dying, 61*(4), 315–332.

Bergeron, D. M. (2023). Time heals all wounds? HRM and bereavement in the workplace. *Human Resource Management Review, 33*(2), 100931.

Berry, J. W. (2006). Contexts of acculturation. In *The Cambridge handbook of acculturation psychology* (Vol. 27, No. 42, pp. 328–336).

Cacciatore, J., & Raffo, Z. (2011). An exploration of lesbian maternal bereavement. *Social Work, 56*(2), 169–177.

Capell, B., Tzafrir, S. S., Enosh, G., & Dolan, S. L. (2018). Explaining sexual minorities' disclosure: The role of trust embedded in organizational practices. *Organization Studies, 39*(7), 947–973.

Cerulo, K. A., & Ruane, J. M. (2021). Future imaginings: Public and personal culture, social location, and the shaping of dreams. Paper presented at the *Sociological Forum, 36*, 1345–1370.

Chan, C. L. W., & Chow, A. Y. M. (2006). *Death, dying and bereavement: A Hong Kong Chinese experience Hong*. Kong University Press.

Davies, P. G., Spencer, S. J., Quinn, D. M., & Gerhardstein, R. (2002). Consuming images: How television commercials that elicit stereotype threat can restrain women academically and professionally. *Personality and Social Psychology Bulletin, 28*(12), 1615–1628.

Davies, P. G., Spencer, S. J., & Steele, C. M. (2005). Clearing the air: Identity safety moderates the effects of stereotype threat on women's leadership aspirations. *Journal of Personality and Social Psychology, 88*(2), 276.

Doka, K. J. (2002). *Disenfranchised grief: New directions, challenges, and strategies for practice*. Research Press Pub.

Doka, K. J., & Martin, T. L. (2011). *Grieving beyond gender: Understanding the ways men and women mourn*. Routledge.

Dugas, C. (2003). Prepaid funeral can have pitfalls. *USA Today*, 3B.

Dulebohn, J. H., Molloy, J. C., Pichler, S. M., & Murray, B. (2009). Employee benefits: Literature review and emerging issues. *Human Resource Management Review, 19*(2), 86–103.

EEOC.gov. (n.d.). *Prohibited employment policies/practices*. www.eeoc.gov/prohibited-employment-policiespractices

Eyetsemitan, F. (1998). Stifled grief in the workplace. *Death Studies, 22*(5), 469–479.

Eyetsemitan, F. E. (2020). *Understanding death and dying: Encountering death, dying, and the afterlife*. Sage.

Eyetsemitan, F. E. (2021). *Death, dying, and bereavement around the world: Theories, varied views and customs*. Charles C Thomas Publisher.

Eysenck, H. J. (1994). Cancer, personality and stress: Prediction and prevention. *Advances in Behaviour Research and Therapy, 16*(3), 167–215.

Fields, J. (2003). Children's living arrangements and characteristics: March 2002. In *Current population reports* (pp. P20–P547). U.S. Census Bureau.

Gibson, J., Gallagher, M., & Jenkins, M. (2010). The experiences of parents readjusting to the workplace following the death of a child by suicide. *Death Studies, 34*(6), 500–528.

Gilmer, M. J., Foster, T. L., Vannatta, K., Barrera, M., Davies, B., Dietrich, M. S., et al. (2012). Changes in parents after the death of a child from cancer. *Journal of Pain and Symptom Management, 44*(4), 572–582.

Gov.au. (2019). *Australian Human Rights Commission Act 1986*. www.legislation.gov.au/Details/C2019C00030

Gov.au. (2021). *Fair work act*. www.legislation.gov.au/Details/C2021C00421

Gov.nz. (n.d.). *Bereavement leave*. www.employment.govt.nz/leave-and-holidays/bereavement-leave/

Gov.uk. (n.d.-a). *Equality act 2010: Guidance*. www.gov.uk/guidance/equality-act-2010-guidance

Gov.uk. (n.d.-b). *Time off for family and dependents*. www.gov.uk/time-off-for-dependants

Greer, S., & Morris, T. (1975). Psychological attributes of women who develop breast cancer: A controlled study. *Journal of Psychosomatic Research, 19*(2), 147–153.

James, J. W., James, J. W., Friedman, R., & Cline, E. (2003). *Grief index: The "hidden" annual costs of grief in America's workplace: 2003 report*. Grief Recovery Institute Educational Foundation, Incorporated.

Laurie, A., & Neimeyer, R. A. (2008). African Americans in bereavement: Grief as a function of ethnicity. *Omega-Journal of Death and Dying, 57*(2), 173–193.

Lizardo, O. (2017). Improving cultural analysis: Considering personal culture in its declarative and nondeclarative modes. *American Sociological Review, 82*(1), 88–115.

Mazerolle, M., Smith, A. M., Torrance, M., & Thomas, A. K. (2021). Understanding older adults' memory distortion in the light of stereotype threat. *Frontiers in Psychology, 12*, 628696.

McGlone, M. S., & Aronson, J. (2006). Stereotype threat, identity salience, and spatial reasoning. *Journal of Applied Developmental Psychology, 27*(5), 486–493.

McNutt, B., & Yakushko, O. (2013). Disenfranchised grief among lesbian and gay bereaved individuals. *Journal of LGBT Issues in Counseling, 7*(1), 87–116.

Parkes, C. M. (1985). Bereavement. *The British Journal of Psychiatry, 146*(1), 11–17.

Parkes, C. M., Laungani, P., & Young, W. (2015). *Death and bereavement across cultures*. Routledge.

Priola, V., Lasio, D., De Simone, S., & Serri, F. (2014). The sound of silence. Lesbian, gay, bisexual and transgender discrimination in 'inclusive organizations'. *British Journal of Management, 25*(3), 488–502.

Raudon, S. (2011). *Contemporary funerals and mourning practices: An investigation of five secular countries*. Winston Churchill Memorial Trust.

Roberson, L., & Kulik, C. T. (2007). Stereotype threat at work. *Academy of Management Perspectives, 21*(2), 24–40.

Rosenblatt, P. C. (2008). Grief across cultures: A review and research agenda. In M. S. Stroebe, R. O. Hansson, H. Schut, & W. Stroebe (Eds.), *Handbook of bereavement research and practice: Advances in theory and intervention* (pp. 207–222). American Psychological Association.

Ross, C. A. (2010). Hypothesis: The electrophysiological basis of evil eye belief. *Anthropology of Consciousness, 21*(1), 47–57.

Russell, G., Ross, M., & Foods, K. (2008). *Work and life in China*. Boston College Center for Work & Family.

Schmidt-Leukel, P. (2006). *Buddhism, Christianity and the question of creation: Karmic or divine?* Ashgate Publishing, Ltd.

SHRM. (n.d.). *Paid leave benchmarking report*. www.shrm.org/resourcesandtools/business-solutions/documents/paid-leave-report-all-industries-all-ftes.pdf

Shulman, L. M. (2020). Emotional traumatic brain injury. *Cognitive and Behavioral Neurology, 33*(4), 301.

Spencer, S. J., Logel, C., & Davies, P. G. (2016). Stereotype threat. *Annual Review of Psychology, 67*, 415–437.

Steele, C. M., & Aronson, J. (1995). Stereotype threat and the intellectual test performance of African Americans. *Journal of Personality and Social Psychology, 69*(5), 797.

Stein, A. J., & Winokuer, H. R. (1989). Monday mourning: Managing employee grief. In *Disenfranchised grief: Recognizing hidden sorrow* (pp. 91–102).

Stroebe, M., & Schut, H. (1999). The dual process model of coping with bereavement: Rationale and description. *Death Studies, 23*(3), 197–224.

Sunoo, J. J., & Sunoo, B. P. (2002). Managing workplace grief—Vision and necessity. *Pepperdine Dispute Resolution Law Journal, 2*, 391.

United States Department of Labor. (n.d.). *Wages and the fair labor standards act*. www.dol.gov/agencies/whd/flsa

van der Klink, M. A., Heijboer, L., Hofhuis, J. G., Hovingh, A., Rommes, J. H., Westerman, M. J., & Spronk, P. E. (2010). Survey into bereavement of family members of patients who died in the intensive care unit. *Intensive and Critical Care Nursing, 26*(4), 215–225.

Walter, T. (2010). Grief and culture. *Bereavement Care, 29*(2), 5–9.

Wilcox, H. C., Mittendorfer-Rutz, E., Kjeldgård, L., Alexanderson, K., & Runeson, B. (2015). Functional impairment due to bereavement after the death of adolescent or young adult offspring in a national population study of 1,051,515 parents. *Social Psychiatry and Psychiatric Epidemiology, 50*, 1249–1256.

Wilson, D. M., Cohen, J., MacLeod, R., & Houttekier, D. (2018). Bereavement grief: A population-based foundational evidence study. *Death Studies, 42*(7), 463–469.

Yeung, N. C. J., & von Hippel, C. (2008). Stereotype threat increases the likelihood that female drivers in a simulator run over jaywalkers. *Accident Analysis & Prevention, 40*(2), 667–674.

Chapter 8
Cultural Factors in Death Anxiety

Death anxiety is a common phenomenon across the lifespan, starting from late childhood when death's finality begins to be comprehended. Death anxiety is triggered by an awareness of one's own mortality (Furer & Walker, 2008; Gonen et al., 2012). It is not just death anxiety for oneself but also death anxiety for loved ones and friends. As defined, death anxiety is the fear of death for self and for others and the fear of dying for self and for others (Lester & Abdel-Khalek, 2003; Dadfar et al., 2015).

Death anxiety has an emotional aspect but also a cognitive and a behavioral component. Researcher Brenda Kenyon (2001) notes that a child's understanding of death, which begins around age 10, includes the following: (1) that death is irreversible, (2) that death has a cause, (3) that death results in the non-functionality of body parts, and (4) that death happens to all living things. Some researchers suggest that in children mortality salience occurs even as young as age 8, based on the child's peculiar experience (Kreitler & Krivoy, 2012). This experience includes a child's encounter with disease and treatment (Corr, 2010; Bonoti et al., 2013). Some studies report on dying children expressing the fear of being alone (e.g., Theunissen et al., 2007) and of being separated from their toys and clothes (Kreitler & Krivoy, 2012). Children, based on their parents' personal or religious beliefs, also learn about an afterlife (Risen, 2016).

In the United States, mass shootings are now a source of death anxiety among children in school. As earlier noted, the awareness of one's own mortality and those of loved ones generates death anxiety. The level of death anxiety could be high or low; when high, death is usually associated with pain, punishment, disconnection with the world, or consequences of transgression in one's faith and beliefs (Abdel-Khalek, 2002). For some, death anxiety results from worries about what becomes of their body when buried beneath the earth's surface and exposed to worms and insects (Suhail & Akram, 2002). Therefore, for those able to afford above-earth burial, a mausoleum becomes a better option.

F. E. Eyetsemitan, *Cultural Influences in Coping with Grief*,
https://doi.org/10.1007/978-3-031-86817-7_8

Researchers Rebecca Lehto and Karen Stein (2009) reviewed the death anxiety literature from 1980 to 2007 and note that death anxiety stems from a stressful environment, from circumstances outside of one's control, from diagnosis with or experience with a life-threatening illness, as well as from other experiences with death and dying.

Cultural Factors That Contribute to Death Anxiety

Each society has specific cultural factors encoded within the themes researchers Rebecca Lehto and Karen Stein (2009) identified as contributing to death anxiety. These include the following:

Life Expectancy

Life expectancy is described as the average number of years that people in a particular society are expected to live from a certain age. In 2021, life expectancy in the United States at birth is 76.4 years. For males, life expectancy is 73.5 years, but for females it is 79.3 years, with a difference of 5.8 years between both genders (CDC, December, 2022). Besides gender differences, there are racial disparities in life expectancy. In the United States, in 2019, the overall life expectancy for the Asian population is 85.7 years; for the Latino population it is 82.2 years; for the white population it is 78.9 years; for the Black population it is 75.3 years; and for the American Indian and Alaska Native (AIAN) population it is 73.1 years (Healthdata.org, June 16, 2022).

Across the world, people in some societies are expected to live longer than those in others. In 2023, the countries where there is low life expectancy include Chad (59.57 years) and Guinea Bissau (64.1 years) and those with high life expectancy include Japan (85 years) and Singapore (86.51 years) (CIA: The World Factbook, accessed May 17, 2023).

Within each society, therefore, cultural life revolves around the average life expectancy of its members, and this perceived time on earth can contribute to death anxiety for self and others.

Based on life expectancy, death anxiety would influence the normative behaviors in a society. These include appropriate time to start a family, to take on adult roles, or to retire from work.

Resources in Society

Death anxiety would be impacted by the available resources in a society. Some societies are richly resourced, whereas others are poorly resourced. Sub-Saharan Africa, for example, has about 18 Western-trained medical doctors per 100,000 persons. In South Africa, there are 60 doctors to 100,000 persons, but in Mozambique there are only 2 doctors per 100,000 persons. To retain African trained medical personnel is a challenge. Within 5 years, approximately 65,000 African trained physicians or about one-fifth of those trained migrate to high-resource countries. The paucity of trained medical personnel is worse in rural areas (Collins et al., 2010). Yet, due to health disparities, in high-resource societies like the United States, minority groups are at a disadvantage. This is a contributary factor to death anxiety among minority group members.

The CDC (n.d.) defines health disparities as *preventable differences in the burden of disease, injury, violence, or opportunities to achieve optimal health that are experienced by populations that have been socially, economically, geographically, and environmentally disadvantaged.* According to the CDC (n.d.), these populations include racial and ethnic minority, immigrants with limited proficiency in English, women, people with disabilities, and people who identify as lesbian, gay, bisexual, transgender, queer, intersex, or other (LGBTQI+). Compared to Whites, these minority groups experience higher rates of diseases including diabetes, hypertension, obesity, asthma, heart disease, and cancer. On average, Blacks or African Americans have a lower life expectancy than Caucasians by 4 years. A factor responsible for health disparities among minority groups is the lack of access to healthcare and use of it. The following are factors that contribute to this barrier:

- Cultural barriers in communication between patient and healthcare provider
- Inequities in treatment of minority group members
- Past historical events that lay the background to mistrust of the healthcare system that include the Tuskegee study of untreated syphilis in African American male and the sterilization of Indian women without their permission
- Living with a chronic and debilitating disease without healthcare or poor access to it

At the height of the COVID-19 pandemic, the entire world community was resource poor, initially. As a result, death across the world took a toll recorded in the millions, and this led to a heightened sense of death anxiety. Being a communicable disease and a public health issue, guidelines for social interactions were set by public officials. People were asked to wear masks, to maintain social distance, and to wash their hands frequently. Many businesses asked their employees to work remotely, and schools held classes remotely as well. However, the discovery of COVID-19 vaccines and other pharmaceuticals led to a drop in death anxiety level. Many businesses went back to normal operations and schools resumed in-person classes. The available resources and access to them made the difference, and death anxiety level was reduced.

Occupations

In any society, work is a very prominent part of adult life. Some occupations carry more risks than others. Culturally, men do risky jobs. For example, more men than women engage in police work, in construction work, as firefighters and in military combat. Risky jobs have been identified as reason for shorter life expectancy in men than in women (Courtenay, 2000; Shmerling, 2016). Risky occupations can contribute to death anxiety among job holders, family members, and friends. At the peak of COVID-19 pandemic, risky jobs were held by frontline workers. Compared to the general populace, death anxiety was higher among medical personnel who were frontline workers (Simione & Gnagnarella, 2020).

Frontline workers include nurses, who are mostly women. Given the circumstance of COVID-19 pandemic, jobs traditionally held by women became risky as well. In the United States, a school teacher's job is mostly held by females. Given mass shootings in schools, a school teacher's job has become risky. Women make up a sizeable number of the teaching profession. In 2017–2018, females make up about 76% of public school teachers, compared to males who constitute 24% (https://nces.ed.gov/programs/coe/indicator/clr/public-school-teachers the United States Center for Education Statistics (NCES, May, 2021).

Public Safety

In the United States, there are public safety concerns in the African American community. Blacks believe that encounters with law enforcement personnel put them at a disadvantage, compared to their White counterparts. High-profile cases such as the George Floyd incident helps to reinforce this belief. Therefore, among minority group members, death anxiety is high when in contact with law enforcement personnel. In his 2023 State of the Union address, United States President Joe Biden noted the case of Tyre Nichols, a Black man who was allegedly beaten to death by law enforcement officers. President Biden mentioned the "talk" that minority parents have to give to their children when in contact with law enforcement officers, which *he* as a White parent would not bother to do.

With regard to the "talk" in his State of the Union speech, President Joe Biden made the following comments:

> Imagine having to worry whether your son or daughter will come home from walking down the street or playing in the park or just driving their car. I've never had to have the talk with my children – Beau, Hunter, and Ashley – that so many Black and Brown families have had with their children. If a police officer pulls you over, turn on your interior lights. Don't reach for your license. Keep your hands on the steering wheel. Imagine having to worry like that every day in America. (The White House, February 7, 2023)

Within the Black community (and other minority groups), the "talk" has become synonymous with death anxiety. In one study, Black men were found to have the highest level of death anxiety followed by Black women, White women, and White men. Between Blacks and Whites, a considerable difference exists in death anxiety (Myers et al., 1980).

Afterlife Beliefs

In most cultures around the world, beliefs about what becomes of life after death are important. Afterlife beliefs create death anxiety as well as help to guide the behavior of the living. Most afterlife beliefs are derived from religious teachings. For example, in the afterlife, Christians believe in heaven and in hell, where people are either rewarded (in heaven) or punished (in hell), based on how they lived their earthly life, including if they accepted Jesus as their lord and savior. With regard to punishment in the afterlife, the Bible in 2 Thessalonians 1:9–10 KJV states the following:

> …who shall be punished with everlasting destruction from the presence of the Lord, and from the glory of his power; when he shall come to be glorified in his saints, and to be admired in all them that believe (because our testimony among you was believed) in that day.

In 2010, Christians of all ages made up 2.18 billion in 195 countries of the world. This represents a third of an estimated global population of 6.9 billion (Pew Research Center, 2011). Islam teaches its followers how to interact with others and establishes Islamic laws (Sharia). In some countries Sharia is the adopted law of the land, and similar to the Bible, the Quran (the holy book of Islam) teaches its followers about an afterlife where good deeds are rewarded in paradise and bad deeds are punished in the afterlife (Quran 2: 81–82). In 2015, worldwide Muslims made up about 1.8 billion people (Pew Research Center, 2017).

Buddhism in its the Four Noble Truths teaches its followers that life is about suffering, pain, and misery; that suffering, pain, and misery arise from selfish desires; that suffering and pain can be eliminated in this world or in the afterlife; and that knowledge about the unsatisfactory nature of life leads to the right mindset and actions. To avoid suffering, therefore, a believer must have right intention, right understanding, right speech, right action, right living, right mindset, right effort, and right concentration (e.g., Puchalski & O'Donnell, 2005). Without these, as punishment, there is no freedom from rebirth. According to the Dhammapada (portions of the Buddha): "Long is the cycle of birth and death to the fool who does not know the true path." In 2010, about 488 million people worldwide practiced Buddhism, and about 99% of these believers lived in Asia (Pew Research Center, 2012). Hinduism also believes in rebirth, but there is good rebirth and there is bad rebirth. A good rebirth is caused by a good karma, whereas a bad rebirth is caused by a bad karma. In life, this means that good actions or bad actions beget good karma or bad karma, respectively (e.g., Lipner, 2012). About 1 billion people worldwide practice Hinduism, and more than 99% of them reside in the Asia-Pacific region (Pew Research Center, 2012). In every religion, one's actions on earth bring about good or bad consequences in the afterlife. Not every practitioner keeps to the teachings of their respective religion, however. For some, religion is a demographic variable used in social interactions. They identify as Christian, Muslim, Hindu, or Buddhist but without truly putting into practice the teachings of their religion. For example, death anxiety was reported among 141 Hong Kong Chinese Buddhists (e.g., Hui & Coleman, 2012).

Conflict in Afterlife Beliefs

Due to acculturation influences, people may hold more than one religious belief and end up with dual beliefs about the afterlife. These individuals exhibit accommodation behavior or, in John Berry's (2006) acculturation model, exhibit *integration* outcomes. Whereas in their daily life these individuals are able to integrate or accommodate both beliefs, these beliefs in contemplating an afterlife may conflict with each other and generate death anxiety. The afterlife belief of one religion may be different from another and with consequences. For example, this author was told about a Muslim traveling on a plane when the flight became very turbulent on air and everyone became frightened and thought the plane was going to crash. Some Christians quickly gathered on one end of the place to pray, while a group of Muslims convened at another corner of the plane to pray. Being a Muslim, this particular individual initially joined the Muslim group but then thought that God might not be a Muslim after all. He then ran to the Christian group. Yet another thought came to him that God might not be a Muslim after all. So until the plane stabilized, he went back and forth both groups. This story illustrates how conflicting dual beliefs about the afterlife could exacerbate death anxiety.

African traditional religion and Christianity have conflicting afterlife beliefs. In African traditional religion, in the afterlife the deceased is believed to exist in spirit form, as an ancestor (Nobles, 2006). Heaven or hell is not part of this belief system, as in Christianity. Christianity regards African traditional religion as a pagan religion. Yet, in 2010, 517 million Christians (and 248 million Muslims) live in sub-Saharan Africa (Pew Research Center, 2015), and over 100 million Africans practice traditional religion across 45 countries (e.g., Lugira, 2009), with a sizeable number holding both Christian and traditional religious beliefs.

Death Causation Beliefs

Within a society, the predominant factors responsible for death causation could lead to death anxiety, especially if resources to prevent or to manage them are lacking. In developing societies the predominant factor responsible for death is communicable disease (e.g., HIV/AIDS). However, in developed societies the predominant cause of death is noncommunicable disease (e.g., heart disease and cancer). In the United

States, across all races, heart disease and cancer (noncommunicable diseases) are the two leading causes of death. However, in communities with poor healthcare system and/or access to it, death anxiety could be palpable.

Usually, medical terms are used to describe death causation (e.g., cancer). Yet death causation can be described in cultural terms as well. Death could be attributed to evil eye, witchcraft, or sorcery. As earlier noted, this is commonplace in non-Western cultures. For example, *Santeria* is an indigenous religion found in Cuba, Puerto Rico, Dominican Republic, Panama, and among some ethnic minority groups in the United States. The followers believe in spiritual factors as cause of death (e.g., Rosario & De La Rosa, 2014).

Cultural beliefs about death causation can lead to death anxiety, and proactive measures can be taken based on such beliefs to prevent death and to reduce death anxiety. The WHO (June 20, 2022) notes that in low-income economies (majority of African countries fall into this category), road traffic injury is the leading cause of death for people ages 5–29 years old. To prevent road traffic accidents, operators of public transportation adorn their vehicles with charms prepared by traditional healers as they believe that evil eye, witchcraft, or sorcery can cause road traffic deaths (Eyetsemitan, 2021). Other proactive steps taken to avoiding death from road traffic accident include holding back information on travel plans for fear of traffic accident deaths caused by sorcery or witchcraft.

Evil eye is also common in the Middle East as cause of death. In order to provide spiritual assistance to a sick person, a traditional healer may request the discontinuation of Western medical treatment (Al-Shahri, 2002). This is because spiritual healing is perceived to be effective against "evil eye" (Qamar, 2013).

Dependence on Others

A person's death anxiety level can reflect that person's level of *dependence* on others. In other words, a high level of dependence on others could lead to a high level of death anxiety. On the contrary, a low level of dependence on others could result in a low level of death anxiety. *Dependence* on others could be cognitive, physical, or emotional. Complicated grief or prolonged grief disorder point to a high level of dependence on the deceased. In the United States, about 7–10% of bereaved individuals experience complicated or prolonged grief. This persistent grief can affect the daily functioning of the survivor. It is accompanied by mental health problems (Dutton & Zisook, 2005), and the survivor persistently worries and ruminates about a future without the deceased (Shear, 2012). As explained by researcher Julie Whetherell (2012), the memory of habits (non-declarative memory) may contribute to complicated grief. Cross-cultural psychologist Harry Triandis (1995) suggests that Western culture is mostly aligned with individualism and non-Western culture with collectivism. With individualism, personal desires are valued, whereas with collectivism group goals are placed ahead of personal desires. Collectivism, unlike individualism, could lead to high level of dependence on others and to death anxiety, as a result. In non-Western cultures, a child's death could result in the loss of future care provision and financial security for the elderly parent (Eyetsemitan & Gire, 2003). In old age, therefore, this leads to a loss in dependence. A study that compared bereaved parents from Switzerland and China found that whereas Swiss parents reported severe grief-related preoccupation, Chinese parents described their experience as empty and meaningless (Xiu et al., 2017).

Coping with Bereavement

Each culture has beliefs on how to respond to a loss, and these beliefs could contribute to death anxiety. Generally, grief models focus on the bereaved (e.g., the four tasks of mourning, meaning making, and the dual process model). These grief models focus on how the bereaved can get back to normalcy following a loss. However, in non-Western cultures, in coping with loss the bereaved gives attention to the deceased, due to beliefs about the decedent's supernatural powers to inflict harm on the living. This attention on the deceased includes providing the deceased with a "proper" burial according to norms and tradition. For the bereaved, when a "proper" burial is not followed, this belief could cause death anxiety. The Afro-Surinamese believe that the spirit of the deceased hovers around for a while before it departs to the afterlife (van der Pijl, 2010). The Creoles in their tradition place items in the decedent's coffin including a handkerchief or an underwear that has the smell of the decedent's widow or widower as decoy that their spouse is with them in the afterlife (van der Pijl, 2016). The Chinese includes in the decedent's coffin something of value such as an expensive jewelry, and they believe that the deceased would visit family members 3 days after a burial (Kemp & Chang, 2002). The Ashantis of Ghana through sacrifices appease their ancestors so that the deceased can join them in the afterlife (van der Geest, 2000). If not appropriately followed in burials, these cultural beliefs could engender death anxiety in survivors. However, Neimeyer and colleagues (Neimeyer et al., 2014) note that due to modernization influences, traditional cultural beliefs may not be shared by everyone.

Life Fulfillment Goals

Each person has life goals against which life fulfillment is benchmarked. These goals may be personal but may be in accordance with cultural expectations as well. In some cultures, the goals for life fulfillment for women may be different from those of men, or both goals may converge. In most cultures, an example of a life goal that cuts across gender is to have offspring. Meeting life goals brings about personal fulfillment and, also, suggests how in death a person is remembered. During funerals (or in obituary notices), the deceased is remembered based on personal or cultural goals that are fulfilled and may include the following statements (Eyetsemitan, 2020, p. 360):

> The deceased lived a good life. She/he raised good children, and they are all successful in life.
> She/he is survived by children, grandchildren, and great grandchildren.
> She/he is survived by a loving spouse and a caring family.
> She/he died at home peacefully surrounded by family and friends.

These examples may reflect personal or cultural goals, yet most times they are aligned with culturally sanctioned life goals. For example, a life lived in isolation from family members and friends is less likely to be mentioned in funerals or in obituary notices.

Therefore, as one advances in age, concerns about not meeting personal or cultural goals can lead to death anxiety. For example, if a personal or cultural goal to have a grandchild is not met, this could lead to death anxiety with advancing age. In other words, an unfinished business can lead to death anxiety.

Coping with Death Anxiety

In the creation or evolution of a culture, the intention is to provide community members with a sense of meaning, of order, and of permanence of existence. Therefore, a cultural worldview would include beliefs about what constitutes personal achievements, a sense of belonging through relationships, the importance of family, and the contemplation of an afterlife (e.g., Greenberg & Arndt, 2012; Strachan et al., 2007). In the words of psychologist John Kotre (1984), "There is no way to outlive the self without the vehicle of culture" (p.269). Thus, cultural worldviews provide people with the confidence to face their mortality salience (e.g., Burke et al., 2010).

Symbolic immortality is the belief that we can transcend death with certain things that point to our existence here on earth after death. The choice of what constitutes symbolic immortality is personal yet could be culturally influenced as well. In some cultures, a child or naming a child after a parent, or having a male child to continue the family name, would constitute symbolic immortality. For example, in India, women face pressure to have a male child. This has resulted in sex selection techniques. In the United States, a study of 65 immigrant Indians by researcher Sunita Puri and colleagues (Puri et al., 2011) found that 40% of the women claimed to have terminated female fetuses, while 89% who were pregnant with female fetuses pursued an abortion. However, in a foreign culture, these immigrant women still hold on to their cultural values, reflective of John Berry's (2006) *separation* outcome in acculturation. Response to mortality salience could be either *proximal* or *distal* (Hayes et al., 2010). In proximal response, immediate action is required. This could take the form of weight loss, exercise, or being more health conscious. In distal response, however, the individual has time in their approach. This could include developing an afterlife belief over time or making plans to establish a foundation ahead of one's death (Steinhauser et al., 2001). Researchers Adam Grant and Kimberly Wade-Benzoni (2009) refer to proximal responses as "hot" because they require immediate action and distal responses as "cold" because they do not require immediate actions but instead rational and deliberative decisions which take time. Death indicates a lack of control. In technologically advanced societies, through biomedical breakthroughs, people have more resources to delay death than their counterparts in less technologically advanced societies. Yet discussions about death anxiety should be culturally sensitive as some cultures are less death accepting than others.

Key Takeaways

1. Death anxiety is a common phenomenon across the lifespan, triggered by an awareness of one's own mortality. This begins in childhood between ages 8 and 10 years. It is not just death anxiety for oneself but also death anxiety for loved ones and friends.
2. Generally, death anxiety stems from a stressful environment, from circumstances outside of one's control, from diagnosis with or encounter with a life-threatening illness, as well as from other experiences with death and dying.
3. Cultural factors do influence death anxiety, including life expectancy in a society, available resources in a society (e.g., healthcare and access to it), risky occupations (usually held by males), and public safety concerns (especially, among minority group members). Others include afterlife beliefs, death causation (medical/cultural beliefs about death causation), dependence on others, traditional beliefs in coping with bereavement, and cultural expectations about what constitutes a fulfilled life.
4. Coping with death anxiety includes *proximal defenses* (what needs to be done now) *or distal defenses (what can be done later).*
5. Symbolic immortality is how an individual wishes to be perpetuated after death (e.g., through an offspring). This could be based on personal choice or cultural expectation.

Critical Cultural Thinking

Joana feels the pressure to have a child for her husband. She is a young professional working full time who aspires to climb up the corporate ladder rapidly. Her husband, James, is advancing in age and has death anxiety about dying without a child as symbolic immortality. What proximal responses or distal responses can Joana make to help reduce her husband's death anxiety? Also, should the child's sex be an issue?

References

Abdel-Khalek, A. M. (2002). Why do we fear death? The construction and validation of the reasons for death fear scale. *Death Studies, 26*(8), 669–680.

Al-Shahri, M. Z. (2002). Culturally sensitive caring for Saudi patients. *Journal of Transcultural Nursing, 13*(2), 133–138.

Berry, J. W. (2006). Contexts of acculturation. *The Cambridge Handbook of Acculturation Psychology, 27*(42), 328–336.

Bonoti, F., Leondari, A., & Mastora, A. (2013). Exploring children's understanding of death: Through drawings and the death concept questionnaire. *Death Studies, 37*(1), 47–60.

Burke, B. L., Martens, A., & Faucher, E. H. (2010). Two decades of terror management theory: A meta-analysis of mortality salience research. *Personality and Social Psychology Review, 14*(2), 155–195.

CDC.gov. (2022, December). *Mortality in the United States, 2021.* www.cdc.gov/nchs/products/databriefs/db456.htm

CDC.gov. (n.d.). *Definitions of terms.* www.cdc.gov/globalhealth/equity/terms.html

CIA: The world Factbook. Accessed May 17, 2023., from www.cia.gov/the-world-factbook/countries/united-states/#people-and-society

Collins, F. S., Glass, R. I., Whitescarver, J., Wakefield, M., & Goosby, E. P. (2010). Developing health workforce capacity in Africa. *Science, 330*(6009), 1324–1325.

Corr, C. A. (2010). Children's emerging awareness and understandings of loss and death. *Children's Encounters with Death, Bereavement, and Coping*, 21–37.

Courtenay, W. H. (2000). Constructions of masculinity and their influence on men's well-being: A theory of gender and health. *Social Science & Medicine, 50*(10), 1385–1401.

Dadfar, M., Lester, D., Vahid, M. K. A., Abdel-Khalek, A. M., Mohammadian, M., Bolhari, J., et al. (2015). Mental disorders signs in Afghan immigrants/refugees. *International Journal of Management and Sustainability, 4*(2), 26.

Dutton, Y. C., & Zisook, S. (2005). Adaptation to bereavement. *Death Studies, 29*(10), 877–903.

Eyetsemitan, F. E. (2020). *Understanding death and dying: Encountering death, dying, and the afterlife*. SAGE Publications.

Eyetsemitan, F. E. (2021). *Death, dying, and bereavement around the world: Theories, varied views and customs*. Charles C Thomas Publisher.

Eyetsemitan, F. E., & Gire, J. T. (2003). *Aging and adult development in the developing world: Applying western theories and concepts*. Greenwood Publishing Group.

Furer, P., & Walker, J. R. (2008). Death anxiety: A cognitive-behavioral approach. *Journal of Cognitive Psychotherapy, 22*(2), 167–182.

Gonen, G., Kaymak, S. U., Cankurtaran, E. S., Karslioglu, E. H., Ozalp, E., & Soygur, H. (2012). The factors contributing to death anxiety in cancer patients. *Journal of Psychosocial Oncology, 30*(3), 347–358.

Grant, A. M., & Wade-Benzoni, K. A. (2009). The hot and cool of death awareness at work: Mortality cues, aging, and self-protective and prosocial motivations. *Academy of Management Review, 34*(4), 600–622.

Greenberg, J., & Arndt, J. (2012). Terror management theory. *Handbook of Theories of Social Psychology, 1*, 398–415.

Hayes, J., Schimel, J., Arndt, J., & Faucher, E. H. (2010). A theoretical and empirical review of the death-thought accessibility concept in terror management research. *Psychological Bulletin, 136*(5), 699.

Healthdata.org. (2022, June 16). *The Lancet: Disparities in life expectancy persist among racial and ethnic groups across the US.* www.healthdata.org/news-release/lancet-disparities-life-expectancy-persist-among-racial-and-ethnic-groups-across-us

Hui, V. K., & Coleman, P. G. (2012). Do reincarnation beliefs protect older adult Chinese Buddhists against personal death anxiety? *Death Studies, 36*(10), 949–958.

Kemp, C., & Chang, B. (2002). Culture and the end of life: Chinese. *Journal of Hospice & Palliative Nursing, 4*(3), 173–178.
Kenyon, B. L. (2001). Current research in children's conceptions of death: A critical review. *OMEGA-Journal of Death and Dying, 43*(1), 63–91.
Kotre, J. (1984). *Outliving the self: Generativity and the interpretation of lives*. Johns Hopkins University Press.
Kreitler, S., & Krivoy, E. (2012). Psychological intervention with the dying child. In *Pediatric psycho-oncology: Psychosocial aspects and clinical interventions* (pp. 209–222).
Lehto, R., & Stein, K. F. (2009). Death anxiety: An analysis of an evolving concept. *Research Theory in Nursing Practice, 23*(1), 23–41.
Lester, D., & Abdel-Khalek, A. (2003). The collett-lester fear of death scale: A correction. *Death Studies, 27*(1), 81–85.
Lipner, J. (2012). *Hindus: Their religious beliefs and practices*. Routledge.
Lugira, A. M. (2009). *African traditional religion*. Infobase Publishing.
Myers, J. E., Wass, H., & Murphey, M. (1980). Ethnic differences in death anxiety among the elderly. *Death Studies, 4*(3), 237–244.
NCES. (2021, May). *Characteristics of public school teachers*. www.nces.ed.gov/programs/coe/indicator/clr/public-school-teachers
Neimeyer, R. A., Klass, D., & Dennis, M. K. (2014). A social constructionist account of grief: Loss and the narration of meaning. *Death Studies, 0*, 1–14.
Nobles, W. W. (2006). *Seeking the sakhu: Foundational writings for an African psychology*. Third World Press.
Pew Research Center. (2011, December 19). *Regional distribution of Christians*. www.pewresearch.org/religion/2011/12/19/global-christianity-regions/
Pew Research Center. (2012, December 18). *The global religious landscape*. www.pewresearch.org/religion/2012/12/18/global-religious-landscape-exec/
Pew Research Center. (2015). *Sub-Saharan Africa*. www.pewresearch.org/religion/2015/04/02/sub-saharan-africa/
Pew Research Center. (2017). *Why Muslims are the world's fastest growing religious group*. www.pewresearch.org/short-reads/2017/04/06/why-muslims-are-the-worlds-fastest-growing-religious-group/
Puchalski, C. M., & O'Donnell, E. (2005). Religious and spiritual beliefs in end of life care: How major religions view death and dying. *Techniques in Regional Anesthesia and Pain Management, 9*(3), 114–121.
Puri, S., Adams, V., Ivey, S., & Nachtigall, R. D. (2011). "There is such a thing as too many daughters, but not too many sons": A qualitative study of son preference and fetal sex selection among Indian immigrants in the United States. *Social Science & Medicine, 72*(7), 1169–1176.
Qamar, A. H. (2013). The concept of the 'evil'and the 'evil eye'in Islam and Islamic faith-healing traditions. *Journal of Islamic Thought and Civilization, 3*(2), 44–53.
Risen, J. L. (2016). Believing what we do not believe: Acquiescence to superstitious beliefs and other powerful intuitions. *Psychological Review, 123*(2), 182.
Rosario, A. M., & De La Rosa, M. (2014). Santería as informal mental health support among US latinos with cancer. *Journal of Religion & Spirituality in Social Work: Social Thought, 33*(1), 4–18.
Shear, M. K. (2012). Getting straight about grief. *Depression and Anxiety, 29*(6), 461–464.
Shmerling, R. H. (2016). Why men often die earlier than women. *Harvard Medical School–Health Blog*.
Simione, L., & Gnagnarella, C. (2020). Differences between health workers and general population in risk perception, behaviors, and psychological distress related to COVID-19 spread in italy. *Frontiers in Psychology, 11*, 2166.
Steinhauser, K. E., Christakis, N. A., Clipp, E. C., McNeilly, M., Grambow, S., Parker, J., & Tulsky, J. A. (2001). Preparing for the end of life: Preferences of patients, families, physicians, and other care providers. *Journal of Pain and Symptom Management, 22*(3), 727–737.

Strachan, E., Schimel, J., Arndt, J., Williams, T., Solomon, S., Pyszczynski, T., & Greenberg, J. (2007). Terror mismanagement: Evidence that mortality salience exacerbates phobic and compulsive behaviors. *Personality and Social Psychology Bulletin, 33*(8), 1137–1151.

Suhail, K., & Akram, S. (2002). Correlates of death anxiety in Pakistan. *Death Studies, 26*(1), 39–50.

Theunissen, J., Hoogerbrugge, P. M., van Achterberg, T., Prins, J. B., Vernooij-Dassen, M., & Van Den Ende, C. (2007). Symptoms in the palliative phase of children with cancer. *Pediatric Blood & Cancer, 49*(2), 160–165.

Triandis, H. C. (1995). A theoretical framework for the study of diversity. In M. M. Chemers, S. Oskamp, & M. A. Costanzo (Eds.), *Diversity in organizations: New perspectives for a changing workplace* (pp. 11–36). Sage Publications.

Van der Geest, S. (2000). Funerals for the living: Conversations with elderly people in kwahu, Ghana. *African Studies Review, 43*(3), 103–129.

Van der Pijl, Y. (2010). Pentecostal-charismatic Christianity: African-Surinamese perceptions and experiences. *Exchange, 39*(2), 179–195.

Van der Pijl, Y. (2016). Death in the family revisited: Ritual expression and controversy in a creole transnational mortuary sphere. *Ethnography, 17*(2), 147–167.

Wetherell, J. L. (2012). Complicated grief therapy as a new treatment approach. *Dialogues in Clinical Neuroscience, 14*(2), 159–166.

White House.gov. (2023, February 7). *Remarks of President Joe Biden-state of the union address as prepared for delivery*. www.whitehouse.gov/briefing-room/speeches-remarks/2023/02/07/remarks-of-president-joe-biden-state-of-the-union-address-as-prepared-for-delivery/

WHO. (2022, June). *Road traffic injuries*. https://www.who.int/news-room/fact-sheets/detail/road-traffic-injuries

Xiu, D., Maercker, A., Yang, Y., & Jia, X. (2017). Prolonged grief, autobiographical memory, and its interaction with value orientations in China and Switzerland. *Journal of Cross-Cultural Psychology, 48*(9), 1369–1388.

Chapter 9
Culture, Resilience, and Coping with Loss

When a death occurs, grief which is a normal occurrence that follows. Yet the level of attachment formed with the deceased person is responsible for grief reaction. In most people grief reaction follows a pattern that would eventually be integrated into their regular daily functioning. The initial grief reaction is called *acute* grief. It is intense and includes shock, sadness, disbelief, fear, anger, and having intrusive thoughts or images of the deceased (Zisook & Shear, 2009). After 6 weeks, however, acute grief becomes less intense. This timeframe could vary from person to person, given the circumstance of death (e.g., expected or unexpected). Acute grief reaction has also been reported in cats, goats, dogs, and elephants in the loss of family members (Nakajima, 2018). *Integrated grief* occurs when the bereaved is able to enter into a new relationship and forge ahead with his or her life, without the hinderance of attachment to the deceased.

At the *integrated grief* stage, the bereaved is able to remember or recall the loss without the reactions associated with acute grief. In the United States, about 7–10% of bereaved persons do not advance to the integrated grief stage. These individuals demonstrate an inability to return to pre-loss functioning and do experience mental health problems (Dutton & Zisook, 2005). This type of grief is known as *prolonged grief disorder* (PGD) or complicated grief. It fits into the description of *traumatic grief*, which is a loss "so great and unexpected that it cannot be defended against, coped with, or managed" (Boss, 2006, p. 35). Traumatic grief has a long-term negative impact on a bereaved person's health (Boelen et al., 2019). In traumatic grief, the bereaved has a disproportionate experience of repeated pain and suffering. In the United States, this experience is reported among racial and ethnic minority groups (Kirmayer et al., 2014; Opara et al., 2020). Furthermore, the unavailability of mental healthcare treatment for ethnic minority groups exacerbates this situation (Dutil, 2019).

F. E. Eyetsemitan, *Cultural Influences in Coping with Grief*,
https://doi.org/10.1007/978-3-031-86817-7_9

History of Trauma Among United States' Ethnic Minority Groups

When trauma is passed on from one generation to another, this becomes historic, and the experience of trauma becomes part of a group's cultural fabric (Denham, 2008). Across generations, various ethnic minority groups in the United States have suffered from emotional injury, with subsequent generations afflicted with mourning pathology and the burdens of sharing in their previous generation's pains (Brave Heart & DeBruyn, 1998; Kellerman, 2001; Raphael et al., 1998). The factors that contribute to historic trauma include systemic racism, poor access to healthcare services, and government policies (Brave Heart & DeBruyn, 1998; Henderson et al., 2020). Consequently, maladaptive reactions that include anger, depression, and violence take hold (Denham, 2008).

When put together, the negative experiences of racial and ethnic minority groups could result in *learned helplessness*, a condition that psychologist Martin Seligman and colleague (Hiroto & Seligman, 1975) describe as an induced trait following repeated inescapable and uncontrollable events. Learned helplessness has been reported in both humans and animals.

Yet the question remains: why do some bereaved individuals experience traumatic grief reactions but not others? The answer may reside in *resilience*. Clinical psychologist Robert Neimeyer and colleague (Neimeyer & Sands, 2011) note that in seeking to handle a helpless state, individuals may look to their community or culture for a roadmap.

What Is Resilience?

Several definitions have emerged for resilience. However, the American Psychological Association (n.d.) suggests that *resilience* is the process that enables a person to adapt well when faced with adversity, trauma, tragedy, or a significant source of stress. Resilience is a process but also a painful experience that could lead to a profound growth. Resilience is not necessarily an endowed trait possessed only by some individuals. Rather it is a way of thinking, believing, and acting that can be learned.

Individual Differences in Resilience

Clinical psychologist George Bonanno and colleague (Mancini & Bonanno, 2006) argue that prior to an adverse event, it is difficult to know a resilient person and that only after an adversity can resilience be determined. Therefore, resilience as an outcome cannot be pre-determinant. Again, George Bonanno and colleagues

(Bonanno et al., 2004) argue further that following a loss, it is easy for the trajectory of a chronic disfunction to be different from resilience. Yet care should be taken to not conflate a normal response to a loss with a lack of resilience.

Some studies point to individual differences in resilience in the face of adversity. For example, individuals with previous experience that fostered resilience tend to fair better than those without prior experience. George Bonanno and colleagues (Bonanno et al., 2002a; Fraley & Bonanno, 2004) note that based on prior experience, resilient individuals exhibit the following traits:

- Self-enhancing biases
- Attachment style
- Repressive coping
- A priori beliefs
- Identity continuity
- Positive emotions

In *self-enhancing bias* the bereaved person takes steps to shore up his self-esteem that a loss could negatively impact (e.g., Taylor & Armor, 1996). For example, the bereaved could suggest that they did everything in their power (including sparing no financial expense) to get the deceased loved one the best medical help and compares himself or herself with someone else that they know whose loved one passed away without as much help that is rendered. Such behavior is called *downward social comparison* (e.g., Helgeson & Taylor, 1993). Regarding *attachment style*, people high in avoidance behavior tend to not have close relationships with others, unlike those low in avoidance behavior and who tend to rely on others (Mikulincer & Shaver, 2007). To cope with adversity, therefore, bereaved individuals who are low in avoidance behavior require social support more than their counterparts who are high in avoidance behavior. With *repressive coping*, an individual tends to avoid stressful situations (e.g., Hock & Krohne, 2004). This is an autonomic response to cope with a stressful situation that does not require cognitive strategies (Bonanno et al., 1995). Some studies suggest that repressive coping has adverse effects on a person's health (e.g., King et al., 1990). Yet other studies point to repressive coping as demonstrating resilience (e.g., Bonanno & Field, 2001). With *a priori beliefs*, an individual can demonstrate resilience if those beliefs are able to explain their loss experience (Gillies & Neimeyer, 2006). A loss explained through the lens of religion or cultural socialization could be based on a priori beliefs. Resilience is helped when an a priori belief is accepting of death (e.g., Gillies & Neimeyer, 2006). Islam teaches that only Allah (or God) decides when a person's time on earth comes to an end. As an a priori belief, this could strengthen resilience in the bereaved in accepting death. But a survivor could hold on to more than one a priori belief that conflicts. For example, whereas Islam teaches that death is in the hands of Allah (or God), another a priori belief based on one's culture is that parents should precede their children in death. In terms of resilience, therefore, one a priori belief may assume saliency over another. Therefore, a priori beliefs and their saliency, if more than one, should be explored for each individual, even within the same religion. For example, a survivor could hold on to their beliefs that only God determines when a person's time on earth will come to an end (e.g., Lichtenthal et al., 2004). Yet, within the same religious faith, he or she asks the question: "If God is such a loving father, as I have been taught in my faith, why would he allow this to happen to me?" Clinical psychologist Robert Neimeyer and colleague (Burke & Neimeyer, 2014), from a study of African Americans who lost loved ones unexpectedly, note "spiritual struggle" among bereaved individuals. In their Inventory of Complicated Spiritual Grief among Christians, Robert Neimeyer and colleagues (Burke et al., 2019) identify several dimensions to spiritual struggle. These include levels of insecurity with God, disaffection with the Christian community, and interference in religious activities.

Following a death, some bereaved individuals feel that a part of them is gone with the deceased (Shuchter & Zisook, 1993). However, with *identity continuation*, a survivor's identity does not change after experiencing a loss. A resilient individual would be someone with multiple identities. If one identity is lost following a death, they are able to maintain identity continuity in areas not affected by the loss. For example, a survivor whose identity is a *married* person will be affected by spousal loss. However, if they also have a professional identity (e.g., a lawyer or a medical doctor), this will not be affected by spousal loss, and they would be able to carry on their identity in that area. The saliency of a remainder identity over a lost identity is important as well. For example, is the identity of married more salient than a professional identity or vice versa for the individual? A survivor can also take on a new identity. They could become the head of family or the bread winner in the family. With *positive emotions,* a resilient survivor is able to exhibit genuine laughter or smile when speaking about their loss (Bonanno & Keltner, 1997). In some cultures, funerals or memorials include jokes or stories told by survivors about the deceased to draw laughter or smiles. Some of them are funny as well. But such light moments should persist beyond funeral or memorial events. In a survivor, resilience comes about when positive emotions have an upside over negative emotions to reduce distress (Tugade & Fredrickson, 2004). As a personality trait, it is also helpful to have an extraversion, an agreeable, or a conscientious disposition (Keltner, 1996).

Based on individual characteristics earlier discussed, a resilient person is better able to manage their adversity than a non-resilient individual. Researcher George Bonanno and colleagues (Bonanno et al, 2002b) followed bereaved individuals several years before and several years after they lost their spouses and found no clinical depression in at least 50% of their study sample. These individuals demonstrate resilience in their loss. This type of resilience could be a *pre-loss resilience*. It could also be a *post-loss resilience*. Post-loss resilience could be based on meaning reconstruction (e.g., Neimeyer & Anderson, 2002), or it comes from growth in new responsibilities such as head of family or breadwinner for the family, as earlier discussed.

Culture and Resilience

In individuals facing adversity, the following cultural practices and models can help to undergird resilience:

Individualist Versus Collectivist Values

With individualist values, the bereaved person in coping with a loss relies on internal resources for resilience. Studies show that individualists tend to be independent and self-contained and seek autonomy. Thus, a person who is high on individualism can by choice be either a *cognitive* griever or an *affective* griever (e.g., Doka & Martin, 2011). Collectivists instead value interdependence, relatedness, and social obligations (e.g., Caffaro et al., 2014). Their grieving style may be constrained by the expectations of others and the need to conform. Social psychologist Harry Triandis (1995) notes a difference in people high on individualism and those high on collectivism in self-perception. Researchers Kenneth Doka and Terry Martin (2011) suggest that cultural values do influence cognitive and affective grieving styles. In coping with a loss, a person's self-perception is associated with resilience (Mancini & Bonanno, 2006). In resilience neither individualism nor collectivism is superior. Instead, resilience is fostered when a grieving style aligns with one's cultural values. For example, an individualist whose grieving style is limited becomes, as the saying goes, "a fish out of water." The same applies to a collectivist. Among Indigenous Australians or Aboriginals (a collectivist group), to cope with the pain of a loss is a communal effort that involves community members who gather to eat, talk, and cry in support of the bereaved (Jones, 2015). Resilience among the Chinese (also a collectivist group) is fostered through the practice of continuing bond with the deceased (Lalande & Bonanno, 2006).

Sociologist Tony Walter (2010), however, notes that the belief systems of minority group members need to be acknowledged within a dominant culture. In other words, in individualist cultures there are minority collectivist cultures and vice versa with collectivist cultures. John Berry (2006) suggests that immigrants who are minorities in host communities could have the following acculturation outcomes:

(1) *Assimilation*: Foreigners assimilate the norms and practices of their host culture.
(2) *Integration:* Foreigners hold on to their indigenous culture and assimilate the norms and practices of the host culture as well.
(3) *Separation:* Foreigners keep their indigenous culture but reject the norms and practices of the host culture.
(4) *Marginalization.* Foreigners embrace neither their indigenous culture nor the host culture.

Autonomy Versus Embeddedness Values

Researcher Shalom Schwartz (2007) in a study of 80 countries from different continents identified polar-opposite cultural values of people. One of such is *autonomy versus embeddedness*. In autonomy people like to express their thoughts, feelings, and preferences unhindered. This can be expressed cognitively or affectively. In embeddedness, however, people have a tendency to conform and to do things in harmony with others (e.g., Kitayama et al., 2006).

Cultural value systems have salutary effects on resilience, especially if they help to build expectations and affirm a person's sense of self.

Resilience and Cultural Resources

As earlier discussed under "History of Trauma Among United States' Ethnic Minority Groups," a cultural group can have negative experience that includes racism, poverty, and discrimination that is pervasive. The reserve capacity model (Gallo & Matthews, 2003) evaluates *resilience* in the United States minority ethnic groups subjected to repeated denial of access to healthcare (e.g., Gallo et al., 2005), to trauma (Sampson et al., 1997), and to racism and discrimination (Brody et al., 2008). Relative to Whites, across the life course African Americans experience more stress and deleterious health outcomes (Myers, 2009). The constant exposure to stressors depletes the reserve capacity of ethnic minority groups to becoming resilient, especially in the absence of opportunity to replenish the depleted reserve capacity (Chen, 2016). Depleted resources are varied. They include savings, childcare, transportation, an optimistic worldview, a perceived control, and an enhanced self-perception. Depleted resources can be both tangible and intangible (e.g., Gallo & Matthews, 2003). Studies show that social support is helpful to mitigating the consequences of stressful situations in low-resourced people (e.g., Chen, 2016).

The "Hispanic Paradox" and the Reserve Capacity Model

The Hispanic population in the United States constitutes a minority group that is subject to stressors including poor access to healthcare, low income, acculturative stress from immigration, and discrimination. According to the United States department of Health and Human Services (n.d.), Hispanics in the United States make up the second largest group and represent 18.9% of the country's total population. In 2020, Mexicans at 61.6% constituted the largest group of the Hispanic population, followed by Puerto Ricans at 9.6%, by Central Americans at 9.3%, by South Americans at 6.4%, and by Cubans at 3.9%. Other Hispanic/Latino groups make up 5.8%. According to the 2019 United States Census Bureau data, compared to Whites at 94.6%, Hispanics were at 71.8% in attainment of a high school diploma or better. For a bachelor's degree or higher, compared to Whites at 40.1%, Hispanics were at 18.8%. Also, for a graduate or advanced professional degree, compared to Whites at 15.1%, Hispanics were at 5.7%. This disparity extends to income for full-time workers. The 2021 United States Bureau of Labor Statistics data had the average household income for Hispanics in 2020 at $55,321 compared to Whites at $74,912. In 2020, 17% of Hispanics were living in poverty compared to Whites at 8.2%. In 2020, Hispanics had private insurance coverage at 49.9% and had the highest uninsured rate in the United States, compared to other racial and ethnic groups.

Yet the Hispanic population often demonstrates equal or better health outcomes and demonstrates higher longevity than Whites. The 2020 Census Bureau projects that by 2060, at birth life expectancy for Hispanics will be 86.5 years, compared to Whites at 85.6 years. Also, by 2060, life expectancy for Hispanic women is projected to be 88.2 years compared to Hispanic men at 84.8 years. Compared to both White women at 85.6 years and White men at 84.0 years, both Hispanic women and Hispanic men are projected to have longer life expectancy. Contrary to the *reserve capacity model* (Gallo & Matthews, 2003), therefore, researchers refer to this puzzling phenomenon by Hispanics as the "Hispanic Paradox" (e.g., Markides & Coreil, 1986). Researchers suggest that the resilience of Hispanics can be explained by cultural factors. Among Hispanic groups, however, variations do occur in health status (CDC, 2008).

The "Hispanic Paradox" and Cultural Factors in Resilience

The diverse Hispanic groups share similar cultural characteristics that help with resilience. They share the following core cultural values (Marin & Marin, 1991):

- Allocentrism
- Simpatia
- Familism
- Power distance
- Personal space
- Time orientation
- Gender roles

In both *allocentrism* and *familism*, the individual's needs are subsumed within those of the family or group. There is a strong attachment to both nuclear and extended family members. This aligns with collectivism. *Simpatia* (or harmony in relationship) is the desire to avoid confrontation with others in interactions. This is aided by a hierarchical structure with respect based on age and gender, contrary to an egalitarian cultural system similar to Shalom Schwartz's (2007) polar-opposite cultural value systems, as discussed earlier. With *personal space,* Hispanics are comfortable in keeping close distances in interactions, and with *gender roles*, there is the general acceptance of male dominance over females. While it is not clear how these core cultural values aid with resilience in adversity, the following inferences could be made, however:

1. Allocentrism and familism can lead to strong social support. Hispanics have large families with strong ties based on loyalty and reciprocity (Gaines et al., 1997).
2. With familism, when confronted with adversity, family members perceive a lower personal burden (e.g., Losada et al., 2006).
3. Simpatia (or harmony in relationship) can engender a *normative* response, in adversity. In the face of adversity, an established ritual to be followed is likely to involve the full participation of family members. This could include a shared belief on the origins of the adversity. There is the general belief that what is going to happen will happen, and if it does happen, it is beyond human control (Cuellar et al., 1995). Belief in *fatalism* could be tied to religiosity. In the face of adversity, belief in fatalism provides a health-protective buffer (e.g., Arrendondo et al., 2005).
4. Close personal space in interaction reduces the desire to be socially distant and be isolated. Due to group interdependence, living in a mostly Hispanic neighborhood is reported to lead to better physical health outcomes (Browning & Cagney, 2002).
5. Usually, hierarchical interactions are based on age and on male dominance, which help to provide structure and leadership in handling adversity.

Death, however, could test a family's coherence. Researchers have identified family types and how likely they are to respond to adversity: *supportive families* have little or no conflicts; *conflict resolving families* have moderate conflict because they work out their differences through open communication; and *intermediate families* have moderate level of cohesion and can become dysfunctional in the face of adversity. Others include *sullen families* where family members lack the desire to support each other and *hostile families,* with low levels of cohesion, where family members reject support from each other (Kissane et al., 2006).

Other Cultural Factors That Contribute to Resilience

In a loss, other cultural factors can aid with resilience. Some of these factors are highlighted in the Hispanic paradox, but others point to the need to carefully understand cultural dynamics that bring about resilience. Psychologist Urie Bronfenbrenner (1979) conceptualized the human-environment interface, based on an ecological model. Although Bronfenbrenner's model focused on child development, his model has relevance in how the environment could influence resilience across the life course. Bronfenbrenner's (1979) ecological model points to the environment in layers, besides the immediate home environment, which are consequential in human development. In Bronfenbrenner's (1979) ecological system, there are the following layers: *microsystem, mesosystem, exosystem, macrosystem, and chronosystem.* The microsystem includes the child's family or neighborhood; the mesosystem includes the environment the child steps into beyond the home, such as the school environment. This system includes parent/teacher interactions that also influence the child's behavior; the exosystem is where the child does not step into yet is capable of influencing the child's development. This includes the parents' workplace (with pay structure and workplace benefits) that impacts on the child's development, and the macrosystem encompasses broad cultural norms and societal socioeconomic imbalances that include racism, poverty, and access to healthcare that can affect the child's development. The last stage, chronosystem, includes historical transitions or experiences influencing human development over the life course. This includes gender or racial discrimination across generations. These environmental layers are interrelated in history, in context, and in culture (Darling, 2007). Therefore, it is difficult to understand one layer in the absence of others.

While the environment can influence the child's development, the child in turn is capable of engaging his or her environment. For example, a child's needs could influence resilience in the mother.

From a qualitative study of the lived experience of bereaved individuals of diverse cultural backgrounds, researcher Jessica Melendez Tyler and colleagues (Tyler et al., 2023) asked study participants to respond to the following: how their culture has been tied to resilience historically, what within their culture is the healing process, within their culture what it means to suffer, and what is most disturbing to them in a traumatic loss. These researchers were able to identify resilience within a culture and synthesized the following subthemes of cultural factors that relate to resilience: *caretaker influence, cultural expectations of suffering, and cultural coping practices.*

Caretaker Influence

A *caretaker influencer* is an individual who models fortitude, resourcefulness, and hardiness in the face of adversity. A likely cue from a caretaker influencer includes that a similar incident has happened in the past and we survived it, and, therefore, the current situation will not be different. This caretaker influencer could be at any level of Bronfenbrenner's ecological model that others look up to and could be a parent, a teacher, a civic leader, or the president of a country.

Cultural Expectations of Suffering

Individuals have personal thresholds for suffering, yet in each culture there is a collective threshold for suffering. Some of the world's happiest people are not in resource-rich societies. It is possible that for the Hispanic paradox earlier discussed, the obverse is the case. Hispanics may have a different understanding to suffering.

Buddhism, for example, teaches its followers that part of life is suffering (Masel et al., 2012). Therefore, in a culture where Buddhism permeates every stratum of Bronfenbrenner's ecological model, the understanding to suffering would be different than in another society where such religious belief is not part of the cultural fabric. However, through acculturation, a non-Buddhist can embrace Buddhism and come to a different understanding to suffering. Researcher Eva Masel and colleagues (Masel et al., 2012) describe an incident in which a Christian patient with pain from cancer visits a Buddha Master who tells her to stop thinking about how long her pain would last. Instead, the Buddha Master asks the patient to admit that pain is part of the experience in this world. With this different perspective, the patient is able to handle her pain.

Cultural Coping Practices

In the face of adversity, different cultures have different practices that help with resilience. They include meaning making, memorializing the loss, avoidance behavior, or seeking forgiveness. Others include continuing bond with the deceased and seeking professional help. Mourning traditions help with resilience because they serve as protective devise for the bereaved (e.g., Boss, 2006) and help to validate the bereaved person's grief as appropriate. Across different cultures, mourning rules are varied and include as examples the following:

- African Americans prefer earth burial over cremation because they believe that only the soul of a non-cremated person would make it to heaven (Lobar et al., 2006). Also, American Americans in handling grief prefer a minister's help over the help of a professional counselor (Taylor et al., 2007). However, African Americans prefer the help of a professional counselor they perceive to understand them or is similar to them. This is to not add to the burden of having to explain themselves to a stranger (Manyam et al., 2020).
- The *Cree nation* (Canada's most populous indigenous group) views death as a transition. Therefore, crying is perceived as preventing the deceased from making a transition to the other world. Instead, death should be marked with prayers, feasts, chants, and songs which strengthen resilience. Additionally, an ongoing relationship with the deceased is maintained (Hampton et al., 2010).
- In difficult times, having a dual religious belief could be helpful with resilience. As earlier discussed, psychologist Robert Neimeyer and colleague (Burke & Neimeyer, 2014) reported that African Americans experience *spiritual struggle* in trying to find meaning to their loss experience. This spiritual struggle could have resulted from having a single religious belief. In Brazil, almost half of the population have dual religious beliefs. While they profess Christianity, they also hold on to Indigenous religious beliefs. They go to church yet visit Umbanda worship centers (Chesnut, 2003). Researcher Regina Bousso and colleagues (Bousso et al., 2011) studied several bereaved Brazilians and reported that in

explaining their loss, one family noted that Christianity failed them where Spiritism helped instead.

- In Ecuador, bereaved persons maintain purposeful continuing bond with the deceased by keeping personal belongings of the deceased or talking to the deceased (Foster et al., 2012).
- Among Indigenous Australians (or Aboriginals), maintaining purposeful continuing bond with the deceased however is discouraged. The decedent's belongings are destroyed, with survivors relocating from the home where the death occurred and the bereaved changing their names if namesake to the deceased (Jones, 2015).
- The Chinese believe that with death comes one less loved one who is physically present. Thus, resilience is based on the strength to move with less number, through family bond and rituals (e.g., Qin & Xia, 2015).
- The Estonians in traditional burial practices take steps to protect the living from the dead. Measures taken include keeping the bath soap used to wash the deceased in the coffin, pouring the water used to wash the deceased at a place nobody goes, and burning the container on which the dead body is washed (Heapost, 2007). As an avoidance behavior, this helps with resilience.

In resilience, the bereaved who is in lockstep with cultural values and expectations is helped, as culture provides a "looking glass" through which the griever evaluates how well they are coping with their loss.

Key Takeaways

1. Grief is a normal response to a loss. Some people fail to eventually integrate their grief into normal daily functioning, which leads to prolonged grief disorder or complicated grief.
2. Some ethnic minority groups have depleted *reserve capacity* due to a history of trauma across generations that includes racism, poor access to healthcare, and prolonged emotional injury. Over time, this experience could lead to learned helplessness. However, culture provides direction for resilience and also acts as a "looking glass" against which a griever can evaluate their resilience in response to adversity.
3. Individual differences could explain resilience to adversity. People with previous experience with adversity are more likely to be resilient than those without.
4. Resilience could be derived from cultural precepts and practices. The "Hispanic paradox" is an example.
5. Urie Bronfenbrenner's (1979) ecological model provides an understanding to how different cultural environmental layers can operate in developing resilience.
6. The cultural elements of individualism/collectivism and autonomy/embeddedness help to explain resilience.

7. Also, in response to adversity, the following cultural elements are important: *caretaker influence, cultural expectations of suffering, and coping practices.*

Critical Cultural Thinking

Within 1 week, John and James experienced the death of close loved ones from COVID-19. Their losses were unexpected. Over a period of time, John is able to integrate his grief into his normal daily functioning, whereas James is unable to do likewise and is experiencing prolonged grief disorder. What individual and cultural factors could help with explaining both situations?

References

American Psychological Association. (n.d.). *Resilience*. www.apa.org/topics/resilience

Arrendondo, E. M., Elder, J. P., Ayala, G. X., & Campbell, N. R. (2005). Is church attendance associated with latinas' health? *American Journal of Health Behavior, 29*(6), 502–511.

Berry, J. W. (2006). Contexts of acculturation. *The Cambridge Handbook of Acculturation Psychology, 27*(42), 328–336.

Boelen, P. A., Olff, M., & Smid, G. E. (2019). Traumatic loss: Mental health consequences and implications for treatment and prevention. *European Journal of Psychotraumatology, 10*(1), 1591331.

Bonanno, G. A., & Field, N. P. (2001). Examining the delayed grief hypothesis across 5 years of bereavement. *American Behavioral Scientist, 44*(5), 798–816.

Bonanno, G. A., Field, N. P., Kovacevic, A., & Kaltman, S. (2002a). Self-enhancement as a buffer against extreme adversity: Civil war in bosnia and traumatic loss in the United States. *Personality and Social Psychology Bulletin, 28*(2), 184–196.

Bonanno, G. A., & Keltner, D. (1997). Facial expressions of emotion and the course of conjugal bereavement. *Journal of Abnormal Psychology, 106*(1), 126–137.

Bonanno, G. A., Keltner, D., Holen, A., & Horowitz, M. J. (1995). When avoiding unpleasant emotions might not be such a bad thing: Verbal-autonomic response dissociation and midlife conjugal bereavement. *Journal of Personality and Social Psychology, 69*(5), 975.

Bonanno, G. A., Wortman, C. B., Lehman, D. R., Tweed, R. G., Haring, M., Sonnega, J., et al. (2002b). Resilience to loss and chronic grief: A prospective study from preloss to 18-months postloss. *Journal of Personality and Social Psychology, 83*(5), 1150.

Bonanno, G. A., Wortman, C. B., & Nesse, R. M. (2004). Prospective patterns of resilience and maladjustment during widowhood. *Psychology and Aging, 19*(2), 260.

Boss, P. (2006). *Loss trauma and resilience*. WW Norton & Company.

Bousso, R. S., Poles, K., Serafim, T. d. S., & Miranda, M. G. d. (2011). Religious beliefs, illness and death: Family's perspectives in illness experience. *Revista da Escola de Enfermagem da USP, 45*, 397–403.

Brave Heart, M. Y. H., & DeBruyn, L. M. (1998). The American Indian holocaust: Healing historical unresolved grief. *American Indian and Alaska Native Mental Health Research, 8*(2), 60–82.

Brody, G. H., Kogan, S. M., Chen, Y., & Murry, V. M. (2008). Long-term effects of the strong African American families program on youths' conduct problems. *Journal of Adolescent Health, 43*(5), 474–481.

Bronfenbrenner, U. (1979). *The ecology of human development: Experiments by nature and design*. Harvard University Press.

Browning, C. R., & Cagney, K. A. (2002). Neighborhood structural disadvantage, collective efficacy, and self-rated physical health in an urban setting. *Journal of Health and Social Behavior*, 383–399.

Burke, L. A., Crunk, E., Neimeyer, R. A., & Bai, H. (2019). Inventory of Complicated Spiritual Grief 2.0 (ICSG 2.0): Validation of a revised measure of spiritual distress in bereavement. *Death Studies*. https://doi.org/10.1080/07481187.2019.1627031

Burke, L. A., & Neimeyer, R. A. (2014). Complicated spiritual grief I: Relation to complicated grief symptomatology following violent death bereavement. *Death Studies, 38*(4), 259–267.

Caffaro, F., Ferraris, F., & Schmidt, S. (2014). Gender differences in the perception of honour killing in individualist versus collectivistic cultures: Comparison between Italy and Turkey. *Sex Roles, 71*(9), 296–318.

CDC.gov. (2008). *Health, United States, 2008*. www.cdc.gov/nchs/data/hus/hus08.pdf

Chen, D. D. (2016). *Stress management and prevention: Applications to daily life*. Routledge.

Chesnut, R. A. (2003). Pragmatic consumers and practical products: The success of pneumacentric religion among women in Latin America's new religious economy. *Review of Religious Research*, 20–31.

Cuellar, I., Arnold, B., & Gonzalez, G. (1995). Cognitive referents of acculturation: Assessment of cultural constructs in Mexican Americans. *Journal of Community Psychology, 23*(4), 339–356.

Darling, N. (2007). Ecological systems theory: The person in the center of the circles. *Research in Human Development, 4*(3–4), 203–217.

Denham, A. R. (2008). Rethinking historical trauma: Narratives of resilience. *Transcultural Psychiatry, 45*(3), 391–414.

Doka, K. J., & Martin, T. L. (2011). *Grieving beyond gender: Understanding the ways men and women mourn*. Routledge.

Dutil, S. (2019). Adolescent traumatic and disenfranchised grief: Adapting an evidence-based intervention for black and latinx youths in schools. *Children & Schools, 41*(3), 179–187.

Dutton, Y. C., & Zisook, S. (2005). Adaptation to bereavement. *Death Studies, 29*(10), 877–903.

Foster, T. L., Roth, M., Contreras, R., Jo Gilmer, M., & Gordon, J. E. (2012). Continuing bonds reported by bereaved individuals in Ecuador. *Bereavement Care, 31*(3), 120–128.

Fraley, R. C., & Bonanno, G. A. (2004). Attachment and loss: A test of three competing models on the association between attachment-related avoidance and adaptation to bereavement. *Personality and Social Psychology Bulletin, 30*(7), 878–890.

Gaines, S. O., Jr., Marelich, W. D., Bledsoe, K. L., Steers, W. N., Henderson, M. C., Granrose, C. S., et al. (1997). Links between race/ethnicity and cultural values as mediated by racial/ethnic identity and moderated by gender. *Journal of Personality and Social Psychology, 72*(6), 1460.

Gallo, L. C., Bogart, L. M., Vranceanu, A., & Matthews, K. A. (2005). Socioeconomic status, resources, psychological experiences, and emotional responses: A test of the reserve capacity model. *Journal of Personality and Social Psychology, 88*(2), 386.

Gallo, L. C., & Matthews, K. A. (2003). Understanding the association between socioeconomic status and physical health: Do negative emotions play a role? *Psychological Bulletin, 129*(1), 10.

Gillies, J., & Neimeyer, R. A. (2006). Loss, grief, and the search for significance: Toward a model of meaning reconstruction in bereavement. *Journal of Constructivist Psychology, 19*(1), 31–65.

Hampton, M., Baydala, A., Bourassa, C., McKay-McNabb, K., Placsko, C., Goodwill, K., et al. (2010). Completing the circle: Elders speak about end-of-life care with aboriginal families in Canada. *Journal of Palliative Care, 26*(1), 6–14.

Heapost, L. (2007). The cemetery of Siksälä: Osteological and paleodemographical analysis. In S. Laul & H. Valk (Eds.), *A community at the frontiers. Iron Age and Medieval* (pp. 213–236). University of Tartu.

Helgeson, V. S., & Taylor, S. E. (1993). Social comparisons and adjustment among cardiac patients 1. *Journal of Applied Social Psychology, 23*(15), 1171–1195.

Henderson, D. X., Jones, J., McLeod, K., Jackson, K., Lunsford, A., & Metzger, I. (2020). A phenomenological study of racial harassment in school and emotional effects among the retrospective accounts of older black adolescents. *The Urban Review, 52*, 458–481.
Hiroto, D. S., & Seligman, M. E. (1975). Generality of learned helplessness in man. *Journal of Personality and Social Psychology, 31*(2), 311.
Hock, M., & Krohne, H. W. (2004). Coping with threat and memory for ambiguous information: Testing the repressive discontinuity hypothesis. *Emotion, 4*(1), 65.
Jones, K. (2015). It is normal to remember: Death and grief in Australia. In *The world of bereavement: Cultural perspectives on death in families* (pp. 243–263).
Kellerman, N. P. (2001). Psychopathology in children of holocaust survivors: A review of the research literature. *Israel Journal of Psychiatry and Related Sciences, 38*(1), 36–46.
Keltner, D. (1996). Facial expressions of emotion and personality. In *Handbook of emotion, adult development, and aging* (pp. 385–401).
King, A. C., Taylor, C. B., Albright, C. A., & Haskell, W. L. (1990). The relationship between repressive and defensive coping styles and blood pressure responses in healthy, middle-aged men and women. *Journal of Psychosomatic Research, 34*(4), 461–471.
Kirmayer, L. J., Gone, J. P., & Moses, J. (2014). Rethinking historical trauma. *Transcultural Psychiatry, 51*(3), 299–319.
Kissane, D. W., McKenzie, M., Bloch, S., Moskowitz, C., McKenzie, D. P., & O'Neill, I. (2006). Family focused grief therapy: A randomized, controlled trial in palliative care and bereavement. *American Journal of Psychiatry, 163*(7), 1208–1218.
Kitayama, S., Mesquita, B., & Karasawa, M. (2006). Cultural affordances and emotional experience: Socially engaging and disengaging emotions in Japan and the United States. *Journal of Personality and Social Psychology, 91*(5), 890.
Lalande, K. M., & Bonanno, G. A. (2006). Culture and continuing bonds: A prospective comparison of bereavement in the United States and the people's republic of China. *Death Studies, 30*(4), 303–324.
Lichtenthal, W. G., Cruess, D. G., & Prigerson, H. G. (2004). A case for establishing complicated grief as a distinct mental disorder in DSM-V. *Clinical Psychology Review, 24*(6), 637–662.
Lobar, S. L., Youngblut, J. M., & Brooten, D. (2006). Cross-cultural beliefs, ceremonies, and rituals surrounding death of a loved one. *Pediatric Nursing, 32*(1), 44–50.
Losada, A., Montorio, I., Knight, B. G., Márquez, M., & Izal, M. (2006). Explanation of caregivers distress from the cognitive model: The role of dysfunctional thoughts. *Psicología Conductual, 14*(1), 115.
Mancini, A. D., & Bonanno, G. A. (2006). Resilience in the face of potential trauma: Clinical practices and illustrations. *Journal of Clinical Psychology, 62*(8), 971–985.
Manyam, S. B., Davis, T. L., & Mitchell, C. D. (2020). Trauma group therapy with african american children and adolescents: A 30-plus year content analysis. *The Journal for Specialists in Group Work, 45*(1), 56–75.
Marin, G., & Marin, B. V. (1991). *Research with Hispanic populations*. Sage Publications.
Markides, K. S., & Coreil, J. (1986). The health of Hispanics in the southwestern united states: An epidemiologic paradox. *Public Health Reports, 101*(3), 253.
Masel, E. K., Schur, S., & Watzke, H. H. (2012). Life is uncertain. Death is certain. Buddhism and palliative care. *Journal of Pain and Symptom Management, 44*(2), 307–312.
Mikulincer, M., & Shaver, P. R. (2007). Boosting attachment security to promote mental health, prosocial values, and inter-group tolerance. *Psychological Inquiry, 18*(3), 139–156.
Myers, H. F. (2009). Ethnicity-and socio-economic status-related stresses in context: An integrative review and conceptual model. *Journal of Behavioral Medicine, 32*, 9–19.
Nakajima, S. (2018). Complicated grief: Recent developments in diagnostic criteria and treatment. *Philosophical Transactions of the Royal Society, B: Biological Sciences, 373*(1754), 20170273.
Neimeyer, R. A., & Anderson, A. (2002). Meaning reconstruction theory. In *Loss and grief: A guide for human services practitioners* (pp. 45–64).

Neimeyer, R. A., & Sands, D. C. (2011). Meaning reconstruction in bereavement: From principles to practice. In R. A. Neimeyer, D. L. Harris, H. R. Winokuer, & G. F. Thornton (Eds.), *Grief and bereavement in contemporary society: Bridging research and practice* (pp. 9–22). Routledge/Taylor & Francis Group.

Opara, I., Assan, M. A., Pierre, K., Gunn, J. F., III, Metzger, I., Hamilton, J., & Arugu, E. (2020). Suicide among black children: An integrated model of the interpersonal-psychological theory of suicide and intersectionality theory for researchers and clinicians. *Journal of Black Studies, 51*(6), 611–631.

Qin, S., & Xia, Y. (2015). Grieving rituals and beliefs of Chinese families. In *The world of bereavement: Cultural perspectives on death in families* (pp. 69–80).

Raphael, B., Swan, P., & Martinek, N. (1998). Intergenerational aspects of trauma for Australian aboriginal people. In *International handbook of multigenerational legacies of trauma* (pp. 327–339).

Sampson, R. J., Raudenbush, S. W., & Earls, F. (1997). Neighborhoods and violent crime: A multilevel study of collective efficacy. *Science, 277*(5328), 918–924.

Schwartz, S. H. (2007). Basic human values: Theory, measurement, and applications. *Revue Française de Sociologie, 47*(4), 929.

Shuchter, S. R., & Zisook, S. (1993). The course of normal grief. In M. S. Stroebe, W. Stroebe, & R. O. Hansson (Eds.), *Handbook of bereavement: Theory, research, and intervention* (pp. 23–43). Cambridge University Press.

Taylor, S. E., & Armor, D. A. (1996). Positive illusions and coping with adversity. *Journal of Personality, 64*(4), 873–898.

Taylor, R. J., Chatters, L. M., & Jackson, J. S. (2007). Religious and spiritual involvement among older African Americans, Caribbean blacks, and non-Hispanic whites: Findings from the national survey of American life. *The Journals of Gerontology Series B: Psychological Sciences and Social Sciences, 62*(4), S238–S250.

Triandis, H. C. (1995). A theoretical framework for the study of diversity. In M. M. Chemers, S. Oskamp, & M. A. Costanzo (Eds.), *Diversity in organizations: New perspectives for a changing workplace* (pp. 11–36). Sage Publications.

Tugade, M. M., & Fredrickson, B. L. (2004). Resilient individuals use positive emotions to bounce back from negative emotional experiences. *Journal of Personality and Social Psychology, 86*(2), 320.

Tyler, J. M., Darrow, N. E. T., Outlaw, A. B., & Guffin, J. P. (2023). Lived experiences of utilizing cultural resiliency to navigate traumatic loss. *Journal of Counseling & Development, 101*(2), 180–192.

United States Department of Health and Human Services. (n.d.). *Hispanic/Latino population information*. https://minorityhealth.hhs.gov/hispaniclatino-health#:~:text=According%20to%202020%20Census%20data,the%20largest%20at%2061.6%20percent

Walter, T. (2010). Grief and culture. *Bereavement Care, 29*(2), 5–9.

Zisook, S., & Shear, K. (2009). Grief and bereavement: What psychiatrists need to know. *World Psychiatry, 8*(2), 67.

Chapter 10
Culture and Coping with Disenfranchised Grief

Disenfranchised: What It Means?

The term "disenfranchised" is a more familiar word in politics. In politics, this refers to a person who is not allowed to vote. At a particular period in the United States, women were not allowed to vote. It was the law back then and women were disenfranchised politically. However, this changed when the United States Congress and state legislatures passed a new law that came into effect on August 18, 1920. The 19th Amendment to the US Constitution states that "The right of citizens of the United States to vote shall not be denied or abridged by the United States or by any state on account of sex" (National Archives, n.d.).

In 1989, researcher Kenneth Doka introduced *disenfranchised grief* into the bereavement lexicon. Doka defined disenfranchised grief as grief denied and not publicly recognized. Unlike politics, however, disenfranchised grief is not codified; rather, it is normative within a cultural context. Accordingly, "Each culture creates its own grieving rules, defining the ways an individual is expected to grieve" (Doka & Martin, 2002, p. 338). Disenfranchised grief could put a limit to obtaining social support, expressing distress, and coping with a loss (Doka, 2008).

Kenneth Doka (2008) provides the following scenarios that could lead to disenfranchised grief in a loss:

Relationship That Is Not Socially Approved (e.g., an Extramarital Affair)

A relationship not socially approved in one culture may be socially approved in another culture. For example, monogamy is legalized in the United States and in most Western societies. Thus, an affair outside of a monogamous conjugal

F. E. Eyetsemitan, *Cultural Influences in Coping with Grief*,
https://doi.org/10.1007/978-3-031-86817-7_10

relationship is publicly frowned at. Similarly, so is an affair with a former spouse. Therefore, to grieve a loss from a previous relationship would call into question one's fidelity to a current relationship. However, in most non-Western societies, polygamous relationship is acceptable, and nothing in their penal code frowns at such a relationship. Therefore, a grief connected to an ex-spouse or an extramarital relationship would have a different understanding. Yet the male being the dominant gender (e.g., Eyetsemitan & Gire, 2003) can openly grieve the loss of an ex-spouse or someone from an extramarital relationship but not the female. In most non-Western cultures, egalitarianism is not a common practice.

Relationship Not Based on Recognizable Kin Ties (e.g., Neighbors, Friends, Coworkers, Companion Animals)

Generally, kin relationships are considered to engender stronger emotional ties than nonkin ties. This is evidenced in how work organizations dispense of paid bereavement leave to their bereaved workers, based on kin ties (Eyetsemitan, 1998). However, in each society, the complexity of the cultural environment should allow for the validation of nonkin ties by certain groups. For example, the African American culture recognizes non-blood relatives as *fictive kins* (Sudarkasa, 1997; Rosenblatt & Wallace, 2005). Also, members of religious groups (e.g., Christianity) refer to each other as "brother" or "sister." Shared beliefs in religious communities bring members closer to each other than blood ties.

Loss That Limits Social Support from Others (e.g., Suicide)

Just as a society evaluates the death of a young child as "off time" and an older person's as "on time," so are some deaths considered "good" and others "bad." As example, a good death would be to die peacefully at home surrounded by loved ones, whereas a bad death would be an unexpected or tragic end. Not only is suicide unexpected but tragic, yet *attribution* is usually made as to its cause. Researchers Harold Kelley and John Michela (1980) note that an attribution is the *perception or inference of cause*. It alludes to *motive* as well. Attribution usually takes one of two forms: (a) situational cause or (b) dispositional cause. With *situational cause*, attribution is made to the action of others, whereas with *dispositional cause* attribution is made to the character or personality of the individual. For example, if a student was absent in class, a professor could make attribution to a situational cause by suggesting that the student's absence was the result of transportation problems. However, with a dispositional cause, the professor could instead suggest that the student missed her class because she overslept. Depending on the culture, suicide could be attributed to either a situational cause or a dispositional cause. With a situational cause, the context that led to the suicide behavior becomes the focus of attention, e.g., lack of parental care or social support. The reckoning would be that something went wrong in the victim's family situation that led to her suicide behavior. Therefore, blame not the victim but the victim's loved ones. In the United States, blame and stigma accompany a suicide (e.g., Range & Thompson, 1987). In the suicide loss of a child, it is commonplace to blame the parents (e.g., Feigelman et al., 2009). A blame based on a situational cause may not attract sympathy or social support from others. Some researchers, however, believe that suicide is a *call for help* because the individual desires to escape from an aversive emotional state. Social psychologist Roy Baumeister (1990) notes that for an adolescent an aversive emotional state is a failure to meet up to the standards set for the teenager by his parents. Thus, parents with standards that led to the suicide become the culprit.

With attribution to dispositional cause, however, the person's characteristics or personality becomes the focus of attention. Some scholars attribute suicide to a faulty thought process. From twin and adoptive studies, between 30% and 55% of suicide behavior is based on inherited factors (Voracek et al., 2007). Yet genetic factors alone without an enabling environment do not explain suicide behavior (Mann, 1999). Family and social support serve as protective factors against suicide. In Venezuela, suicidal ideations among teenagers have been linked to loneliness (e.g., Granero et al., 2008). In Taiwan, Thailand, and the Philippines, suicidal behaviors among adolescents have also been linked to loneliness (e.g., Page et al., 2006). However, studies show that young people who experience love and support from parents and adults are less likely to commit suicide. In 1994–1995, the United States National Longitudinal Survey of Adolescent Health followed over 20,000 teenagers into adulthood for 15 years and found the importance of parental love and care in preventing suicide. Parental love and care serve as buffer against suicidal behavior in teenagers (e.g., Winfree & Jiang, 2010). Across all age groups, suicide is common among people who are less likely to be socially integrated (Durkheim, 1897; Williams, 2007).

In China, however, suicide has been reported as a *face-saving* behavior. Similar reports have been documented in Sri Lanka and in Japan (e.g., Lee et al., 2016; Turner et al., 2002; Vijayakumar et al., 2005). Most Asian cultures have high expectations for their young people to succeed vocationally, financially, or socially (e.g., Sue et al., 1995). Therefore, an individual who is unable to meet these expectations may commit suicide to keep the group's high expectations intact. Asian cultures have collectivist value system (Markus & Kitayama, 1991). Suicide as a face-saving act to maintain group harmony may not make sense in an individualist culture. Instead, suicide in an individualist culture may reflect a rejection of the group. And, as earlier referenced, there is the tendency to blame the group (e.g., family) in the case of suicide (Baumeister, 1990). Suicide is "the ultimate rejection," as a survivor parent in the United States coined it. Thus, based on cultural expectations, disenfranchised grief from suicide would be relative. Also, within the same culture, disenfranchised grief would be influenced by context. For example, researcher Tony Walter and colleague (Walter & Bailey, 2020) noted that in the United Kingdom nonfamily members did not perceive their grief as disenfranchised when not given the same consideration as family members of the deceased, in seating arrangement during funerals.

Grieving Styles Not Approved by a Culture, e.g., Male Grieving as "female" or Female Grieving as "male"

Psychiatrists Simon Zisook and Katherine Shear (2009) note that in death the initial response includes intense pain, sadness, and crying, a preoccupation with the thoughts and memories of the deceased, and a disinterest in normal daily functioning. This is the *acute stage* of grief. The totality of this grief response is physical, cognitive, emotional, and behavioral. In most cultures people are socialized along gender lines, including appropriate grieving styles. Generally males, unlike females, do not display excessive emotions. Males are expected to be "strong for others" and therefore to keep their emotions in check. A male whose grieving style includes an excessive display of emotion may be regarded as lacking in control. Such a grieving style would not be socially approved. Generally, females are allowed excessive display of emotions during grief. Therefore, it may be perceived as inappropriate if following a loss a female holds back on her emotions. Yet, in a loss, a female could take on the role of breadwinner, head of household, or become a single parent. In her new role, therefore, the female may be forced to keep her emotions in check to be strong for others (Eyetsemitan, 2021). Given this circumstance, her grieving style may become acceptable. Kenneth Doka and colleague (Doka & Martin, 2011) describe two types of grievers not necessarily based on gender: the *intuitive* griever who is more emotional and the *instrumental* griever who is more cognitive and tries to master the problem that arises from a loss.

Disenfranchised Grief and a Layered Cultural Environment

The cultural environment is not monolithic but has different layers (Bronfenbrenner, 1979). At each layer, there are *influencers* capable of influencing the grief outcomes of the bereaved.

Bronfenbrenner's Ecological Model

As discussed in Chap. 9, psychologist Urie Bronfenbrenner's (1979) ecological environment is made up of layers that include the *microsystem, mesosystem, exosystem, macrosystem, and chronosystem.* When applied to grief, Bronfenbrenner's ecological model could be understood as follows:

The *microsystem* is the bereaved person's immediate cultural environment made up of family, friends, and neighbors. At this level the bereaved person's grief could be validated or disenfranchised. Based on prior good relationships with others, a bereaved person's grief would be acknowledged, and they would receive social support from family members, friends, and neighbors, even if his or her grief is disenfranchised at a different environmental layer. This validation of the bereaved person's grief and the provision of social support by others may be based on obligation or reciprocity. For example, in the past the bereaved person might have been there to support family members, friends, or neighbors during their own time of grief. Yet the bereaved person's grief may be disenfranchised, based on prior poor relationships with people that constitutes his microsystem. The *mesosystem* is where the bereaved person steps into in his daily interactions and includes people at the grocery store or at the gas station in his local community. Also, based on prior relationships formed with the people at these places in his community, the bereaved person's grief may be either validated or disenfranchised. The *exosystem* is where the bereaved person lacks a direct influence, yet what happens at this level can either validate or disenfranchise his or her grief. This would include the bereavement leave policy at his workplace and the work schedule of family members, friends, or neighbors that would prevent or allow them to provide social support or acknowledge the survivor's grief in a tangible way. Family members, friends, or neighbors may work two jobs or shift jobs that could limit their availability, and their nonavailability may disenfranchise the bereaved person's grief.

The *macrosystem* encompasses the broad cultural norms regarding grief rules and types of grief that are validated. At earlier environmental layers, due to close relationships with or obligations to the bereaved, people may not necessarily follow cultural norms set at the macrosystem. For example, in the United States some states have laws banning abortion. Based on this ban, abortion is against the law, and these states do not provide support or resources for a person involved in an abortion. Yet, as earlier discussed, an individual with an abortion may find support or validation at a previous layer. Also, opposition to the legal ban on abortion may come from the people who support abortion at a previous ecological level. Thus, a grief disenfranchised at one environmental layer may be enfranchised at another environmental layer and vice versa.

The last stage is the *chronosystem* which includes the historical transitions or experiences over the life course that could impact on disenfranchised grief. As society undergoes changes, a grief not acknowledged 20 years ago could be acknowledged today. In the United States, over historical times, same-sex couples have experienced disenfranchised grief. However, a law signed by the governor of the state of New York in 2010 states that:

> No employer who extends to its employees funeral or bereavement leave for the death of an employee's spouse or the child, parent or other relative of the spouse shall deny the same leave to an employee for the death of the employee's same-sex committed partner or the child, parent or other relative of the committed partner. (New York State Government (2010): N.Y. Civ. Rights Law § 79-N" N.Y. Civ. Rights Law § 79-N)

Psychologist Urie Bronfenbrenner's (1979)'s ecological layered environment provides with a nuanced understanding to disenfranchised grief.

Disenfranchised Grief and a Culture of Tradition Versus Modernity

Within a cultural environment, both tradition and modernity can coexist. However, most times, tradition gives way to modernity. Researcher Ryan Schram (2007) reports the following situation among the Auhelawa tribe in Papua New Guinea: The tribe decided to change its traditional practices to modern ways of burial and mourning. They found their traditional ways were too time-consuming and expensive and hindered a quick return to normalcy. This might reflect a disenfranchised grief or a "stifled grief" (Eyetsemitan, 1998).

Tradition Versus Modernity

Tradition refers to how things are done or known to be done over historic times, whereas modernity represents a new way of thinking and acting. Thus, tradition and modernity may not move in the same direction (Eyetsemitan, 2021).

To move from tradition to modernity would require a cognitive shift, as was done by the Auhelawa tribal people of Papua New Guinea. Psychologist Jean Piaget (1976) refers to a cognitive shift as movement from assimilation to accommodation. To solve their problem, the Auhelawa tribal people of Papua New Guinea moved from an old way of thinking (assimilation) to a new way of thinking (accommodation), with the possible outcome of disenfranchised grief or stifled grief.

Over time, traditional practice helps to define who a person is and becomes integrated into that person's sense of self. Therefore, a shift away from traditional practice becomes a transformational experience. Some individuals with traditional views perceive abortion as wrong and would not provide social support to a person who commits an abortion nor acknowledge their grief. To do otherwise is to challenge how they perceive of themselves.

Institutions have traditional beliefs/practices as well. For example, historically the Catholic Church believes that abortion is wrong. Yet institutions (or people) can embrace modernity, if they believe that it would enhance who they are or be of benefit to them. The Auhelawa tribal people of Papua New Guinea, mentioned earlier, is an example. Traditionally, the Catholic Church has strong pro-life beliefs and practices. However, in embracing modernity, the Catholic Church acknowledges the grief of people who commit abortion and offers its support. In an article that appeared in the publication of the United States Conference of Catholic Bishops, Joanne Angelo (n.d.) states that Pope John Paul II in his encyclical letter *Evangelium Vitae* (EV), the Gospel of Life, had the following message for women who had committed an abortion:

> Certainly what happened was and remains terribly wrong. But do not give in to discouragement and do not lose hope. (EV, 99)

In 2010, the Catholic Church had a worldwide followership of nearly 1.1 billion believers (Pew Research Center, 2013). The Pope, as leader of the Catholic Church worldwide, has a pervasive influence on his followers with his stance on abortion.

Disenfranchised Grief and the Cultural Values of Individualism and Collectivism

Researcher Geert Hofstede (1980) proposes two major value systems that undergird cultures around the world. The value of individualism is mostly found in Western societies, whereas the value of collectivism is reported in most non-Western societies. However, due to acculturation influences, there are people in Western societies who value collectivism and those in non-Western societies who value individualism. When individuals uphold more than one value system, this is referred to as "accommodation" behavior (Eyetsemitan, 2021). As sociologist Tony Walter (2010) notes, within every society, there are heterogenous belief systems.

Individualists prefer autonomy, independence, and self-containment and also value freedom and wish to be treated equally (Caffaro et al., 2014).

Therefore, in the context of individualism, to limit or to deny a person's choice of grief is to disenfranchise their grief.

Collectivists value norms, duties, and obligation and prioritize relatedness based on tribe, clan, ethnicity, caste, village, or nation (Triandis, 1995). Therefore, a grief can be disenfranchised if it violates cultural norms or group members' position.

Disenfranchised Grief and Morality

Morality is about how decisions are made on complex matters by an individual or a cultural group. The decision to not recognize a grief may border on moral judgment. As earlier discussed, researcher Kenneth Doka (1987) identifies disenfranchised grief in the following situations in a loss: a relationship that is not socially approved (e.g., an extramarital affair), a relationship not based on a recognizable kin ties (e.g., neighbors, friends, coworkers, companion animals), a loss that limits social support from others (e.g., suicide), and a grieving style not approved by a culture, e.g., male grieving as "female" or female grieving as "male."

From a literature review, researcher Molley Crockett (2013) describes an approach to morality that is based on two acceptable rules: (1) morality based on set rules (or *deontological* judgment) such as killing is bad and (2) morality based on outcomes (or *consequential* judgement) such as killing is bad but toward what end? In the case of suicide, for example, a moral dilemma could be: *is it morally bad to take one's life (deontological judgment), or it is morally bad to take one's life for the good of others (consequential judgement)?* On the issue of abortion, a moral dilemma could be : *is it morally bad to commit an abortion (deontological judgment), or is it morally bad to commit an abortion to save the life of the mother (consequential judgment)?*

In stage theories, stage skipping or stage irreversibility is problematic. However, several decades ago psychologist Lawrence Kohlberg (1958) proposed a stage-based developmental theory of morality that has relevance to disenfranchised grief today. In Kohlberg's (1958) theory of moral development, there are three stages: (1) pre-conventional level, (2) conventional level, and (3) post-conventional level. At the *pre-conventional level*, the child responds to set cultural rules as good or bad, based on reward or punishment. The external enforcers of these set rules include people in the child's world such as parents, adult loved ones, and teachers. In other words, they are authority figures. At the *conventional level*, the individual is both supportive of and loyal to set rules, because they help to achieve law and order in the society. These set rules are internalized and help to regulate the person's own behavior and, also, provide a lens through which their behaviors and those of others are judged. This occurs around early adolescence to adulthood. At the *post-conventional level*, the individual fails to identify with what is customary in society. Instead the individual has wishes of what they think the society could become in the future, based on personal values. Personal values may be acquired from own experience, from others' experience, or from a philosophical/religious viewpoint. In the United States, as earlier noted, there was a time women were not allowed to vote. During that period, the law of the land influenced moral judgment. This is at the conventional level. Yet this law was later changed by the United States Congress on June 4, 1919. Without the personal values of people who operated at the *post-conventional level* of morality, this could not have happened. The United States National Archives (n.d.) notes that:

> The 19th amendment legally guarantees American women the right to vote. Achieving this milestone required a lengthy and difficult struggle—victory took decades of agitation and protest.

> Kenneth Doka's (1987) disenfranchised grief is related to morality construction at both personal and societal levels.

Disenfranchised Grief, Niche-Picking, and Human Agency

In researchers Sandra Scarr and Kathleen McCartney's (1983) concept of *niche-picking* , humans exercise agency by choosing to interact with the environment that suits their disposition or natural proclivity. Psychologist Albert Bandura (2006) describes *self-efficacy* as the belief in oneself able to act on the environment.

While researchers Scarr and McCartney's (1983) model is about gene-environment interaction, a parallel can be made of a bereaved individual who is able to make a choice on how to interact with aspects of the environment that validates their grief.

Researcher Paige Toller (2008) conducted research on bereaved parents who wanted to remain parents to their deceased children. The study involved 53 bereaved parents (17 men and 36 women), who had experienced the loss of a child at least 6 months prior to start of the study.

Friends and loved ones did not recognize the bereaved parents' grief because they wanted the bereaved parents to move on with their lives. But to the bereaved parents, their identity as *parent* was important, and they continued to render parental caregiving by tending to the grave of their deceased child. Friends and family members thought this behavior was pathological and avoided them.

The bereaved parents then explored situations in their environment that would validate their grief and maintained two identities: an *outsider identity* with friends and family members and an *insider identity* with like-minded people who were supportive of their grave-tending behavior. To *enfranchise* their grief, therefore, the bereaved parents developed the following strategies:

(a) Limit interactions with non-supportive people
(b) Be selective on who to tell what information
(c) Spend more time with supportive people
(d) Counterbalance interactions with non-supportive people with supportive individuals

Key Takeaways

1. Disenfranchised grief is grief denied and not publicly recognized.
2. Each culture creates its own grieving rules that bereaved members are expected to follow.
3. People who experience disenfranchised grief may be limited in obtaining social support, expressing distress, or coping with loss.
4. Cultural expectations are relative: a grief not recognized in one culture may be recognized in another. The cultural values of individualism and collectivism could provide insights into this difference.
5. A culture's environment is not monolithic but layered, according to psychologist Urie Bronfenbrenner (1979). Thus, a grief disenfranchised at one cultural layer may be enfranchised at another.
6. Historically, a culture undergoes change from tradition to modernity. Therefore, a grief currently recognized could have been disenfranchised in the past.
7. Morality relates to disenfranchised grief at personal and societal levels.
8. Humans are not entirely at the mercy of their environment. They can exercise agency and "niche-pick" their environment to circumvent grief rules that disfranchises their grief and participate in aspects of the environment that recognize their grief.

Critical Cultural Thinking

John's teenage son died from suicide. John came to see a bereavement counselor because his grief was disenfranchised, based on his culture's "grief rules." John wondered quietly if these grief rules would have been different in another culture. He also asked his bereavement counselor if his grief could still be recognized within own culture. What would you tell John?

References

Angelo, J. E. (n.d.). *A special word to women who have had an abortion*. www.usccb.org/issues-and-action/human-life-and-dignity/abortion/post-abortion-healing/a-special-word-to-women-who-have-had-an-abortion

Bandura, A. (2006). Toward a psychology of human agency. *Perspectives on Psychological Science, 1*(2), 164–180.

Baumeister, R. F. (1990). Suicide as escape from self. *Psychological Review, 97*(1), 90.

Bronfenbrenner, U. (1979). *The ecology of human development: Experiments by nature and design*. Harvard University Press.

Caffaro, F., Ferraris, F., & Schmidt, S. (2014). Gender differences in the perception of honour killing in individualist versus collectivistic cultures: Comparison between Italy and Turkey. *Sex Roles, 71*(9), 296–318.

Crockett, M. J. (2013). Models of morality. *Trends in Cognitive Sciences, 17*(8), 363–366.

Doka, K. J. (1987). Silent sorrow: Grief and the loss of significant others. *Death Studies, 11*(6), 455–469.

Doka, K. J. (2008). Disenfranchised grief in historical and cultural perspective. In M. S. Stroebe, R. O. Hansson, H. Schut, & W. Stroebe (Eds.), *Handbook of bereavement research and practice: Advances in theory and intervention* (pp. 223–240). American Psychological Association.

Doka, K. J., & Martin, T. L. (2002). How we grieve: Culture, class, and gender. In *Disenfranchised grief: New directions, challenges, and strategies for practice* (pp. 337–347).

Doka, K. J., & Martin, T. L. (2011). *Grieving beyond gender: Understanding the ways men and women mourn*. Routledge.

Durkheim, E. (1897). *Le suicide: Étude de sociologie*. Félix Alcan.

Eyetsemitan, F. (1998). Stifled grief in the workplace. *Death Studies, 22*(5), 469–479.

Eyetsemitan, F. E. (2021). *Death, dying, and bereavement around the world: Theories, varied views and customs*. Charles C Thomas Publisher.

Eyetsemitan, F. E., & Gire, J. T. (2003). *Aging and adult development in the developing world: Applying western theories and concepts*. Greenwood Publishing Group.

Feigelman, W., Gorman, B. S., & Jordan, J. R. (2009). Stigmatization and suicide bereavement. *Death Studies, 33*(7), 591–608.

Granero, R., Poni, E., & Poni, C. (2008). Suicidal ideation among students of the 7th, 8th, and 9th grades in the state of Lara, Venezuela: The global school health survey. *Puerto Rico Health Sciences Journal, 27*(4).

Hofstede, G. (1980). Culture and organizations. *International Studies of Management and Organization, 10*(4), 15–41.

Kelley, H. H., & Michela, J. L. (1980). Attribution theory and research. *Annual Review of Psychology, 31*(1), 457–501. https://doi.org/10.1146/annurev.ps.31.020180.002325

Kohlberg, L. (1958). *The development of modes of moral thinking and choice in the years 10 to 16*. Dissertation, The University of Chicago.

Lee, C. S., Anderson, J. R., & Klimes-Dougan, B. (2016). Potentially traumatic experiences, academic performance, and psychological distress: The role of shame. *Journal of Counseling & Development, 94*(1), 41–50.

Mann, J. J. (1999). Role of the serotonergic system in the pathogenesis of major depression and suicidal behavior. *Neuropsychopharmacology, 21*(2), 99S–105S.
Markus, H. R., & Kitayama, S. (1991). *Cultural variation in the self-concept* (pp. 18–48). *Interdisciplinary Approaches*.
National Archives. (n.d.). *19th amendment to the US constitution: Women's right to vote (1920)*. www.archives.gov/milestone-documents/19th-amendment
New York State Government. (2010). *N.Y. Civ. Rights Law § 79-N" N.Y. Civ. Rights Law § 79-N*. www.casetext.com/statute/consolidated-laws-of-new-york/chapter-civil-rights/article-7-miscellaneous-rights-and-immunities/section-79-n-multiple-versions-funeral-or-bereavement-
Page, R. M., Yanagishita, J., Suwanteerangkul, J., Zarco, E. P., Mei-Lee, C., & Miao, N. (2006). Hopelessness and loneliness among suicide attempters in school-based samples of Taiwanese, Philippine and Thai adolescents. *School Psychology International, 27*(5), 583–598.
Pew Research Center. (2013). *The global Catholic population*. www.pewresearch.org/religion/2013/02/13/the-global-catholic-population/
Piaget, J. (1976). *Need and significance of cross-cultural studies in genetic psychology*. Springer.
Range, L. M., & Thompson, K. E. (1987). Community responses following suicide, homicide, and other deaths: The perspective of potential comforters. *The Journal of Psychology, 121*(2), 193–198.
Rosenblatt, P. C., & Wallace, B. R. (2005). Narratives of grieving African-Americans about racism in the lives of deceased family members. *Death Studies, 29*(3), 217–235.
Scarr, S., & McCartney, K. (1983). How people make their own environments: A theory of genotype→ environment effects. *Child Development*, 424–435.
Schram, R. (2007). Sit, cook, eat, full stop: Religion and the rejection of ritual in auhelawa (papua new guinea). *Oceania, 77*(2), 172–190.
Sudarkasa, N. (1997). African American families and family values. In H. P. McAdoo (Ed.), *Black families* (pp. 9–40). Sage Publications. (Reprinted in modified form from N. Sudarkasa et al (Eds.), "Exploring the African-American Experience," Lincoln, PA: Lincoln University Press.
Sue, S., Sue, D. W., Sue, L., & Takeuchi, D. T. (1995). Psychopathology among Asian Americans: A model minority? *Cultural Diversity and Mental Health, 1*(1), 39.
Toller, P. W. (2008). Bereaved parents' negotiation of identity following the death of a child. *Communication Studies, 59*(4), 306–321.
Triandis, H. C. (1995). A theoretical framework for the study of diversity. In M. M. Chemers, S. Oskamp, & M. A. Costanzo (Eds.), *Diversity in organizations: New perspectives for a changing workplace* (pp. 11–36). Sage Publications.
Turner, J. E., Husman, J., & Schallert, D. L. (2002). The importance of students' goals in their emotional experience of academic failure: Investigating the precursors and consequences of shame. *Educational Psychologist, 37*(2), 79–89.
Vijayakumar, L., John, S., Pirkis, J., & Whiteford, H. (2005). Suicide in developing countries (2) risk factors. *Crisis, 26*(3), 112–119.
Voracek, M., Loibl, L. M., Egle, J., Schleicher, S., & Sonneck, G. (2007). Correlates, item-sequence invariance, and test-retest reliability of the beliefs in the inheritance of risk factors for suicide scale (BIRFSS). *Psychological Reports, 101*(3_suppl), 1107–1117.
Walter, T. (2010). Grief and culture. *Bereavement Care, 29*(2), 5–9.
Walter, T., & Bailey, T. (2020). How funerals accomplish family: Findings from a Mass-Observation study. *OMEGA – Journal of Death and Dying, 82*(2), 175–195.
Williams, K. D. (2007). Ostracism: The kiss of social death. *Social and Personality Psychology Compass, 1*(1), 236–247.
Winfree, L. T., Jr., & Jiang, S. (2010). Youthful suicide and social support: Exploring the social dynamics of suicide-related behavior and attitudes within a national sample of US adolescents. *Youth Violence and Juvenile Justice, 8*(1), 19–37.
Zisook, S., & Shear, K. (2009). Grief and bereavement: What psychiatrists need to know. *World Psychiatry, 8*(2), 67.

Chapter 11
Culture, Rituals, and Coping with Loss

Conventional grief models and theories appear to be either basic or applied in approach. Some grief models explain the bereaved person's experiences, while others prescribe steps the bereaved person needs to take to return to normal functioning. Psychoanalyst Sigmund Freud (1917) suggests that the bereaved needs to break ties with the deceased to return to normalcy. Unlike Freud (1917), however, William Worden (2018) proposes a stage-like process for moving to normalcy, referred to as the four tasks of mourning. These are tasks the bereaved must attend to (in no particular order) in returning to normalcy. The first task is to acknowledge the loss (e.g., attend the funeral or view the deceased); the second task is to feel the pain of the loss (e.g., cry or deny yourself of some pleasures); the third task is to replace the role(s) of the deceased (e.g., becoming a breadwinner); and the fourth task is to move on with your life (e.g., form new relationships), after memorializing the deceased.

Researcher Margaret Stroebe and colleague's (Stroebe & Schut, 2006) dual process model takes away the burden that a task model imposes on the bereaved, who might believe that they have to make progress on Worden's (2018) four tasks in returning to normalcy. Stroebe and Schut's (2006) model instead explains that in coping with a loss, the bereaved *oscillates* between attending to the loss (or *loss orientation*) and moving forward with their life (or *restoration orientation*). The bereaved is assumed to make progress when he or she spends less time on loss orientation but more time on restoration orientation. Researcher Kenneth Doka and colleague (Doka & Martin, 2011) suggest two types of grievers: the *intuitive* griever who is inclined toward emotional expressions in grief and the *instrumental* griever who tries to master the challenges of the loss cognitively. Another grief model involves meaning making (or meaning reconstruction) in a loss (Gillies & Neimeyer, 2006). While important, these grief models do not *explicitly* point to grief rituals in coping with the pain of a loss and/or in making it less burdensome on bereaved persons to move on with their lives. Yet, around the world, in people's cultural and religious lives, grief rituals are important and emphasized.

F. E. Eyetsemitan, *Cultural Influences in Coping with Grief*,
https://doi.org/10.1007/978-3-031-86817-7_11

For example, researcher Robert Neimeyer and colleague (Neimeyer & Harris, 2023) note that the common grief ritual in North America is funeral. Funerals are collective acts. However, in coping with a loss, grief rituals could be personal to the bereaved.

Importance of Grief Rituals

Researcher Alison Wood Brooks and colleagues (Brooks et al., 2016) define rituals as predetermined set of acts, which are usually formal and repetitive. Also, rituals tend to be rigid and allow little or no room for substitution or dilution. For example, the prayers said prior to a meal cannot be substituted with the prayers said after a meal. Yet some researchers argue that, in exercise of agency, humans can adapt rituals to suit their purpose (Moran, 2017; Robarchek & Robarchek, 2005).

Also, rituals are not random acts but have meaning to the person performing them. An act performed in one culture with a meaning becomes a random behavior in another culture. For example, on special occasions in the African culture, to spill a drink on the floor before every guest takes a sip is a ritual to seek the blessings of deceased ancestors for the event. Yet in another culture without a similar belief, it becomes a random or an accidental act. Whereas in the African culture this act of spilling a drink is called a *libation*, in another culture it is considered a waste of resource.

Rituals are used in several spheres of life, including in sports and in entertainment. Researcher Alison Wood Brooks and colleagues (Brooks et al., 2016) report that tennis star Serena Williams bounces her ball five times before her first serve, but before her second serve she bounces it two times. Also, these researchers report that singer Beyonce before every performance listens to the same playlist of songs with her entire band members. Researcher Alison Wood Brooks et al. (2016) note that in situations where people feel that they lack control, rituals help to reduce anxiety and provide reassurance. The death of a loved one is a situation where people feel they lack control and need reassurance (Neimeyer & Harris, 2023). In their study, researchers Michael Norton and Francesca Gino (2014) find that rituals help to mitigate grief, when bereaved participants are either asked to reflect on past rituals or are assigned novel rituals. These researchers report that bereaved participants experienced lower levels of grief, even when they have no prior beliefs in the effectiveness of rituals. Furthermore, the bereaved participants report an increased feeling of regaining control over their situation. Yet the acts of ritual assigned to these participants are different. Another study finds that Catholics who recite the rosary and attend church regularly tend to recover faster from grief than those who do not (Ahler & Tamney, 1964). Among Turkish women, also, research connects grief rituals to gaining a sense of control in loss (Aksoz-Efe et al., 2018). Taiwan is a society where the word "death" is hardly mentioned. It is a taboo word. Yet a study of Taiwanese women with stillborn babies demonstrates that through rituals, these women are able to regain control of their grief. Rituals not only help these bereaved mothers to acknowledge the death of their still born babies, but they were able to mention the taboo word "death" as well. The rituals helped the bereaved mothers to believe that their deceased children are in a safe place, to avoid parental guilt, and that any likely misfortune from failing to honor their deceased children in the future is now prevented (Tseng et al., 2018).

Rituals as Learned Behavior

As earlier defined, rituals are repetitive acts. Habits are repetitive behaviors as well. Out of habit, you may wake up every morning at 5:00 am. You are able to do this because your body has been so accustomed. Habit is an unconscious act that affects your conscious behavior. It is in your *non-declarative (implicit) memory* in the long-term memory store that also includes memory for procedures, skills, and conditioned responses (Ciccarelli & White, 2014).

Unlike habits, however, rituals convey meaning. It is the meaning attached to rituals that helps to promote *beliefs* in regaining control over uncertain situations such as in a loss (Ahler & Tamney, 1964; Aksoz-Efe et al., 2018; Tseng et al., 2018).

Russian physiologist Ivan Pavlov (1927), whose work impacted on the psychology of learning, elucidates on how as learned behavior rituals do serve utility purpose. In his classical conditioning experiment, Ivan Pavlov (1927), whose original study was on the physiology of digestion, noticed that his footsteps elicited salivation in his experimental dog. The dog's natural reaction is salivate to food (not footsteps), but the dog has learned to attach a meaning to Pavlov's footsteps, a cue that food is at hand (Pavlov went on to conduct a formal experiment with a bell sound). Pavlov named this type of learning *classical conditioning*. He further established that a primary conditioned behavior (like footsteps) could be the source of a secondary conditioned act. Pavlov called this learning *higher order conditioning*. An example would be a soccer player who associates wearing a pair of yellow socks with winning a game (conditioned learning). However, to win a game, that pair of socks has to be worn at 2:00 pm and not 3:00 pm (higher order learning). The pair of socks (the primary conditioned act) influences 2:00 pm (the secondary conditioned act), as time to wear the socks. Thus, a ritual could be a singular act or a multiplicity of acts. Researcher Bronislaw Malinowski (1954) notes that in their fishing expedition, the Trobriand Islanders tend to perform several rituals when traveling in rough waters in the open ocean.

Also, a ritual could be transferable from one situation to another if, to an individual, both situations appear to be similar. Psychologist John Watson (1913) conducted an experiment on little Albert to find out if this child could transfer learning from one situation to another. First, little Albert was made familiar to a white rat. The white rat was later paired with a loud sound that made little Albert to become afraid, and this changed his response to the white rat. Little Albert learned to associate the white rat with an uncomfortable situation (loud noise), and consequently, little Albert extended the same fear response to any furry object that appeared similar to the white rat. This learning is known as *stimulus generalization.*

Thus, a ritual that was performed to cope with a job loss could be transferred to cope with the loss of a loved one if, in the judgment of the bereaved, both losses appear similar.

Rituals could be learned through the observation of others, especially those who are significant in a person's life or in a position of authority, e.g., parents, grandparents, relatives, teachers, or clergy. Social psychologist Albert Bandura and colleague (Bandura & Walters, 1963) refer to this kind of learning as *observational learning* or learning by modeling. It leads to the acquisition of attitudes, values, and cognitive styles. An effective way that rituals could be passed on from one generation to another is through observational learning. Observational learning is effective in the acquisition of cultural values (e.g., Lave & Wenger, 1991; Rogoff et al., 2007). By observing adults in group rituals and activities, children can acquire a sense of self-identity within their culture (e.g., Miller & Goodnow, 1995). However, observational learning (or learning by modeling) requires attention, storage and recall of information, and the motivation to put into action and replicate what has been observed. So observational learning may not have a similar outcome for everyone.

An adolescent is different from a young child in how self-identity is developed. Researcher Erik Erickson (1963) identifies the adolescent stage as a period when the teenager seeks to discover a sense of self that is different from that of childhood but formed outside of parental influence. In doing this, the adolescent spends more time with peers and friends and less time observing parents. To do otherwise is to become confused in search for self-identity. Erickson (1963) calls this the *identity versus role confusion* stage. Researchers Monica Anderson and Jingjing Jiang (2018), in a 2018 Pew Research Center study, note that in the United States 95% of teenagers (ages 13–17 years) claim to have smartphones and almost 45% of them report being online regularly. With technology, a teenager's spheres of influence beyond the home environment become easier. Yet external influence could cause conflicts between teenagers and parents, who want to pass on their values to the next generation. Developmental psychologist Karen Fingerman and colleagues (Birditt et al., 2010) refer to this conflict type as *developmental schism*, spurred on in part by an independent-seeking teenager. Thus, a teenager could acquire grief rituals from their peers that do not reflect those of their parents. Also, in a situation where the law is on the teenager's side in recognizing their independence, it is difficult for parents to enforce personal values. For example, the "Mature Minor" doctrine recognizes the capacity of people aged 16 years (or even younger) to make healthcare decisions for themselves, without prior parental consent (e.g., Sigman & O'Connor, 1991).

Grief Rituals as Verbal or Nonverbal Acts

Around the world, grief rituals are verbal or nonverbal acts. Researcher Alfred Radcliffe-Brown notes that rituals have either *expressive* or *symbolic* elements (Radcliffe-Brown, 2014). Grief rituals include taking care of remains of the deceased, which varies from culture to culture, by age of the deceased, or based on the decedent/loved ones' financial resources (Reeves, 2011).

Latinos are mainly Catholic which influences their grief rituals. Before a funeral and during a funeral service, the rosary is recited, and family members and friends offer group prayers to the soul of the deceased. After a funeral, the rosary is also recited each day for 9 days (Diaz-Cabello, 2004). *Mexicans* maintain a family altar for their deceased children that sometimes include photos of the deceased children and have keepsakes and dolls dressed in the children's clothing to entice the spirit of the deceased to return home (Doran & Downing Hansen, 2006). In *Puerto Rican* culture, deceased children are dressed in white and their faces painted to resemble angels, with flowers placed inside and outside of the casket (Parkes et al., 2015). The color white represents the children's innocence and purity. Some Latinos believe that the 9 days of post-funeral prayers for the forgiveness of sin for adults should exclude children who are believed to be innocent (Brooten et al., 2016; Parry & Shen Ryan, 1995). In *African American* culture, there are chanting, singing, and praying to enable the decedent's spirit make a smooth transition to another type of life (Baloyi, 2014). During funerals food is shared as comfort to the survivors (Holloway, 2002). In the *Jamaican culture*, there is free expression of emotion that includes dizziness, fainting, and wailing to demonstrate one's closeness to the deceased (McIlwain, 2001).

In Africa, among the *Yoruba* of Southwestern Nigeria and the *Shona* of Zimbabwe, appropriate grief rituals have to the followed. Otherwise, as believed, the deceased can cause harm to the living (Spellman, 2014; Mupinda, 1995). The Yoruba men of Nigeria express their grief through drumming. The drum instrument is known as the *talking drum* (Eyetsemitan, 2022). The drum rhythms for washing the body are different from those for lowering the body into the grave (Lund, 2017).

The United States government recognizes over 500 *Native American* nations (Wilkinson, 2005). Yet, as diverse as they are, various tribal groups believe in the ability of the dead to cause harm to the living. Fueled by this fear, therefore, grief rituals include disposal of the dead person's belongings and, in discussions, avoiding the mention of the dead person's name during the mourning period. It is believed that when mentioned the dead person's name can provoke the deceased person's anger (e.g., Cox & Fundis, 2022). Similarly, among the *Indigenous Australians*, during the mourning period which could last up to 6 months, the deceased person's name is never mentioned. Also, a person with a namesake to the deceased has to change their name, at least during the mourning period. Personal belongings of the deceased are destroyed, including clothing, and people relocate from the house where the death occurred (Jones, 2015). These steps are to enable the survivor to cope with the pain of their loss. As ritual, these avoidance behaviors may be adaptive as long as they enable the bereaved to have control over their environment (e.g., Hofmann & Hay, 2018).

Most *Middle Eastern* societies have Islamic religious influences on their death culture. For example, burial is done on the same day as death, and cremation is avoided. Without embalming, the dead body in burial is wrapped with a white cloth and made to come in contact with the earth (Mehraby, 2003). This burial approach is irrespective of the dead person's or their loved one's economic resources. It is meant to reflect a life of simplicity to which the Muslim religion calls on its followers. Control in death is yielded to God or Allah who, as believed, knows a person's appointed time to die. In grief, therefore, the bereaved through his or her belief in Allah's supreme control derives vicarious control over death. Therefore, in Islam, "death" is not a taboo word (Kristiansen & Sheikh, 2012); rather, death is an opportunity to draw closer to Allah who, in knowing all things, would exercise mercy on the bereaved. *Haitians* in grief rituals observe a tradition of the *nine night*, based on the belief that the ninth day is when the soul of the deceased finally departs this world to its final resting place. Prior to the nine night, on each day prayers are said to usher the deceased into the afterlife, who then becomes the guide and protector of the living (e.g., Simpson, 1980). The *Hindu Balinese*, as researcher Carol Warren (1993) notes, perform rituals that enable the decedent's soul to fuse with the collective souls of their ancestors. This act helps to protect the living from any harm that could occur as the decedent's soul moves between two worlds.

The *Afro Surinamese* believe that the decedent's spirit does not depart from the world of the living immediately. This is unsettling to survivors as the decedent's spirit is believed to have supernatural powers that could cause harm to the living. Thus, to expedite the departure of the decedent's spirit, grief rituals are set into motion to exercise control. These rituals include covering of mirrors, paintings, or photos (van der Pijl, 2010).

Researcher Alina Mihaela (2015) notes that traditional *Romanians*, based on pagan beliefs, have death rituals influenced by mythologies. Traditional Romanians believe that the dead person's soul integrates with the universe. Unlike adults, a child's soul, due to a child's innocence, is easily integrated with the universe. Thus, for an adult, a priest has to offer prayers to help his or her soul integrate with the universe. The deceased person's soul is believed to hover around the world of the living for a period between 3 and 40 days. Thus, a lit candle is required to help guide the deceased person's spirit from darkness into the life beyond. Traditional Romanians believe that people whose deaths are sudden do die without a lit candle. Therefore, November 21st (called *ovidenie*) is a day set aside to light a candle for these individuals. This action exemplifies a *redemptive* grief ritual.

Grief Rituals and Dual Belief Systems

About 50–80% of Haitians incorporate elements of vodou culture or practice into another religion, especially Roman Catholicism (CIA World Factbook, 2023). Approximately 98% of Haitians are professed Catholic, yet Vodou, a West African religion, is a common practice (Huggins & Hinkson, 2019). Vodou practitioners believe in several gods, who act as intermediary for the Almighty God. As Catholics seek the Almighty God's intervention through saints, so do Vodou worshippers seek the Almighty God's intervention through lesser gods (e.g., Rey & Stepick, 2013).

The Afro-Surinamese combine Christianity and traditional African beliefs in grief rituals. Researcher van der Pijl (2016) notes that during the wake (or *dede oso*), a white table, a glass of water, and a lit candle are set on a table. In the tradition of African religion, these items connect the living and the dead, whereas in Christianity, they symbolize purity (water) and hope for a resurrection (lit candle). On the 40th day, after burial, another mourning takes place. In the African traditional religion, this is when the spirit of the deceased is believed to depart this world, but in Christianity, it is a reminder of Jesus' ascension after death into heaven (van der Pijl, 2016). In dual belief systems grief rituals that are similar are helpful to the bereaved. They prevent cognitive dissonance, if the bereaved has to make a choice between both belief systems.

Researcher Sandra Lobar and colleagues (Lobar et al., 2006) studied bereaved participants from different cultures and note the following common themes in grief rituals: (a): the type of grief ritual is tied to beliefs about what becomes of the deceased person's soul and (b): the stronger the beliefs, the *appropriate* grief rituals would be performed.

Generally, beliefs about what becomes of the decedent's soul centers around the perceived *location* of the deceased and the perceived *abilities* of the deceased in the afterlife by the survivor. Around the world, these beliefs are influenced by either religious teachings or traditional values.

Grief Rituals Based on Perceived Afterlife Location of the Deceased

Grief rituals are influenced by perceived afterlife location of the deceased. Christians believe that in the afterlife the deceased is located in either heaven or hell. Therefore, during a funeral the participation of a Christian clergy who affirms the decedent's afterlife location (usually heaven) is included in grief ritual. Readings from John 14:2–3 in the Bible, where Jesus promises Christians that heaven would be their dwelling place after death, might be part of the grief ritual. Muslims believe in "paradise," and this would be emphasized in the eulogy for a deceased Muslim. Grief rituals for practitioners of Buddhism and Hinduism would reflect beliefs in rebirth. Practitioners of African traditional religion believe that departed loved ones are domiciled on earth, as reflected by libation poured to the ground in reverence to departed ancestors on special occasions.

Grief Rituals Based on Perceived Afterlife Abilities of the Deceased

In death, the deceased is believed to take on a *spirit* persona. A spirit is believed to have abilities humans do not possess. Unlike humans who dwell in bodily form, a spirit is unseen and is ubiquitous (Loorits, 1949). A spirit, also, is believed to inhabit inanimate objects that include mirrors. Therefore, in several cultures, soon after a death mirrors are covered, as it is believed that on seeing himself/herself in a mirror, the living could join the dead (Loorits, 1949). As believed, a spirit's supernatural abilities can be used for either good or bad. Thus, people can have either *avoidance* or *embracement/consultation* response to the supernatural abilities of the spirit of the dead.

Avoidance Grief Rituals

Avoidance grief rituals include acts that discourage the spirit of the deceased. To the spirit of the dead, these acts are to send a message that they are *unwelcome* in the world of the living. For example, the avoidance grief rituals of traditional Estonians include placing the soap/bath whisk used to wash the decedent's body in the coffin, pouring water used to wash the decedent's body at a place nobody goes, fumigating the room where the dead body was kept, and avoiding the decedent's name during the mourning period (Heapost, 2007).

Embracement/Consultation Grief Rituals

In embracement/consultation grief rituals, the message to the spirit of the dead is that they are *welcome* to the world of the living. The decedent's spirit is perceived as a guide and protector of the living (Simpson, 1980). For example, in Chinese culture, the spirit of the deceased is expected to visit loved ones within 3 days after a funeral. As earlier mentioned, Mexicans maintain a practice that entices the spirit of their deceased children to visit home (Doran & Downing Hansen, 2006).

Embracement rituals include consultations with the decedent's spirit. For example, the Bible in 1 Samuel 28:3–25 states that Saul, the first king of Israel, was concerned about a war he was going to wage with the Philistines. Saul then approached a female sorcerer, the *Witch of Endor*, who conjured up the spirit of the prophet Samuel to find out about the outcome of the war. The spirit of the dead prophet Samuel, identified by Saul, said that the Philistines would defeat the Israeli army and that Saul and his three sons would die in that war (Bible.com;1SA.28.3–25).

Consultation with spirit of the dead occurs in contemporary times as well. In a survey of 18,607 people drawn from the United States and from 13 European countries, 25% of survey participants reported having sought an encounter with the spirit of the dead (Harraldsson & Houtkooper, 1991).

Prospective Acts as Grief Rituals

From earlier discussions, usually grief rituals take place after a death. Yet as people contemplate their death in the future and have concerns about what becomes of their loved ones and legacy, they begin to set in place certain acts which could become *prospective grief* rituals for the survivor. Additionally, being mentally compromised and unable to make decisions in the future becomes an issue of concern. Therefore, in exercise of control over an uncertain future, certain actions are put in place prior to death. Sometimes these actions are backed by law to secure a person's rights and preferences. Such proactive acts by the decedent could become proactive grief rituals that enable a survivor to gain control over a loved one's death. The following proactive actions can become prospective grief rituals:

Last Will and Testament: As a legal instrument, a last will and testament includes a person's wishes after they are gone for loved ones. In a last will and testament, the *testator* (the owner of the will) names an *executor* (who represents the testator), with an indication on how the testator wishes that his or her assets be distributed after death. A will could be contested for reasons that include perceived undue influence on the testator, mental incompetence of the testator, or forgery. Absent these, a last will and testament provides a survivor with an understanding of the decedent's thinking and enables the survivor to better cope with their loss. An abridged sample of a last will and testament is provided below:

11.1: Abridged sample of a last will and testament

LAST WILL AND TESTAMENT

I, [NAME], resident in the City of [CITY], County of [COUNTY], State of [STATE], being of sound mind, not acting under duress or undue influence, and fully understanding the nature and extent of all my property and of this disposition thereof, do hereby make, publish, and declare this document to be my Last Will and Testament and hereby revoke any and all other wills and codicils heretofore made by me.

1. EXPENSES AND TAXES. *I direct that all my debts and expenses of my last illness, funeral, and burial be paid as soon after my death as may be reasonably convenient, and I hereby authorize my Personal Representative to settle and discharge at their discretion any claims made against my estate.*

I further direct that my Personal Representative shall pay out of my estate any and all estate and inheritance taxes payable by reason of my death in respect of all items included in the computation of such taxes, whether passing under this Will or otherwise. Said taxes shall be paid by my Personal Representative as if such taxes were my debts without recovery of any part of such tax payments from anyone who receives any item included in such computation.

2. PERSONAL REPRESENTATIVE. *I nominate and appoint [NAME], of [CITY], County of [COUNTY], State of [STATE] as Personal Representative of my estate, and I request that (he/she) be appointed temporary Personal Representative if (he/she) applies. If my Personal Representative fails or ceases to so serve, then I nominate [NAME] of [CITY], County of [COUNTY], State of [STATE] to serve.*

3. DISPOSITION OF PROPERTY. *I devise and bequeath my property, both real and personal and wherever situated, as follows:*

1st Beneficiary: *[NAME], currently of [ADDRESS], as my [RELATION] whose last four (4) digits of their Social Security Number (SSN) are xxx-xx-[SSN] with the following property: [PROPERTY TO BE BEQUEATHED]*

2nd Beneficiary: *[NAME], currently of [ADDRESS], as my [RELATION] whose last four (4) digits of their Social Security Number (SSN) are xxx-xx-[SSN] with the following property: [PROPERTY TO BE BEQUEATHED]*

If any of my beneficiaries have pre-deceased me, then any property that they would have received if they had not pre-deceased me shall be distributed in equal shares to the remaining beneficiaries.

If any of my property cannot be readily sold and distributed, it may be donated to any charitable organization(S) of my Personal Representative's choice. If any property cannot be sold or donated, my Personal Representative may dispose of such property. I authorize my Personal Representative to pay administration expenses of my estate.

4. GOVERNING LAW. *This document shall be governed by the laws of the State of [STATE].*

I, the undersigned [NAME], do hereby declare that I sign and execute this instrument as my last Will, that I sign it willingly in the presence of each of the undersigned witnesses, and that I execute it as my free and voluntary act for the purposes herein expressed, on this [DAY] day of [MONTH], 20[YEAR].

_______________________________ -

____

Testator Signature *Testator (Printed Name)*

The foregoing instrument was, on this [X] day of [MONTH], 20[X], subscribed on each page and at the end thereof by [NAME], the above-named Testator, and by (him/her) signed, sealed, published, and declared to be (his/her) LAST WILL AND TESTAMENT, in the presence of us and each of us, who thereupon, at (his/her) request, in (his/her) presence, and in the presence of each other, have hereunto subscribed our names as attesting witnesses thereto.

_______________________________ -

____

Witness SignatureAddress

_______________________________ ------------------------

____

Witness SignatureAddress

Source: https://eforms.com/wills/#sample

Verbal Instructions: Before a death, a loved one could *verbally* make their wishes known to family members and friends. This is helpful in a society with a high rate of illiteracy. Yet, irrespective of a society's literacy rate, some important matters may be left out in a formal document because they can only be effectively communicated through verbal instructions. For example, CBS News (2018) reported that late United States senator John McCain's son-in-law recalled how, prior to his death, the late senator hugged him and told him to "take care of Meghan," the late senator's daughter to whom he was married. This instruction may not find a place in a formal last will and testament document. Also, a verbal instruction is a way of saying *goodbye* which may not be included in a last will and testament. The survivor may reciprocate the dying person's goodbye with assurances to honor their request. And the late senator's son-in-law said he did.

1. **Living will:** A living will is a legal document that states how a person wishes to be treated in the future, if unable to make that decision. For example, a person may indicate that they would not want be on a life-sustaining machine or that procedures that prolong life without a cure should not be used on them. He or she can appoint a *healthcare proxy* to act on their behalf, and the attending physician is made known of the dying person's preferences. The *five wishes* on which a living will should be based include (1) the person I want to make decisions for me when I cannot; (2) the kind of medical treatment I both want or do not want; (3) how comfortable I should be; (4) how people should treat me; and (5) what my loved ones should know (fivewishes.org; retrieved, April 29, 2023).

A living will places the choice of life or death on the individual. This reflects an individualist value system different from a culture of collectivism. Researchers Subrarta Chatoopadhyay and Alfred Simon (2008) note that in India (a society that values collectivism) an attending physician is more likely to yield to the wishes of the family rather than the wishes of the dying person. In Latino culture (also a culture that values collectivism), end-of-life decisions for the seriously ill are referred to the family (Kelley et al., 2010).

End-of-life decision, whether made by the dying person or by the dying person's family, gives the survivor a sense of control over the uncertainties that could result from a loved one's death.

Also, a grief ritual that precedes a death can be influenced by religious practices. For example, in preparation for heaven, Catholics administer the *last rites* to a dying person. In Chinese Buddhism, in preparation for a good rebirth, the dying person recites the Sutra (statements of beliefs). The Hindus, as death is approaching, avoid mind-altering medications like narcotics. They believe that, for the prospects of a good rebirth, a dying person should face death with a clear mind (Sharma et al., 2013). Also, the Hindus believe that to complete an unfinished business prior to death enhances the prospects for a good rebirth. An unfinished business include doing good deeds, offering apology and reconciling differences with others, or distributing personal belongings to heirs and charities (e.g., Firth, 2005).

Retroactive Acts as Grief Rituals

In some cultures and religions, a grief ritual not done at the appropriate time can be done retroactively. Practitioners of Chinese Taoism believe that, to experience peace and balance, it is never too late to voice appreciation or right wrongs with the deceased (Qin & Xia, 2015). Researcher Shirley Firth (2005) reported on a Hindu family that could not have the last rites administered on their loved one prior to death, because doctors switched off her life support machine. Yet, generations later, before engaging in any social activities such as family weddings, this family performed those last rites to seek penance.

Grief Rituals and Body Disposal Method

Grief rituals are reflected in the choice of body disposal methods, which is influenced by either secular or non-secular beliefs. Among people who believe in rebirth, a common practice is cremation, as it helps to hasten the release of the decedent's spirit in rebirth. But the choice of cremation (e.g., green cremation) may be out of concern for the environment as well. In green cremation, the corpse is placed in a water solution of potassium hydroxide, which reduces the body to the bones, and the bones are then pulverized into ashes.

Christians who believe in bodily resurrection prefer whole-body burial and hold on to the traditional earth burial in body disposal. Yet, for people who prefer continuity of their lives in others, body organ donation or entire body donation to science becomes a choice.

Key Takeaways

1. Grief rituals are important in the cultural (and religious) lives of people around the world. Yet conventional grief models do not *explicitly* point to grief rituals, in coping with the pain of a loss, and/or in making it less burdensome on bereaved persons to move on with their lives.
2. A ritual is not a random act but has meaning to the person performing it.
3. In a situation of uncertainty as occurs after a loss, grief rituals help to provide control and reassurance to the survivor.
4. Rituals are learned behavior and could be verbal or nonverbal acts.

5. Through learning, a grief ritual is passed on from one generation to another. Yet individuals may have their own personal rituals.
6. When a survivor has more than one belief system (e.g., traditional religious beliefs and Christian beliefs), grief rituals may conflict with each other. However, when in both belief systems a survivor finds common grounds, grief rituals become easier. A bereavement counselor/healthcare professional could help with exploring common grounds or help with finding the saliency of one belief system over the other.
7. Some grief rituals are never too late; when performed after the appropriate time has elapsed, they serve a *redemptive* rituals to the survivor. Also, a bereavement counselor/healthcare professional could help in exploring a *redemptive* ritual with a survivor.
8. A prospective act done by the deceased before death (e.g., a last will and testament, a living will, or a verbal instruction) could help with gaining control and reassurance in grief by the survivor. It becomes a prospective grief ritual. A bereavement counselor/healthcare professional could help with exploring a decedent's prospective acts with the survivor.

Critical Cultural Thinking

After a death, and not being able to afford an elaborate funeral, John and Paul separately wrapped their deceased loved ones in a white cloth and buried them without a casket. The corpses were in direct contact with the earth, and the actions of John and Paul were similar. Afterward, John felt good about the burial of his loved one, but not so Paul. Paul felt his deceased loved one should have had a different burial but for financial constraints. How can Paul cope with his grief through either a prospective grief ritual or a retroactive grief ritual?

References

Ahler, J. G., & Tamney, J. B. (1964). Some functions of religious ritual in a catastrophe. *Sociological Analysis, 25*(4), 212–230.

Aksoz-Efe, I., Erdur-Baker, O., & Servaty-Seib, H. (2018). Death rituals, religious beliefs, and grief of turkish women. *Death Studies, 42*(9), 579–592.

Anderson, M., & Jiang, J. (2018). Teens, social media & technology 2018. *Pew Research Center, 31*(2018), 1673–1689.

Baloyi, M. E. (2014). Distance no impediment for funerals: Death as a uniting ritual for African people-A pastoral study. *Verbum Et Ecclesia, 35*(1), 1–7.

Bandura, A., & Walters, R. H. (1963). *Social learning and personality development.* Holt, Reinhardt, Wintston Co.

Bible.com/bible/compare/1SA.28.3-25. 1 Samuel 28:3–25 NLT

Birditt, K. S., Fingerman, K. L., & Zarit, S. H. (2010). Adult children's problems and successes: Implications for intergenerational ambivalence. *The Journals of Gerontology. Series B, Psychological Sciences and Social Sciences, 65*(2), 145–153.
Brooks, A. W., Schroeder, J., Risen, J. L., Gino, F., Galinsky, A. D., Norton, M. I., & Schweitzer, M. E. (2016). Don't stop believing: Rituals improve performance by decreasing anxiety. *Organizational Behavior and Human Decision Processes, 137*, 71–85.
Brooten, D., Youngblut, J. M., Charles, D., Roche, R., Hidalgo, I., & Malkawi, F. (2016). Death rituals reported by white, black, and Hispanic parents following the ICU death of an infant or child. *Journal of Pediatric Nursing, 31*(2), 132–140.
CBS News. (2018, April 30). *Son-in-law says John McCain told him to "take care" of his daughter.* www.cbsnews.com/news/john-mccain-son-in-law-says-senator-told-him-to-take-care-of-daughter-report/
Chattopadhyay, S., & Simon, A. (2008). East meets west: Cross-cultural perspective in end-of-life decision making from Indian and German viewpoints. *Medicine, Health Care and Philosophy, 11*(2), 165–174.
CIA: The World Factbook. Accessed May 17, 2023., from www.cia.gov/the-world-factbook/countries/
Ciccarelli, S. K., & White, J. N. (2014). *Psychology: Dsm 5*. Pearson.
Cox, G. R., & Fundis, R. J. (2022). *Spiritual, ethical, and pastoral aspects of death and bereavement*. Routledge.
Diaz-Cabello, N. (2004). The Hispanic way of dying: Three families, three perspectives, three cultures. *Illness, Crisis & Loss, 12*(3), 239–255.
Doka, K. J., & Martin, T. L. (2011). *Grieving beyond gender: Understanding the ways men and women mourn*. Routledge.
Doran, G., & Downing Hansen, N. (2006). Constructions of Mexican American family grief after the death of a child: An exploratory study. *Cultural Diversity and Ethnic Minority Psychology, 12*(2), 199.
Erickson, E. H. (1963). *Childhood and society*. Norton.
Eyetsemitan, F. E. (2022). Bereavement theories and models. In *The deceased-focused approach to grief: An alternative model* (pp. 59–76).
Firth, S. (2005). End-of-life: A Hindu view. *The Lancet, 366*(9486), 682–686.
Fivewishes.org. Five wishes. www.fivewishes.org/
Freud, S. (1917). Mourning and melancholia. *The Standard Edition of the Complete Psychological Works of Sigmund Freud, 14*(1914–1916), 237–258.
Gillies, J., & Neimeyer, R. A. (2006). Loss, grief, and the search for significance: Toward a model of meaning reconstruction in bereavement. *Journal of Constructivist Psychology, 19*(1), 31–65.
Haraldsson, E., & Houtkooper, J. M. (1991). Psychic experiences in the multinational human values study: who reports them. *The Journal of the American Society for Psychical Research, 85*(2), 145–165.
Heapost, L. (2007). The cemetery of Siksälä: Osteological and paleodemographical analysis. In S. Laul & H. Valk (Eds.), *A community at the frontiers. Iron age and medieval* (pp. 213–236). University of Tartu.
Hofmann, S. G., & Hay, A. C. (2018). Rethinking avoidance: Toward a balanced approach to avoidance in treating anxiety disorders. *Journal of Anxiety Disorders, 55*, 14–21.
Holloway, K. F. (2002). *Passed on*. Duke University Press.
Huggins, C. L., & Hinkson, G. M. (2019). Contemporary burial practices in three Caribbean Islands among Christians of African descent. *OMEGA-Journal of Death and Dying, 80*(2), 266–279.
Jones, K. (2015). It is normal to remember: Death and grief in Australia. In *The world of bereavement: Cultural perspectives on death in families* (pp. 243–263).
Kelley, A. S., Wenger, N. S., & Sarkisian, C. A. (2010). Opiniones: End-of-life care preferences and planning of older Latinos. *Journal of the American Geriatrics Society, 58*(6), 1109–1116.

Kristiansen, M., & Sheikh, A. (2012). Understanding faith considerations when caring for bereaved Muslims. *Journal of the Royal Society of Medicine, 105*(12), 513–517.

Lave, J., & Wenger, E. (1991). Learning in doing: Social, cognitive, and computational perspectives. *Situated Learning: Legitimate Peripheral Participation, 10*, 109–155.

Lobar, S. L., Youngblut, J. M., & Brooten, D. (2006). Cross-cultural beliefs, ceremonies, and rituals surrounding death of a loved one. *Pediatric Nursing, 32*(1), 44–50.

Loorits, O. (1949). Grundz¸ge des estnischen Volksglaubens, 1. (Skrifter utgivna av Kungl. *Gustav Adolfs Akademien f'r Folklivsforskning,* 18: 1.) Lund.

Lund, D. (2017). *Death and bereavement around the world: Reflective essays, 5.*

Malinowski, B. (1954). *Magic, science and religion, and other essays, etc.* Doubleday & Company.

McIlwain, C. D. (2001). Death in black and white: A study of family differences in the performance of death rituals. *Communication Quarterly, 49*(3), Q1.

Mehraby, N. (2003). Psychotherapy with Islamic clients facing loss and grief. *Psychotherapy in Australia, 9*(2), 30–34.

Mihaela, A. S. (2015). The vision of death in Romanian culture. In *The world of bereavement: Cultural perspectives on death in families* (pp. 121–128).

Miller, P. J., & Goodnow, J. J. (1995). Cultural practices: Toward an integration of culture and development. In J. J. Goodnow, P. J. Miller, & F. Kessel (Eds.), *Cultural practices as contexts for development* (pp. 5–16). Jossey-Bass/Wiley.

Moran, M. H. (2017). Missing bodies and secret funerals: The production of "safe and dignified burials" in the Liberian ebola crisis. *Anthropological Quarterly*, 399–421.

Mupinda, M. (1995, November). Loss and grief among the Shona: The meaning of disappearances. In Paper presented at the *VII International Symposium on Torture as a Challenge to the Medical Profession.*

Neimeyer, R. A., & Harris, D. L. (2023). Bereavement and grief. In H. S. Friedman & C. H. Markey (Eds.), *Encyclopedia of mental health* (Vol. 1, pp. 204–211). Elsevier, Academic Press.

Norton, M. I., & Gino, F. (2014). Rituals alleviate grieving for loved ones, lovers, and lotteries. *Journal of Experimental Psychology: General, 143*(1), 266.

Parkes, C. M., Laungani, P., & Young, W. (2015). *Death and bereavement across cultures.* Routledge.

Parry, J. K., & Ryan, A. S. (1995). *A cross-cultural look at death, dying, and religion.* Wadsworth Publishing.

Pavlov, I. P. (1927). *Les réflexes conditionnels: Étude objective de l'activité nerveuse supérieure des animaux F.* Alcan.

Qin, S., & Xia, Y. (2015). Grieving rituals and beliefs of Chinese families. In *The world of bereavement: Cultural perspectives on death in families* (pp. 69–80).

Radcliffe-Brown, A. R. (2014). *Taboo.* Cambridge University Press.

Reeves, N. C. (2011). Death acceptance through ritual. *Death Studies, 35*(5), 408–419.

Rey, T., & Stepick, A. (2013). *Crossing the water and keeping the faith: Haitian religion in Miami.* NYU Press.

Robarchek, C., & Robarchek, C. (2005). Waorani grief and the witch-killer's rage: Worldview, emotion, and anthropological explanation. *Ethos, 33*(2), 206–230.

Rogoff, B., Moore, L., Najafi, B., Dexter, A., Correa-Chávez, M., & Solís, J. (2007). Children's development of cultural repertoires through participation in everyday routines and practices. In J. E. Grusec & P. D. Hastings (Eds.), *Handbook of socialization: Theory and research* (pp. 490–515). The Guilford Press.

Sharma, H., Jagdish, V., Anusha, P., & Bharti, S. (2013). End-of-life care: Indian perspective. *Indian Journal of Psychiatry, 55*(Suppl 2), S293.

Sigman, G. S., & O'Connor, C. (1991). Exploration for physicians of the mature minor doctrine. *The Journal of Pediatrics, 119*(4), 520–525.

Simpson, G. E. (1980). Ideas about ultimate reality and meaning in haitian vodun. *Ultimate Reality and Meaning, 3*(3), 187–199.

Spellman, W. M. (2014). *A brief history of death.* Reaktion Books.

Stroebe, M., & Schut, H. (2006). Complicated grief: A conceptual analysis of the field. *OMEGA-Journal of Death and Dying, 52*(1), 53–70.

Tseng, Y., Hsu, M., Hsieh, Y., & Cheng, H. (2018). The meaning of rituals after a stillbirth: A qualitative study of mothers with a stillborn baby. *Journal of Clinical Nursing, 27*(5-6), 1134–1142.

Van der Pijl, Y. (2010). Pentecostal-charismatic Christianity: African-Surinamese perceptions and experiences. *Exchange, 39*(2), 179–195.

Van der Pijl, Y. (2016). Death in the family revisited: Ritual expression and controversy in a creole transnational mortuary sphere. *Ethnography, 17*(2), 147–167.

Warren, C. (1993). *Adat and dinas: Balinese communities in the Indonesian state*. Oxford University Press.

Watson, J. B. (1913). Psychology as the behaviorist views it. *Psychological Review, 20*(2), 158.

Wilkinson, C. F. (2005). *Blood struggle: The rise of modern Indian nations*. WW Norton & Company.

Worden, J. W. (2018). *Grief counseling and grief therapy: A handbook for the mental health practitioner*. Springer Publishing Company.

Index

F. E. Eyetsemitan, *Cultural Influences in Coping with Grief*,
https://doi.org/10.1007/978-3-031-86817-7

The manufacturer's authorised representative in the EU is Springer
Nature Customer Service Centre GmbH, Europaplatz 3, 69115 Heidelberg,
Germany. If you have any concerns regarding our products, please
contact ProductSafety@springernature.com

Printed and bound by CPI Group (UK) Ltd, Croydon, CR0 4YY
30/09/2026
02225513-0010